Utilize este código QR para se
cadastrar de forma mais rápida:

Ou, se preferir, entre em:
www.richmond.com.br/ac/livroportal
e siga as instruções para ter acesso
aos conteúdos exclusivos do
Portal e Livro Digital

CÓDIGO DE ACESSO:

A 00044 CHALLENGE3 U 64907

Faça apenas um cadastro. Ele será válido para:

12103491   Aluno

CB053121

From trees to books, *sustainability all the way*

Da semente ao livro,
sustentabilidade por todo o caminho

Planting forests

The wood used as raw material for our paper comes from planted forests, that is, it is not the result of deforestation. This practice generates thousands of jobs for farmers and helps to recover environmentally degraded areas.

Making paper and printing books

The entire paper production chain, from pulp production to book binding, is certified, complying with international standards for sustainable processing and environmental best practices.

Creating content

Our educational solutions are developed with life-long goals guided by editorial values, diverse viewpoints and socio-environmental responsibility.

Developing life projects

Richmond educational solutions are an act of commitment to the future of younger generations, enabling partnerships between schools and families in their mission to educate!

Plantar florestas

A madeira que serve de matéria-prima para nosso papel vem de plantio renovável, ou seja, não é fruto de desmatamento. Essa prática gera milhares de empregos para agricultores e ajuda a recuperar áreas ambientais degradadas.

Fabricar papel e imprimir livros

Toda a cadeia produtiva do papel, desde a produção de celulose até a encadernação do livro, é certificada, cumprindo padrões internacionais de processamento sustentável e boas práticas ambientais.

Criar conteúdos

Os profissionais envolvidos na elaboração de nossas soluções educacionais buscam uma educação para a vida pautada por curadoria editorial, diversidade de olhares e responsabilidade socioambiental.

Construir projetos de vida

Oferecer uma solução educacional Richmond é um ato de comprometimento com o futuro das novas gerações, possibilitando uma relação de parceria entre escolas e famílias na missão de educar!

Apoio:
www.twosides.org.br

Scan the QR code to learn more.
Access *richmond.com.br/quem-somos/praticas-sustentaveis/*

Fotografe o código QR e
conheça melhor esse caminho.
Saiba mais em *richmond.com.br/quem-somos/praticas-sustentaveis/*

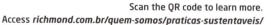

Challenge

3RD edition

Eduardo Amos

Elisabeth Prescher

Ernesto Pasqualin

Richmond

Richmond

Direção editorial: Sandra Possas

Edição executiva de inglês: Izaura Valverde
Gerência de *design* e produção: Christiane Borin
Edição executiva de conteúdos digitais: Adriana Pedro de Almeida
Coordenação de arte: Raquel Buim
Coordenação de multimídia: Claudiner Corrêa Filho

Edição de texto: Giuliana Gramani
Edição de conteúdo digital: Gabrielle Navarro
Elaboração de conteúdo: Paulo Machado (*Reading, ENEM Practice* e *Extra Reading*)
Revisão: Amanda de Lima Lassak, Ana Curci, Ana Paula Felippe, Barbara Yumi Lemos, Carolina Waideman, Daniele Crema, Elaine Moreira, Evelyn Zaidam Porting, Flora Vaz Manzione, Frederico Helou Doca de Andrade, Kandy Saraiva, Lívia Mantovani, Marina Andrade, Natasha Montanari, Rafael Gustavo Spigel, Raura Monique Ikeda, Raymond Shoulder, Rhennan Felipe Siqueira Santos, Roberta Moratto Risther, Sheila Saad, Tássia Carvalho, Vivian Cristina de Souza
Áudio: Maximal Studio

Projeto gráfico: Gustavo Moraes
Edição de arte: Fabiane Eugenio, APIS design integrado
Edição de arte multimídia: Daniel Favalli
Diagramação: APIS design integrado
Capa: Amanda Savoini, Camila Ranelli
Criações: APIS design integrado, Gustavo Moraes, Hulda Melo, Matheus Banti, Mônica Oldrine
Ilustrações: Erika Onodera, Leonardo Teixeira, Orlandeli, Zuba
Iconografia: Joanna Heliszkowski, Lourdes Guimarães, Nicolle Bizelli, Sara Alencar
Coordenação de *bureau*: Américo Jesus
Tratamento de imagens: Denise Feitoza Maciel, Marina M. Buzzinaro, Rubens M. Rodrigues
Pré-impressão: Alexandre Petreca, Everton L. de Oliveira, Fabio N. Precendo, Hélio P. de Souza Filho, Marcio H. Kamoto, Vitória Sousa
Impressão e acabamento: BMF Gráfica e Editora
Lote: 295514

Todos os *sites* mencionados nesta obra foram reproduzidos apenas para fins didáticos. A Richmond não tem controle sobre seu conteúdo, o qual foi cuidadosamente verificado antes de sua utilização.

Websites mentioned in this material were quoted for didactic purposes only. Richmond has no control over their content and urges care when using them.

Embora todas as medidas tenham sido tomadas para identificar e contatar os detentores de direitos autorais sobre os materiais reproduzidos nesta obra, isso nem sempre foi possível. A editora estará pronta a retificar quaisquer erros dessa natureza assim que notificada.

Every effort has been made to trace the copyright holders, but if any omission can be rectified, the publishers will be pleased to make the necessary arrangements.

Dados Internacionais de Catalogação na Publicação (CIP)
(Câmara Brasileira do Livro, SP, Brasil)

Amos, Eduardo
    Challenge / Eduardo Amos, Elisabeth Prescher, Ernesto Pasqualin. – 3. ed. – São Paulo : Moderna, 2016.

    Bibliografia.

    1. Inglês (Ensino médio) I. Prescher, Elisabeth. II. Pasqualin, Ernesto. III. Título.

16-02451   CDD-420.7

Índices para catálogo sistemático:
1. Inglês : Ensino médio   420.7

ISBN 978-85-16-10349-1 (LA)
ISBN 978-85-16-10350-7 (LP)

RICHMOND
EDITORA MODERNA LTDA.
Rua Padre Adelino, 758 – Belenzinho
São Paulo – SP – Brasil – CEP 03303-904
Central de atendimento ao usuário: 0800 771 8181
www.richmond.com.br
2021
Impresso no Brasil

Contents

Contents

Grammar Diagnostic Test

In files 1 to 10, choose the correct alternative. If you need help, go to pages 10-11.

File 1 (To Be – Present Form)

1 It _____ summer, but it _____ hot.
   a ☐ is – isn't   b ☐ am – is   c ☐ are – are

2 Paul and I _____ already late for school.
   a ☐ am   b ☐ are   c ☐ is

3 His car _____ brand new.
   a ☐ are   b ☐ aren't   c ☐ is

4 _____ he ready for the exam?
   a ☐ Am   b ☐ Isn't   c ☐ Are

5 The doctor _____ worried because the patients _____ fine.
   a ☐ isn't – are   b ☐ aren't – is   c ☐ are – aren't

6 _____ I a good student?
   a ☐ Is   b ☐ Isn't   c ☐ Am

File 2 (To Be – Past Form)

1 Where _____ they yesterday?
   a ☐ was   b ☐ wasn't   c ☐ were

2 In the fall of 1998 Mary and I _____ in Canada.
   a ☐ was   b ☐ were   c ☐ are

3 My uncle _____ an architect. He _____ an engineer.
   a ☐ wasn't – was   b ☐ were – was   c ☐ weren't – isn't

4 _____ they at the party?
   a ☐ Is   b ☐ Was   c ☐ Weren't

5 The dog _____ sick, only the cat _____.
   a ☐ wasn't – was   b ☐ weren't – weren't   c ☐ aren't – was

6 Hi, kids! _____ you OK while your father and I _____ at work?
   a ☐ Were – were   b ☐ Was – wasn't   c ☐ Is – were

File 3 (There to Be – Present and Past Forms)

1 **Mike:** Last night I saw a movie about a small city in the Midwest of the United States.

    Paul: What was it about?

    Mike: _____ any museums or art galleries in the city, but the masked thief was there because _____ two unguarded banks.

    a ☐ There is – there were   b ☐ There are – there weren't   c ☐ There weren't – there were

2 **Paul:** Two unguarded banks! _____ really a masked thief in the movie?

    Mike: Sure! And _____ a hotel right in front of one of the banks.

    a ☐ Was there – there was   b ☐ Is there – there aren't   c ☐ Was there – there were

3 **Paul:** _____ a police station?

    Mike: No! And no squad car!

    a ☐ Was there   b ☐ Aren't there   c ☐ Are there

4 **Paul:** Hey, let's go to that new coffee shop so you can tell me more about the movie.

    Mike: Good idea! _____ a bus stop near here?

    a ☐ Is there   b ☐ There is   c ☐ Aren't there

5 **Paul:** _____ one on the corner of Franklin and Madison.

    Mike: Let's go!

    a ☐ There was not   b ☐ There is   c ☐ There aren't

File 4 (Demonstrative Pronouns)

1 Look! _____ is my high school yearbook.

    a ☐ This   b ☐ These   c ☐ Those

2 _____ woman on the right wasn't a secretary. She was Ms. Windsor, the principal.

    a ☐ That   b ☐ Those   c ☐ These

3 Look at _____ other four pictures.

    a ☐ that   b ☐ these   c ☐ this

4 _____ three men were my teachers. _____ one on the left was my English teacher.

    a ☐ These – This   b ☐ This – Those   c ☐ That – These

5 _____ are my parents. Mom was very happy and so was Dad.

    a ☐ That   b ☐ This   c ☐ These

6 _____ little girl in the back is my sister. She was only three.

    a ☐ These   b ☐ Those   c ☐ That

File 5 (Indefinite Articles)

1   Is _____ American university located in Europe or in the United States?

   a ☐ an   b ☐ a

2   Troy is _____ front desk manager and Kendra is _____ operator. They work in a hotel.

   a ☐ a – an   b ☐ an – an

3   _____ human body was seen near the bridge, but the police hasn't arrived there yet.

   a ☐ A   b ☐ An

4   _____ European bank is the best place to buy euros.

   a ☐ An   b ☐ A

5   I saw _____ job ad on the internet about _____ hour ago. They are looking for _____ university professor. Call and see if it is interesting.

   a ☐ a – an – an   b ☐ a – an – a   c ☐ an – a – an

6   Yesterday I went to _____ huge park for a walk and saw _____ honest man giving back _____ woman's wallet, which he had found on the floor.

   a ☐ a – a – a   b ☐ an – an – a   c ☐ a – an – a

File 6 (Plural of Nouns)

1   This is my school. There are two _____.

   a ☐ building   b ☐ buildings   c ☐ buildinges

2   We all have lockers and all our _____ are in _____ inside them.

   a ☐ thing – box   b ☐ things – boxs   c ☐ things – boxes

3   Our _____ are excellent. Mrs. Barter, for example, taught us how to do all our Chemistry _____.

   a ☐ teacher – activitys   b ☐ teachers – activities   c ☐ teachers – activityes

4   Mr. Jesterfield is the _____ and Sonia and Maggy are his _____.

   a ☐ principal – secretaries   b ☐ principals – secretarys   c ☐ principal – secretares

5   The green building is where I study. There are twenty-five _____ in my classroom: thirteen _____ and twelve _____.

   a ☐ students – girls – boys   b ☐ student – girl – boy   c ☐ studentes – girls – boyes

6   These are the _____ that take us to school and that is our orchard, where we plant _____ and plums.

   a ☐ buses – peachs   b ☐ bus – peachies   c ☐ buses – peaches

File 7 (Genitive Case)

1 My _____ were lost. Dad was worried because his laptop was in one of his _____. My uncle was very upset too.

a ☐ suitcase's family – suitcase's brothers   c ☐ family's suitcases – brother's suitcases

b ☐ family suitcase's – brother suitcase's

2 My _____ was also very sad because of the lost luggage.

a ☐ brother's girlfriend   c ☐ brothers's girlfriends

b ☐ brothers' girlfriends

3 _____ was in her suitcase. She was sad because it was a gift from Grandma.

a ☐ Dad' shoes   c ☐ My brother's glasses

b ☐ Mom's necklace

4 We lost our bags at JFK airport. My _____ were big and red, while my _____ was small and grey.

a ☐ parents' bags – sister's bag   c ☐ parents' bags – sister' bags

b ☐ parents's bag – sisters's bag

File 8 (Interrogative Words)

1 Can you tell me _____ the subway station is, please?

a ☐ which   b ☐ when   c ☐ where

2 _____ car is that in front of the library?

a ☐ Whose   b ☐ Who's   c ☐ Who

3 Amanda is an art collector. _____ isn't she here for the auction?

a ☐ Why   b ☐ When   c ☐ Where

4 _____ are the sandwich and the fruit salad?

a ☐ How much   b ☐ How many   c ☐ What

5 _____ times do I have to repeat this order?

a ☐ How much   b ☐ How long   c ☐ How many

6 _____ do you prefer: the green jacket or the blue one?

a ☐ Whose   b ☐ Who   c ☐ Which

File 9 (Personal Pronouns: Subject)

1   **Ann:** What is Sally doing?

   David: _____ don't know what _____ is doing.

   a ☐ She – you   b ☐ I – he   c ☐ I – she

2   **Ann:** Who was looking for me?

   David: Cindy and I were.

   Ann: Who was?

   David: _____ were! Cindy and I were looking for you.

   a ☐ They   b ☐ We   c ☐ You

3   **Ann:** Ask Sally where Tom is.

   David: _____ doesn't know where _____ is.

   a ☐ She – he   b ☐ He – she   c ☐ You – I

4   **Ann:** Where are the kids?

   David: _____ are in the yard playing with Tom.

   Ann: Oh, Tom is there too!

   David: Yes, _____ is.

   a ☐ He – we   b ☐ They – he   c ☐ They – we

File 10 (Modal Verb: *Can*)

1   What can I _____ to protect myself from catching the flu?

   a ☐ did   b ☐ does   c ☐ do

2   You can _____ a mask when in close contact with someone who is sick.

   a ☐ wear   b ☐ to wear   c ☐ wearing

3   **Patrick:** _____ I travel?

   Rose: If you have any symptoms, you should not travel.

   a ☐ Am   b ☐ Can   c ☐ Is

4   You _____ at home and avoid going to crowded places.

   a ☐ can to stay   b ☐ can't stay   c ☐ can stay

5   You can rest and _____ plenty of fluids.

   a ☐ drink   b ☐ drank   c ☐ to drink

Grammar Diagnostic Files

File 1 — To Be (ser, estar) – Present Form

Afirmativa	Negativa	Interrogativa
I **am** (I'**m**)	I **am not** (I'**m not**)	**Am** I?
You **are** (You'**re**)	You **are not** (You **aren't**)	**Are** you?
He **is** (He'**s**)	He **is not** (He **isn't**)	**Is** he?
She **is** (She'**s**)	She **is not** (She **isn't**)	**Is** she?
It **is** (It'**s**)	It **is not** (It **isn't**)	**Is** it?
We **are** (We'**re**)	We **are not** (We **aren't**)	**Are** we?
You **are** (You'**re**)	You **are not** (You **aren't**)	**Are** you?
They **are** (They'**re**)	They **are not** (They **aren't**)	**Are** they?
I **am** a student.	She **is not** a teacher.	**Are** they here?

File 2 — To Be (ser, estar) – Past Form

Afirmativa	Negativa	Interrogativa
I **was**	I **was not** (I **wasn't**)	**Was** I?
You **were**	You **were not** (You **weren't**)	**Were** you?
He **was**	He **was not** (He **wasn't**)	**Was** he?
She **was**	She **was not** (She **wasn't**)	**Was** she?
It **was**	It **was not** (It **wasn't**)	**Was** it?
We **were**	We **were not** (We **weren't**)	**Were** we?
You **were**	You **were not** (You **weren't**)	**Were** you?
They **were**	They **were not** (They **weren't**)	**Were** they?
I **was** a student.	She **was not** a teacher.	**Were** they here?

File 3 — There to Be (haver, existir) – Present and Past Forms

Presente	Passado
There is (há, existe) – **There is** a dog in the backyard.	**There was** (havia, existia) – **There was** a notebook here.
There are (há, existem) – **There are** dogs in the backyard.	**There were** (havia, existiam) – **There were** notebooks here.

File 4 — Demonstrative Pronouns

Singular	Plural
This (este, esta, isto) – **This** is my car.	**These** (estes, estas) – **These** are my books.
That (aquele, aquela, aquilo) – **That** is my father.	**Those** (aqueles, aquelas) – **Those** are my sisters.

File 5 — Indefinite Articles

a (um, uma) – usado antes de palavras no singular iniciadas por:

- sons consonantais – **a** cat, **a** girl, **a** bus
- **h** aspirado – **a** horse, **a** house, **a** huge park
- som de **y** e **w** – **a** European, **a** uniform, **a** week, **a** year, **a** university

an (um, uma) – usado antes de palavras no singular iniciadas por:

- sons vocálicos – **an** egg, **an** eraser, **an** ugly picture
- **h** mudo – **an** hour, **an** honest person, **an** heir

Obs.: *a*/*an* não são usados antes de substantivos incontáveis – **some** bread, **some** coffee

File 6 — Plural of Nouns

Regra geral	Particularidades
O plural em inglês é formado acrescentando-se **-s** ao substantivo. chair – chair**s** girl – girl**s**	• Substantivos terminados em **s**, **sh**, **ch**, **x**, **z** e **o** recebem **-es** para formar o plural. kiss – kiss**es** peach – peach**es** topaz – topaz**es** brush – brush**es** fox – fox**es** potato – potato**es** • Substantivos terminados em **y** precedido de consoante fazem o plural com a substituição do **y** por **i** e o acréscimo de **-es**. baby – bab**ies** lady – lad**ies** city – cit**ies**

File 7 — Genitive Case

O *genitive case* é indicado por **'s** ou **'**, que são acrescentados ao substantivo para indicar posse. Ele é geralmente usado para pessoas ou animais.

• **'s** é usado quando o substantivo não termina em **s** – the man**'s** hat

• **'** é usado quando o substantivo termina em **s** – the girls**'** dresses

File 8 — Interrogative Words

What* (o que, qual)
What do you want?

Which** (que, qual – usado para indicar uma escolha específica)
Which color do you prefer?

Where (onde)
Where do you live?

Why (por que)
Why are they here?

When (quando)
When did she arrive?

Whose (de quem)
Whose book is this?

Who* (quem)
Who did you call?

How (como)
How are you?

How much/many (quanto, quantos)
How much is this book?
How many girls are there?

*Quando a pergunta for sobre o sujeito do verbo, não se usa verbo auxiliar.

What caused the accident?   **Who** saw you?

**Usado em perguntas nas quais há um número fixo ou limitado de respostas ou possibilidades.

Which bus do you take to school?   **Which** is more important: money or character?

File 9 — Personal Pronouns: Subject

Os pronomes pessoais são usados como sujeito da oração.

I (eu)	**I** am sorry.	It (ele, ela)	**It** runs fast.
You (tu, você)	**You** look tired.	We (nós)	**We** like coffee.
He (ele)	**He** dances well.	You (vós, vocês)	Kids, **you** are late.
She (ela)	**She** loves me.	They (eles, elas)	**They** are at school.

File 10 — Modal Verb: *Can* (poder)

Afirmativa	Negativa	Interrogativa
I **can**	I **cannot** (I **can't**)	**Can** I?
You **can**	You **cannot** (You **can't**)	**Can** you?
He **can**	He **cannot** (He **can't**)	**Can** he?
She **can**	She **cannot** (She **can't**)	**Can** she?
It **can**	It **cannot** (It **can't**)	**Can** it?
We **can**	We **cannot** (We **can't**)	**Can** we?
You **can**	You **cannot** (You **can't**)	**Can** you?
They **can**	They **cannot** (They **can't**)	**Can** they?

Can é seguido por um verbo no infinitivo sem *to*:

I **can** work.	He **can** travel.	They **can** stay here.

1 The World's Trash

Look at the picture and answer orally.

1 What does the picture tell you about this unit?

2 What do you know about recycling?

3 What do you do about recycling?

4 Can we really throw trash away? Where is "away"?

Language in Context

1 **Take a look at the cartoon.**

2 **Give your opinion about the cartoon.**

1 What is it about?

2 Why is the father proud of Tim?

3 The mother looks surprised. Why?

3 **Read, think, and answer orally.**

Now, I'm making posters.

Alex is working on a recycling project.

We're collecting things for the campaign!

1 What do the sentences have in common?

2 Is it possible to know when the actions happen?

Vocabulary

proud: orgulhoso(a)
recycling: reciclagem
What's going on?: O que está acontecendo?

Language Practice

Present Continuous

Presente do verbo **to be** + verbo terminado em **-ing**	
I **am**	
You **are**	
He **is**	**Afirmativa:** He **is working**.
She **is**	**Interrogativa: Is** he **working**?
It **is** (working.)	**Negativa:** He **is not working**.
We **are**	**Formas abreviadas: isn't** (is not)
You **are**	**aren't** (are not)
They **are**	

Uso

Expressa ações que estão ocorrendo na atualidade.

I **am working** on a project.

He **is making** posters.

They **are reading** a magazine.

Expressa ações que estão ocorrendo no exato momento em que se fala. Pode ser usado com *now, at this moment, at present* (*time adverbs*).

It **is raining** now.

We **are waiting** for her call at this moment.

Ortografia

Alguns verbos não sofrem modificações ao receber a terminação **-ing**.

try – try**ing**   ski – ski**ing**   agree – agree**ing**

Em verbos terminados em um único **e**, elimina-se esse **e** e acrescenta-se **-ing**.

love – lov**ing**   have – hav**ing**   write – writ**ing**

Exceção: be – be**ing**

Em verbos terminados em **ie**, substitui-se o **ie** por **y** e acrescenta-se **-ing**.

die – d**ying**   tie – t**ying**   lie – l**ying**

Em verbos terminados em **consoante** + **vogal** + **consoante** em que a última sílaba é a sílaba tônica, dobra-se a última consoante e acrescenta-se **-ing**.

swim – swim**ming**   run – run**ning**   begin – begin**ning**

1 Circle the correct alternative.

1 The children **is have** / **are having** breakfast now.

2 We **are not studying** / **is studying** Portuguese at this moment.

3 Jennifer **is try** / **is trying** to help you.

4 My sister **is running** / **is run** in the park.

2 Complete the sentences using the verbs in parentheses in the Present Continuous.

1 Julie _____ (wash) her hair now. She can't answer the phone.

2 My friends _____ (ski) down the mountain.

3 The detectives _____ (try) to solve the mystery.

4 Dad _____ (work) in his office at the moment.

5 I _____ (write) them an e-mail to explain the situation.

3 Unscramble the words to make sentences.

1 the – crying – is – now – baby – right
The baby is crying right now. _____

2 moment – working – the – computer – is – my – not – at

_____

3 cleaning – I – the – am – garage

_____

4 doing – not – now – they – their – homework – are – Math

_____

4 Write the sentences below in the interrogative form.

1 He is playing tennis with his older sister.

_____

2 The girls are swimming in the lake.

_____

3 We are thinking of the same person.

_____

4 I am trying to find a solution to the problem.

_____

5 **Give complete answers to the questions.**

1 **A:** Is Peter lying to his father?

   B: No, _____ .

2 **A:** Are the girls helping their mother?

   B: Yes, _____ .

3 **A:** Is he trying to make breakfast?

   B: Yes, _____ .

4 **A:** Are the boys running?

   B: No, _____ .

5 **A:** Are you starting the Math test?

   B: Yes, _____ .

6 **A:** Are they making a poster?

   B: No, _____ .

6 **Use the words in parentheses and give complete answers to the questions.**

1 **A:** What are you doing now? (write)

   B: _____

2 **A:** What are your friends studying now? (English)

   B: _____

3 **A:** What is the teacher correcting? (a test)

   B: _____

4 **A:** Who is talking on the phone? (Peter and Jim)

   B: _____

5 **A:** Who is doing the dishes? (John)

   B: _____

Go to page 32 for Extra Practice.

Before Reading

1 **Discuss the questions below in Portuguese.**

1 How much waste do you produce in a day?

2 What are some possible destinations for the waste you produce?

3 Do you practice the 3 Rs (reduce, reuse, recycle)?

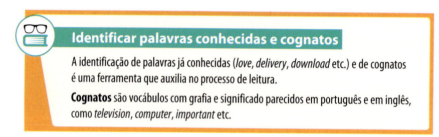

Identificar palavras conhecidas e cognatos

A identificação de palavras já conhecidas (*love, delivery, download* etc.) e de cognatos é uma ferramenta que auxilia no processo de leitura.

Cognatos são vocábulos com grafia e significado parecidos em português e em inglês, como *television, computer, important* etc.

2 Underline the cognates in the texts on page 19. Then say in Portuguese what you understand from them.

3 **Match the words in the box to their equivalent in English.**

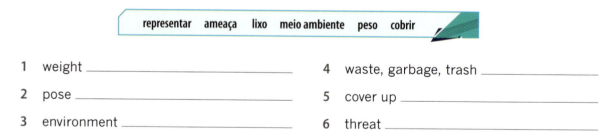

representar   ameaça   lixo   meio ambiente   peso   cobrir

1 weight _____

2 pose _____

3 environment _____

4 waste, garbage, trash _____

5 cover up _____

6 threat _____

Text A

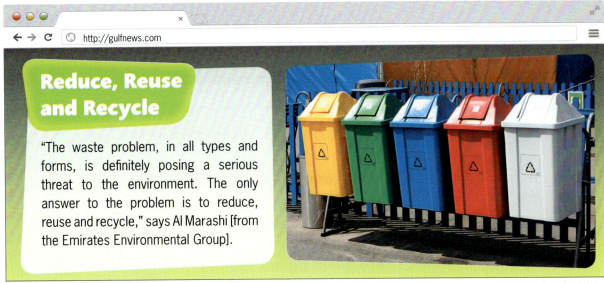

Reduce, Reuse and Recycle

"The waste problem, in all types and forms, is definitely posing a serious threat to the environment. The only answer to the problem is to reduce, reuse and recycle," says Al Marashi [from the Emirates Environmental Group].

Available at <http://gulfnews.com/in-focus/earthwatch-2.813/reduce-reuse-and-recycle-1.27233>.
Accessed on July 27, 2015.

Text B

2.6 Trillion Pounds of Garbage: Where Does the World's Trash Go?

This year, the world will generate 2.6 trillion pounds of garbage – the weight of about 7,000 Empire State Buildings. What kind of trash is it? Where does it all go?

[…]

[What's in the global garbage can?] Mostly food and paper. Organic trash – food we eat, food animals eat, horticultural waste – makes up about half of global solid waste, and paper and plastic add another 27%. […]

In both rich and poor countries, the vast majority of our waste goes into landfills, where it's (often) covered up.

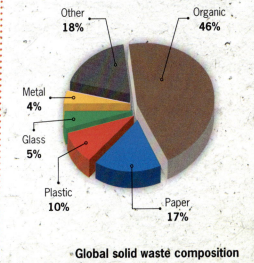

Other 18%
Organic 46%
Metal 4%
Glass 5%
Plastic 10%
Paper 17%

Global solid waste composition

Available at <www.theatlantic.com/business/archive/2012/06/26-trillion-pounds-of-garbage-where-does-the-worlds-trash-go/258234>.
Accessed on August 1, 2015.

Vocabulary

food: comida
glass: vidro

half: metade
often: geralmente

After Reading

1 **Match the columns to define the words.**

1 reduce   a [ ] to turn used objects and materials into something new

2 reuse   b [ ] to cut down on the waste that we produce

3 recycle   c [ ] to find ways of using again our unwanted items

2 **Write the meaning of the terms in bold. Use the words/expressions in the box.**

> constitui   lata   reduzir   libras   principalmente   aterros sanitários

1 The vast majority of our waste goes into **landfills**. _____

2 The global garbage **can** contains **mostly** food and paper. _____

3 The only answer to the problem is to **reduce** the use. _____

4 The world will generate 2.6 trillion **pounds** of garbage. _____

5 Organic trash **makes up** about half of global solid waste. _____

3 **Check the correct information according to the graph in text B.**

1 Most of the solid waste in the world consists of _____.

    a [ ] organic trash

    b [ ] paper

    c [ ] plastic

2 _____ and _____ are the two recyclable materials most present in global waste.

    a [ ] Glass – metal

    b [ ] Paper – plastic

    c [ ] Paper – glass

3 Recyclable materials are found _____ organic products in the waste produced around the world.

    a [ ] more frequently than

    b [ ] as frequently as

    c [ ] less frequently than

Vocabulary Expansion

1 **Read the box and write new words.**

1 to think _____

2 definition _____

3 to consider _____

4 construction _____

5 to organize _____

6 to create _____

> **Prefix re-**
>
> O prefixo *re-* é acrescentado a verbos e substantivos e indica repetição.
>
> **re**use   **re**action

2 **Rewrite the sentences adding a prefix to the words in bold. Make the necessary changes to the sentences.**

1 Are they **writing** their Science paper again?

   Are they rewriting their Science paper?

2 We are **organizing** the groups again.

   _____

3 My company is **making** that old movie again.

   _____

4 The festival is **creating** a 1960s atmosphere again.

   _____

3 **Read the box and complete the sentences.**

1 The boys are playing _____ their mother's bed.

2 My dog is running _____ the house.

3 Bob and Alice are playing _____ the living room.

4 Billy is learning _____ garbage and its impact _____ our health.

5 The teachers are talking _____ the new students.

> **about:** sobre, a respeito de
> **around:** em volta de, ao redor
> **in:** em, dentro de
> **on:** sobre, em cima de

2

Healthy Colors

Look at the picture and answer orally.

1　What does the picture tell you about this unit?

2　What is a balanced diet?

3　How would you describe your eating habits?

4　Do you think you can improve your eating habits? How?

Language in Context

1 **Take a look at the dialogue and the notes.**

🎧 (4)

Mr. Robins: What do you do in the morning, Gloria?

Gloria: I go to school.

Mr. Robins: Do you have the afternoons free?

Gloria: Yes, I do.

Mr. Robins: We have two afternoon positions: salad assistant and dishwasher. What do you know about salads?

Gloria: A good salad is fresh and colorful.

Gloria Elliot

- She goes to school in the morning.

- She has the afternoons free.

- Good candidate.

Vocabulary

assistant: assistente
dishwasher: lavador(a) de pratos

2 **Give your opinion about the dialogue.**

1 Do you think Gloria did well in the interview?

2 In your opinion, will she get the job? Why?

3 **Read, think, and answer orally.**

A	B
She goes to school in the morning. She has the afternoons free.	I go to school in the morning. I have the afternoons free.

1 What do the sentences in column A have in common?

2 What is the difference between the two groups of sentences?

Language Practice

Simple Present

Infinitivo sem *to*
3ª pessoa do singular recebe -s

I walk.	
You walk.	
He walk**s**.	
She walk**s**.	I walk in the morning.
It walk**s**.	He walk**s** in the morning.
We walk.	They walk in the morning.
You walk.	
They walk.	

Uso

Pode expressar verdades universais e ações futuras agendadas.

Dogs **bark**.

Wood **floats**.

Your bus **comes** at 4:15 p.m.

Expressa ações habituais ou que se repetem no presente.

Geralmente usado com *always, often, usually, frequently, sometimes, never, seldom, every day, on Mondays* etc.

I <u>always</u> **arrive** early.

He **calls** her late at night <u>every day</u>.

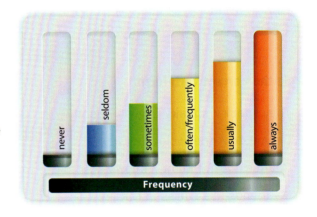

Ortografia

A maioria dos verbos forma a 3ª pessoa do singular com o acréscimo de **-s**.

work – work**s**   live – live**s**   play – play**s**

Se o verbo termina em **ss**, **sh**, **ch**, **x**, **z** ou **o**, acrescenta-se **-es**.

kiss – kiss**es**   teach – teach**es**   buzz – buzz**es**

wash – wash**es**   fix – fix**es**   do – do**es**

Se o verbo termina em **y** precedido de **consoante**, troca-se o **y** por **ies**.

try – tr**ies**   study – stud**ies**   hurry – hurr**ies**

A 3ª pessoa do singular do verbo *have* é **has**.

She **has** many friends at school.

Verbos auxiliares

Do/Does

Afirmativa	You work.	He works.
Interrogativa	**Do** you work?	**Does** he work?
Negativa	You **do not** work.	He **does not** work.
Formas abreviadas	**don't** (do not)	**doesn't** (does not)

Nota
Do e **does** não têm tradução quando possuem a função de auxiliares.

1 Circle the verbs in the 3rd person singular.

I work in a bank and my friend John works there too. I walk to work, but John goes by bus. We sometimes meet at the cafeteria and have a cup of coffee together. After work, I go to night school and study until late. John has more fun. He plays football with his friends or goes dancing. But I want a better job, so while he plays, I learn.

2 Circle the correct verb form.

1 They **speak** / **speaks** English fluently.

2 Do you **do** / **does** voluntary work?

3 Charles doesn't **know** / **knows** how to use the computer.

4 My friends **live** / **lives** in Dublin.

5 He **is** / **are** a doctor and **work** / **works** in a large hospital.

6 My brother **don't like** / **doesn't like** his job.

3 Complete the sentences using the verbs in parentheses in the Simple Present.

1 My brother _____ (hurry) to school every morning.

2 Janet _____ (work) from 8:00 a.m. to 6:00 p.m.

3 In her free time she _____ (play) rugby.

4 I often _____ (have) to work on Saturdays.

5 What do you _____ (do) in the morning?

6 We _____ (wash – neg.) our dog every week.

4 Complete the sentences.

1 (apples/pears)

He doesn't like apples. He _____ likes pears _____.

2 (morning/afternoon)

They don't swim in the morning. They _____.

3 (Chemistry/Physics)

She doesn't study Chemistry. She _____.

4 (pub/restaurant)

We don't work in a pub. We _____.

5 (French/English)

I _____. I speak English.

6 (meat/sardines)

My cat _____. It eats sardines.

5 Check the correct question.

1 Jimmy reads books after school.

a ☐ When does Jimmy read books?

b ☐ What is Jimmy doing?

2 Yes, I do. I use the computer every day.

a ☐ What do you do every day?

b ☐ Do you use the computer every day?

3 Denise works at the hospital.

a ☐ When does Denise work at the hospital?

b ☐ Where does Denise work?

4 We go to school in the morning.

a ☐ Where do you go in the morning?

b ☐ Do you go to school in the morning?

5 No, he doesn't have coffee in the morning.

a ☐ Does he have coffee in the morning?

b ☐ When does he have coffee?

Go to page 32 for Extra Practice.

Before Reading

Relacionar experiências pessoais, imagens e texto

As experiências de vida auxiliam o contato do leitor com o texto. Os elementos visuais, por sua vez, podem ajudar na compreensão do vocabulário e das ideias presentes no texto.

1 Check the statements that are true for you.

1 ☐ I like all types of food, including fruits, vegetables, and grains.

2 ☐ Fast food is my favorite kind of food. I eat it a lot.

3 ☐ I don't like to eat green food.

2 Look at the text and the pictures. Then write the meaning of the food items below.

1 strawberry _____

2 carrot _____

3 cauliflower _____

4 beet _____

5 grapes _____

6 tomato _____

3 Write the meaning of the words below. Use the glossary.

1 bone _____

2 blood _____

3 heart _____

4 bowel _____

Healthy Food

Some people classify food according to the food pyramid: fats, sugars, proteins, fibers, and grains. Others classify them according to food types: fruit, meat, fish, and vegetables. Modern dieticians go back to the teachings of our great-grandmothers and say that food has to be colorful.

The color of food is determined by pigments. Pigments not only color fruit, vegetables, and other foods, but also protect our organism against diseases.

Purple food
- Contains anthocyanin.
- Delays aging.

beet
grapes
cabbage
plum
fig

Red food
- Contains lycopene, a potent antioxidant.
- Protects against some types of cancer.
- Stimulates blood circulation.

watermelon
strawberry
tomato
cherry
guava

White food
- Contains potassium and vitamin C.
- Helps reduce the risk of cancer.

cauliflower
banana
milk
rice
cheese
potato
mushrooms

Green food
- Contains vitamin A.
- Helps in the formation and maintenance of bones.

green vegetables and herbs

Brown food
- Contains vitamins B and E.
- Prevents anxiety and depression.
- Reduces the risk of cancer and heart diseases.
- Provides for better bowel functioning.

nuts
chestnut
cereal
oatmeal

Orange/ Yellow food
- Contains beta-carotene.
- Protects the eyes and the skin.

mango
peach
apricot
papaya
carrot
pumpkin
orange

Based on <www.naturalwellness.com/nwupdate/colorful-nutrition-top-5-purple-foods>; <www.naturalwellness.com/nwupdate/rainbow-nutrition-10-red-foods-to-enhance-your-health>; <www.diabetesforecast.org/2011/aug/eating-colorful-food-has-health-benefits.html>; <www.organicfacts.net/health-benefits/other/health-benefits-of-oatmeal.html>. Accessed on July 27, 2015.

 Vocabulary

delay: retardar	**functioning:** funcionamento	**maintenance:** manutenção	**provide for:** propiciar

After Reading

1 **Read the magazine article on pages 28 and 29 and find seven cognates.**

_____

_____

2 **Write the meaning of the terms in bold. Use the words in the box.**

| envelhecimento | doenças | colorida | previne |

1 Dieticians say that food has to be **colorful**. _____

2 Pigments protect our organism against **diseases**. _____

3 Purple food, such as beet and plum, delays **aging**. _____

4 Brown food **prevents** anxiety and depression. _____

 Scanning

Fazer _scanning_ significa passar os olhos rapidamente pelo texto para encontrar informações como dados específicos, nomes, datas etc.

3 **Read the text and complete the sentences.**

1 _____White food_____ helps reduce the risk of cancer.

2 _____ helps in the formation of bones.

3 _____ stimulates blood circulation.

4 _____ protects the eyes and the skin.

5 _____ reduces the risk of heart diseases.

4 **Answer the questions according to the magazine article.**

1 What is lycopene?

_____

2 What does orange/yellow food contain?

_____

3 What types of food reduce the risk of cancer?

_____

4 What type of food delays aging?

_____

Scan this QR code to learn about five items of food you can eat to make your diet healthier.

Vocabulary Expansion

1 **Read the box. Then make new words using the ones in parentheses to complete the sentences.**

1 Children love to play with _____ (color) toys.

2 A _____ (success) businesswoman will speak at the conference.

3 Our country is _____ (beauty), especially its beaches.

4 Be _____ (care)! This vase is made of glass!

2 **Fill in the blanks with the prepositions from the box.**

1 He's _____ all kinds of prejudice.

2 This is important for the functioning _____ the heart.

3 They go _____ Santos to São Paulo every day.

against: contra
from: de (origem)
of: de (posse, parte)

3 **Read the information in the box and complete the sentences.**

Phrasal Verb	To go
Um *phrasal verb* é um verbo acrescido de uma partícula que lhe dá um significado diferente do seu significado original.	**go back** = return (voltar)
	go by = pass (passar – tempo)
	go on = continue (continuar)
	go out = leave (sair)

1 My grandma is 78 and still _____ a lot.

2 I can't _____ sleeping so little: I'm too exhausted.

3 It's late. I have to _____ home.

4 A vacation always _____ quickly.

4 **Check the opposite of the words in bold.**

1 Brown food **reduces** the risk of cancer.

a ☐ equals   b ☐ increases   c ☐ diminishes

2 Vegetables and fruits **protect** our organism.

a ☐ look after   b ☐ take care   c ☐ attack

3 This procedure **prevents** risks.

a ☐ blocks   b ☐ poses   c ☐ stops

attack: atacar
increase: aumentar
pose: representar

Extra Practice 1

1 **Answer the questions to describe the scene below.**

1 What are Gary and Janet doing?

_____

2 What's Susan washing?

_____

3 Who's making posters?

_____

4 Where's Carla writing letters?

_____

2 **Ask questions about the expressions in bold. Use the box for help.**

1 The baby is crying **at the front door**.

_____

2 The dog is **running after** the cat.

_____

3 Stella is eating **a sandwich**.

_____

3 Complete the text using the verbs in parentheses in the Present Continuous.

From the top of the hill I can see the village in the valley: the houses, the streets, everything. The children _____ (play) in the schoolyard.

Mr. Gardner _____ (talk) to a friend.

Some ladies _____ (walk) to church. Some people _____ (run) around the lake.

The Taylors _____ (open) their store now and Mrs. Swanson _____ certainly _____ (buy) some bread for breakfast.

It's 8 a.m. now and the sun _____ (shine) brightly. I am here on the top of the hill.

I _____ (think) about my life.

Vocabulary

everything: tudo, todas as coisas
schoolyard: pátio da escola
shine: brilhar
top of the hill: topo da colina

4 **Check the correct synonym for the words in bold.**

1 Londoners are recycling their **waste**.

a ☐ campaign

b ☐ garbage

c ☐ project

2 Institutions are collecting great **quantities** of used paper.

a ☐ some

b ☐ ton

c ☐ amounts

3 The amount of garbage is **growing** around the world.

a ☐ increasing

b ☐ starting

c ☐ collecting

4 Governments are trying to **diminish** the quantity of garbage.

a ☐ learn

b ☐ launch

c ☐ reduce

5 Tarsila do Amaral is **regarded** as one of the major artists of the 20th century.

a ☐ protected

b ☐ considered

c ☐ combined

6 My cousin works in a **large**, modern office downtown.

a ☐ near

b ☐ big

c ☐ select

7 Carol is **determined** that this semester things will be different.

a ☐ lazy

b ☐ quiet

c ☐ insistent

5 **Write these sentences in the negative form.**

1 He needs to eat more white food to protect his bones.

   _____

2 They want to have a sandwich for lunch.

   _____

3 She prefers salad for dinner.

   _____

6 **Write these sentences in the interrogative form. Then answer them using short forms.**

1 He always eats salad.
   Does he always eat salad?
   Yes, he does.

2 We usually arrive late.

   _____

   _____

3 It rarely eats fish.

   _____

   _____

4 The kids frequently wash their hands.

   _____

   _____

5 Alice doesn't go to school in the afternoon.

   _____

   _____

7 **Complete the sentences using the Simple Present or the Present Continuous.**

1 This pigment _____ (reduce) the risk of cancer.

2 They _____ (go) to school by bus today.

3 Marian never _____ (eat) fish.

4 Alice _____ (read) the newspaper every morning.

5 Look! Sylvia _____ (make) bread for the children.

8 Read the text about Janet. Then write a similar one about Chuck. Use the information in the fact file.

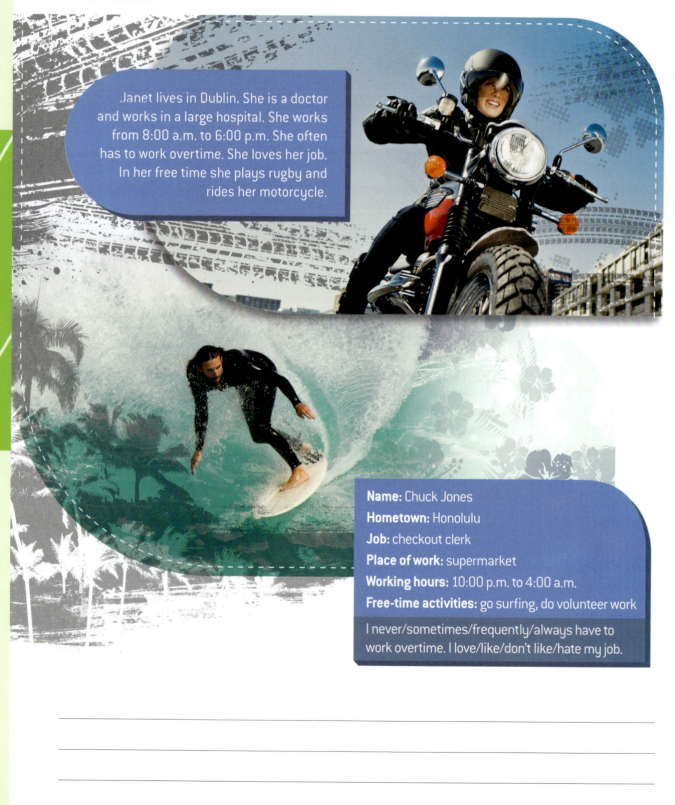

Janet lives in Dublin. She is a doctor and works in a large hospital. She works from 8:00 a.m. to 6:00 p.m. She often has to work overtime. She loves her job. In her free time she plays rugby and rides her motorcycle.

Name: Chuck Jones
Hometown: Honolulu
Job: checkout clerk
Place of work: supermarket
Working hours: 10:00 p.m. to 4:00 a.m.
Free-time activities: go surfing, do volunteer work

I never/sometimes/frequently/always have to work overtime. I love/like/don't like/hate my job.

CV

A CV or résumé is an important part of getting a job. It gives you an opportunity to sell yourself to potential employers.

Submit your résumé with a cover letter and one or more letters of reference.

GEORGE JAMESON

Brazilian, single,

18 years old

(address)

(telephone number)

(e-mail address)

Objective

✔ Seeking a position as a receptionist in a department that rewards hard work.

Education

✔ (name and address of the school) High school diploma, 2015

Work Experience

✔ (year and name of the company) Receptionist

Skills

✔ Receive phone calls and direct them to the appropriate departments.
✔ Arrange appointments between clients and employees.
✔ Receive and distribute mail and messages to appropriate departments and employees.

References

✔ References and letters of recommendation available on request.

Based on <www.essortment.com/example-good-resume-bad-one-34357.html>.
Accessed on July 27, 2015.

Vocabulary

appointment: compromisso
available: disponível
CV: *curriculum vitae*
employee: empregado(a)
request: solicitação
résumé: currículo
reward: recompensar
seek: procurar

3

Amazon River Dolphin

Look at the picture and answer orally.

1   What does the picture tell you about this unit?

2   What do you know about the Amazon rainforest?

3   Which animals can be found there?

4   Is deforestation a problem in the region? Why?

Language in Context

1 Take a look at the cartoon.

2 Give your opinion about the cartoon.

1 Where are they?

2 Are the girls going fishing together?

3 Why is one of the boys frightened?

3 Read, think, and answer orally.

What are you going to do today?
I'm going to get out of here!

1 What do the sentences have in common?

2 Do the sentences refer to the present, the past, or the future?

Language Practice

Future with *Going to*

Presente do verbo *to be* + *going to* + verbo	
I **am** You **are** He **is** She **is** It **is** We **are** You **are** They **are**	**going to** swim.

Afirmativa: He **is going to** swim.

Interrogativa: Is he **going to** swim?

Negativa: He **is not going to** swim.

Formas abreviadas: isn't (is not)

aren't (are not)

Uso

Expressa intenção futura provável de se concretizar ou ação futura planejada.

She **is going to travel** in two weeks.

They **are going to study** tomorrow.

I **am going to play** volleyball after class.

We **are going to meet** Paul tonight.

Geralmente vem acompanhado de advérbios de tempo como *tomorrow*, *next…*, *in…* etc.

What is going to happen next?

---

1 **Complete the sentences using the future with *going to*.**

1 I am not studying now. I _____ am going to study _____ later.

2 She is not swimming now. She _____ tomorrow.

3 They are not reading at this moment. They _____ after lunch.

4 We are not leaving now. We _____ in twenty minutes.

5 It is not raining now, but it _____ in the afternoon.

2 Match the pictures to the sentences.

1 ☐ She is going to buy some bread.

2 ☐ She is going to write her mother an e-mail.

3 ☐ We are going to have a picnic.

4 ☐ She is going to have dental treatment.

5 ☐ I am going to study for my Geography test.

Object Pronouns

Subject Pronouns	Object Pronouns
I	me
you	you
he	him
she	her
it	it
we	us
you	you
they	them

Uso

Funcionam como objeto da oração. São usados após um verbo ou uma preposição.

I love **her**.

She always talks about **me**.

Quando o verbo tem dois objetos, usa-se uma destas construções:

Give the book to **her**.

Give **her** the book.

3 Circle the correct pronoun.

1 Leo wants to talk to **we** / **us**, but **we** / **us** don't want to talk to **he** / **him**.

2 **She** / **Her** is waiting for **me** / **I**.

3 Do you want to see **him** / **he**?

4 **I** / **Me** meet **she** / **her** at the cafeteria every day.

5 The children are sick. Don't let **them** / **they** go to the park.

4 **Use the appropriate object pronoun to complete the sentences.**

1 I want that book. Can you buy _____ for me, please?

2 I never visit the Johnsons. I don't know _____ very well.

3 I really like Brenda. I always speak to _____ during the break.

4 Do you want Jason to help you? Then be nice to _____.

5 Wait a minute, Frank. I have to talk to _____.

6 We want to know all about your trip, so don't forget to write to _____.

Imperative

Infinitivo sem *to*

Afirmativa: Wash your hands!

Negativa: Don't wash the dog here!

Uso

Expressa ordem, comando ou pedido.

> **Don't come** home late.
>
> **Call** me tonight.
>
> **Close** the door, please.

5 **Write sentences using the Imperative.**

1 Ask a friend to open the window.
   Open the window, please.

2 Ask a friend to bring you the Science book.

3 Tell your friend not to copy your homework.

4 Tell your friend not to close the door.

5 Tell your friend not to forget to call you.

6 Ask your friend to send you a postcard.

Go to page 58 for Extra Practice.

Reading

Before Reading

1 **Discuss the questions below in Portuguese.**

1 Have you ever seen a pink dolphin?

2 Are pink dolphins really pink?

3 Can you name at least one factor that can endanger this species?

> **Fazer antecipações**
>
> Fazer antecipações sobre o conteúdo de um texto ativa os conhecimentos do leitor sobre o assunto, contribuindo para a compreensão do texto.

2 **The texts on page 45 are about the Amazon river dolphin. Check the words you might find in them.**

- [ ] brain
- [ ] fishermen
- [ ] forest
- [ ] freshwater
- [ ] hunter
- [ ] hydroelectric
- [ ] ocean
- [ ] repellent
- [ ] sunscreen
- [ ] swim
- [ ] tourists
- [ ] zoo

> **Identificar características e tipo de texto**
>
> Identificar os elementos que caracterizam determinado tipo de texto ajuda o leitor a contextualizá-lo e compreendê-lo.

3 **Look at text A and check its characteristics.**

a [ ] A single topic discussed by different writers.

b [ ] Formal language.

c [ ] Regular posts by a single writer about a topic.

d [ ] Presence of date and time in each segment.

e [ ] Writers identified by nicknames and avatars.

4 **A text with the characteristics that you checked in activity 3 can be considered…**

a [ ] a blog.

b [ ] an online forum.

c [ ] an online magazine.

Text A

TRAVELING TIPS

AdventurousPete | Aug. 20, 2015, 7:48 p.m.
Exploring the Amazon River, Need Tips!
Hey, guys! I'm going on a cruise on the Amazon river, then I'm going to visit some cities near Manaus. What should I wear? Do you have any tips for me?

ExpertTraveler | Aug. 20, 2015, 8:52 p.m.
Wear long pants and long-sleeved shirts. Bring a hat and stay covered. Don't forget to wear sunscreen and bug repellent as well.

mike_on_the_road | Aug. 21, 2015, 9:15 a.m.
Your trip sounds great, AdventurousPete. My girlfriend and I are going to travel to Manaus next month. Do you guys think we are going to see river dolphins?

chris_around_the_world | Aug. 21, 2015, 11:36 a.m.
Go by car to Novo Airão, on the banks of Rio Negro, not far from Manaus (180 km). It is the land of the pink dolphins.

nicks_trips | Aug. 21, 2015, 5:56 p.m.
I'm going to swim with pink dolphins on my next trip! Did you know that most of them are actually pink?! Their color varies from grey to pink according to their age and the characteristics of the water. Besides being very cute, pink dolphins are also very smart! Their brain capacity is 40% larger than that of humans!

Text B

www.wwf.org

Amazon/Pink River Dolphin

The Amazon river dolphin is a freshwater dolphin found in the Amazon and Orinoco Rivers, in South America. Also known as *boto*, it is one of the world's three dolphins that only inhabit freshwater.

5 Historically, the *boto* has not been persecuted by humans because of the belief that it has special powers. Today, however, it is increasingly viewed by fishermen as an unwanted competitor for fish. It can also get caught in fishing nets or get hurt by colliding with boats.

In addition to this, its habitat is currently threatened by river development projects. Hydroelectric and irrigation schemes separate rivers in bodies of waters, which may reduce
10 the species' range and its ability to breed.

Adapted from <wwf.panda.org/what_we_do/endangered_species/cetaceans/about/river_dolphins/pink_river_dolphin>.
Accessed on August 27, 2015.

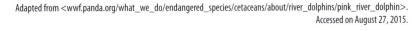

Vocabulary

bank: margem	**fisherman:** pescador	**range:** alcance
belief: crença	**freshwater:** água doce	**sunscreen:** protetor solar
bug repellent: repelente de insetos	**long-sleeved:** de manga longa	**threaten:** ameaçar

After Reading

1 Match the words to their definition.

1	tips	☐	at the present time
2	inhabit	☐	live in
3	persecuted	☐	annoyed or hurt
4	unwanted	☐	useful pieces of advice or suggestions
5	currently	☐	procreate; reproduce
6	breed	☐	not desired

2 Write T (true) or F (false), according to text B.

1 ☐ Pink dolphins are found in rivers and oceans.

2 ☐ *Botos* are believed to have special powers, which helps the species to survive.

3 ☐ There is currently more than one threat to the survival of pink dolphins.

4 ☐ Some power generation processes may make it difficult for *botos* to reproduce.

3 Answer in Portuguese.

1 Why do some fishermen view the pink dolphin as a competitor?

_____

2 How do hydroelectric and irrigation schemes threaten pink dolphins?

_____

_____

4 Check the correct alternative.

1 The word "however" in "*Today, **however**, it is increasingly viewed by fishermen as an unwanted competitor for fish*" (text B, lines 5-6) conveys the idea of...

a	☐ addition.	c	☐ contrast.
b	☐ consequence.	d	☐ time.

2 The word "also" in "*It can **also** get caught in fishing nets [...]*" (text B, lines 6-7) expresses the idea of...

a	☐ addition.	c	☐ contrast.
b	☐ consequence.	d	☐ time.

Vocabulary Expansion

1 Look at the pictures, read the box, and complete the sentences.

1 Lucy is _____ Paul and John.

2 The table is _____ the window.

3 The cat is _____ the stool.

4 The girl is _____ her brother.

Prepositions of Place

behind: atrás   **near:** perto de
between: entre   **under:** embaixo de

2 Substitute the words in bold for an opposite. Use the box for help.

1 The hotel is **behind** the school. _____

2 There are clothes **on** the chair. _____

3 They are going to live **near** the library. _____

4 The papers are **on** her desk. _____

5 There is a river **near** the camping site. _____

far from: longe de
in front of: na frente de
under: embaixo de

3 Read the box and complete the sentences using *by* or *on*.

1 She always travels _____ car.

2 My sister is going to the beach _____ bus.

3 The children usually go to school _____ foot.

4 We are going to visit the countryside next week. We are going _____ bus.

5 He is afraid of traveling _____ plane.

6 Kylie and her son go to the park _____ foot every day.

Means of Transportation

by bus: de ônibus   **by plane:** de avião
by car: de carro   **on foot:** a pé

4 Prejudice

Look at the picture and answer orally.

1   What does the picture tell you about this unit?

2   How would you define "prejudice"?

3   What kinds of prejudice can you think of?

4   How can prejudice affect a person's life?

Language in Context

1 Take a look at the cartoon.

2 Give your opinion about the cartoon.

1 What kind of prejudice is represented in the cartoon?

2 Were the boys sexist? How do you know?

3 Read, think, and answer orally.

Look! He twisted and jumped. Cool!

1 What do the verbs in the sentence have in common?

2 Does the sentence refer to the present, the past, or the future?

Language Practice

Simple Past – Regular Verbs

Verbo + **-ed/-d**	
I You He She It We You They	**worked**.	**Afirmativa:** He work**ed**. **Interrogativa: Did** he **work**? **Negativa:** He **did not work**. **Forma abreviada: didn't** (did not)

Uso

Expressa hábitos passados.

> I **walked** to school when I was a child.

> Every year they **traveled** to Bahia for their summer vacation.

Expressa ações passadas que já foram concluídas ou que ocorreram em um momento definido no passado.

É geralmente usado com *yesterday*, *last…*, *… ago*, *in…* etc.

> She **arrived** late <u>yesterday</u>.

> <u>Last night</u> they **called** to cancel the meeting.

Ortografia

Alguns verbos não sofrem modificações na grafia: apenas acrescenta-se a terminação **-ed** a eles. No caso dos verbos terminados em **e**, acrescenta-se apenas **-d**.

play – play**ed**	love – love**d**
want – want**ed**	agree – agree**d**

Em verbos terminados em **y** precedido de consoante, elimina-se esse **y** e acrescenta-se **-ied**.

study – stud**ied**	carry – carr**ied**
cry – cr**ied**	try – tr**ied**

Em verbos terminados em **consoante** + **vogal** + **consoante** em que a última sílaba é a sílaba tônica, dobra-se a última consoante e acrescenta-se **-ed**.

permit – permit**ted**	occur – occur**red**
stop – stop**ped**	drop – drop**ped**

1 Write the verbs below in the Simple Past.

1 admire _____

2 miss _____

3 prefer _____

4 try _____

5 match _____

6 identify _____

7 admit _____

8 rain _____

9 share _____

10 act _____

11 pause _____

12 compose _____

2 Complete the sentences using the verbs in parentheses in the Simple Past.

1 Yesterday we _____ (dance) the whole evening at the party.

2 Julie _____ (ignore) me after the concert.

3 He _____ (shower) and _____ (dress) quickly because he was already late.

4 Last Saturday they _____ (wait) for Linda, but she didn't show up.

5 The kids _____ (watch) TV and _____ (play) video games two days ago.

6 I _____ (clean) the kitchen before going to bed.

3 Rewrite the sentences in the negative form.

1 The scientists developed a new theory.

   _____

2 Martha answered her e-mails this morning.

   _____

3 She checked the time of the flight before leaving.

   _____

4 I listened to the band's new album last night.

   _____

5 He promised to find a solution to the problem.

   _____

6 They failed their History test last week.

   _____

4 **Rewrite the sentences using the Simple Past.**

1 My mother loves Japanese food.

　　_____

2 They never ask the waitress about reservations.

　　_____

3 My girlfriend calls me every day.

　　_____

4 Do you travel to the island by boat?

　　_____

5 He stops at the grocery store and asks for some sandwiches.

　　_____

5 **Check the correct question for each of the answers below.**

1 Baron de Coubertin helped revive the Olympic Games.

　a ☐ What did Baron de Coubertin help revive?

　b ☐ When did Baron de Coubertin help revive the Olympic Games?

2 No, the police didn't identify the criminal.

　a ☐ Who did the police identify?

　b ☐ Did the police identify the criminal?

3 We studied Geography in the library yesterday.

　a ☐ Did you study yesterday?

　b ☐ Where did you study Geography yesterday?

4 Yes, they did.

　a ☐ Did the children wash their hands before dinner?

　b ☐ When did the children wash their hands?

5 Brenda arrived home after lunch.

　a ☐ Did Brenda arrive home after lunch?

　b ☐ When did Brenda arrive home?

Go to page 58 for Extra Practice.

Reading

Before Reading

1 **Discuss the questions below in Portuguese.**

1 Have you ever experienced a situation of prejudice?

2 Do you think prejudice is learned or innate?

3 Is one type of prejudice worse than the others?

2 **Check the cognates in the list below.**

☐ prejudice   ☐ discrimination   ☐ mistaken

☐ belief   ☐ disabilities   ☐ homophobic

☐ make up   ☐ town   ☐ innate

☐ actually   ☐ former   ☐ skin

☐ stereotypes   ☐ monkey   ☐ noticed

> 👓 **Identificar o objetivo principal do texto**
>
> Identificar qual é o objetivo principal de um texto é uma habilidade fundamental para o processo de leitura. Saber por que e para quem o texto foi escrito pode ajudar em sua compreensão.

3 👓 **Look at the five texts on the next page. Then check the correct alternative.**

1 Altogether, the texts are mostly...

a ☐ critical.   b ☐ informative.   c ☐ opinative.

2 Which text presents the definition of a word?

a ☐ Text A.   c ☐ Text C.   e ☐ Text E.

b ☐ Text B.   d ☐ Text D.

3 Which text is based on an academic study?

a ☐ Text A.   c ☐ Text C.   e ☐ Text E.

b ☐ Text B.   d ☐ Text D.

Text A

PREJUDICE

Prejudice refers to the belief that one group of people is in some way inferior to another. The word "prejudice" comes from the Latin *prae-* (in advance) and *judicium* (judgment), so it means to judge before. When we "pre-judge" someone, we make up our minds about who they are before we actually get to know them. Prejudice often originates from stereotypes and leads to different kinds of discrimination, based on characteristics like gender, race, age, sexual orientation, social class, and disabilities.

Adapted from <www.ehow.com/list_7467177_different-types-prejudice.html>. Accessed on September 2, 2015.

Text B

> When they called me a 'stinking black' and 'black trash' I put up with it, but when they started making monkey noises, it was too much.

Goalkeeper Aranha, in a statement after the game

Available at <http://fusion.net/story/69547/abuse-by-gremio-fans-highlighted-the-fact-that-racism-is-doing-just-fine-in-brazil>. Accessed on September 2, 2015.

Text C

Taliban militants attacked Malala Yousafzai, a fourteen-year-old campaigner for education for girls in Mingora, a town in Pakistan. "She was just the girl who wanted to go to school," the former editor of the Urdu Web site of BBC World Service said.

Adapted from <www.newyorker.com/news/news-desk/the-girl-who-wanted-to-go-to-school>. Accessed on September 2, 2015.

Text D

NEWS FATHER AND SON MISTAKEN FOR GAY COUPLE ATTACKED BY HOMOPHOBIC MEN

Based on <http://oglobo.globo.com/brasil/pai-filho-sao-confundidos-com-casal-gay-agredidos-por-grupo-em-sao-joao-da-boa-vista-sp-2714592>. Accessed on September 2, 2015.

Text E

PREJUDICE: INNATE OR LEARNED?

According to Robinson and Bowman (1997), differences in skin color are first noticed when children are about two or three years old, even though they do not attach meaning to these differences. Young children often play
5 together and make friends regardless of cultural, racial, and social backgrounds. Unfortunately, prejudice is learned and by the time they are in the fourth or fifth grade, these same children often separate in traditional racial/cultural groups.

Adapted from <http://ag.arizona.edu/sfcs/cyfernet/nowg/sc_valdiv.html>. Accessed on September 2, 2015.

Vocabulary

actually: na verdade, de fato
attach: atribuir
disability: deficiência
former: anterior, ex-
mistake: confundir
prejudice: preconceito
skin: pele
town: cidade

After Reading

1 **According to text A, an act of prejudice is...**

a ☐ the result of inferior thinking.

b ☐ a consequence of discrimination.

c ☐ a possible result of stereotypes.

> **Scan this QR code to learn about the prejudice behind some English expressions.**

2 **Texts B, C, and D mention discrimination against which groups of people?**

_____

3 **Based on text D, it is possible to affirm that...**

a ☐ homophobic men are homosexuals.

b ☐ some men believed the father and the son were homosexuals.

c ☐ some men believed the father and the son were homophobic.

d ☐ the father and the son are homosexuals.

e ☐ the father and the son attacked homosexual men.

> **Reconhecer o significado de conectivos**
>
> Identificar o significado de palavras de ligação auxilia no reconhecimento da relação entre as frases, facilitando a percepção de como a argumentação foi desenvolvida.

4 **What is the best definition of the expression "regardless of" (text E, line 5)?**

a ☐ because of

b ☐ contrary to

c ☐ without the influence of

d ☐ resulting in

5 **Write T (true) or F (false), according to text E.**

1 ☐ Children that notice racial differences the most are below the age of three.

2 ☐ Different racial characteristics don't prevent three-year-olds from being friends.

3 ☐ Robinson and Bowman believe prejudice is innate.

4 ☐ Children in the fifth grade often get together in similar ethnic groups.

Vocabulary Expansion

Suffixes *-ion* and *-ation*

Os sufixos *-ion* e *-ation* formam substantivos, indicando "ato de" ou "estado de".
opt – opt**ion**   gradu**ate** – gradu**ation**

1 **Read the box and write new words.**

1 act _____
2 create _____
3 attract _____
4 operate _____

5 separate _____
6 irritate _____
7 protect _____
8 invent _____

2 **Read the information in the box. Then write the meaning of "just" in the sentences below.**

1 Wait **just** a moment, please. _____
2 You didn't pay a **just** price for this book. _____
3 It's **just** impossible to finish this task on time. _____
4 He's not angry. He's **just** tired. _____
5 The coach is a **just** person. _____
6 I have **just** enough money to buy a car. _____

Just

fair: He is a **just** man.
only: We are **just** friends.
simply: It's **just** beautiful.

3 **Read the information in the box. Then match the correct meaning of "like" to the sentences below.**

1 ☐ She is a nurse, but she sings **like** a professional singer.
2 ☐ He **liked** his girlfriend a lot, everyone could see it.
3 ☐ Did you **like** the new episode of the series?
4 ☐ I cried **like** a child watching that movie yesterday.
5 ☐ They acted **like** they didn't believe anything we were saying.

Like

a gostar
b como se fosse

4 **Complete the sentences with the words from the box.**

| make up   noticed   backgrounds   unfortunately |

1 _____, he didn't have time to explain the situation before he left.
2 He _____ something was wrong when he saw the look on their faces.
3 The class had students from different social and cultural _____.
4 You have to _____ your mind and choose one of the options.

Extra Practice 2

1 **Complete the sentences.**

1 I hear them but _____ *they don't hear me* _____.

2 She likes him but _____.

3 They can see us but _____.

4 You love her but _____.

5 He listens to her but _____.

6 The kids help me but _____.

2 **Rewrite the sentences in the negative form.**

1 Give her this letter, please.

    _____

2 Write it in your notebook.

    _____

3 Help him choose a shirt.

    _____

4 Call me after dinner.

    _____

3 **Complete the note below using the verbs in parentheses in the Imperative.**

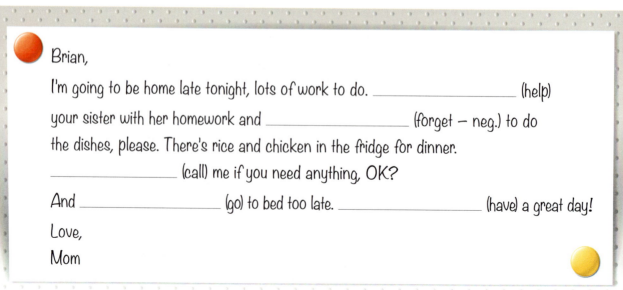

Brian,

I'm going to be home late tonight, lots of work to do. _____ (help)
your sister with her homework and _____ (forget – neg.) to do
the dishes, please. There's rice and chicken in the fridge for dinner.
_____ (call) me if you need anything, OK?
And _____ (go) to bed too late. _____ (have) a great day!
Love,
Mom

4 Rewrite the sentences in the negative and interrogative forms.

1 He is going to have dinner at home.

He is not/isn't going to have dinner at home.

Is he going to have dinner at home?

2 Robert is going to visit his friends in Italy.

_____

_____

3 They are going to work on their Science project tomorrow.

_____

_____

4 He is going to play volleyball with his friends next Wednesday.

_____

_____

5 Marian is going to move to Paris next year.

_____

_____

6 I am going to live with my grandma in Curitiba.

_____

_____

5 What are their New Year's resolutions?

1 Patricia is 22 years old. She wants to run the New York marathon in November, but she smokes one pack of cigarettes a day.

(quit/smoking) She's going to quit smoking.

2 Jane is 18 years old. She eats a lot of fast food and is having health problems.

(eat/healthy food) _____

3 Raphael is 17 years old. He wants to study in England, but he speaks little English.

(study/hard) _____

4 Peter is 25 years old. He wants to buy a house, but he spends a lot of money.

(save/more money) _____

6 **What about you? What are your resolutions for this year?**

_____

_____

7 **Write questions using the words in parentheses.**

1 They are going to read a novel in the library.

(Where) Where are they going to read a novel? ____

2 Linda is going to help me fill in this form.

(Who) _____

3 He is going to have a garage sale on Sunday.

(What) _____

4 We are going to visit grandpa next week.

(What) _____

5 Lauren is going to stay at her cousin's house.

(Where) _____

6 My parents are going to come back tonight.

(When) _____

8 **Rewrite the sentences using _going to_ and adjusting the time adverbs.**

1 He usually works in the morning.
   He's going to work tomorrow morning. ____

2 She always travels to Bahia in January.

   _____

3 They often watch a lot of movies in the summer.

   _____

4 He always takes a nap in the afternoon.

   _____

5 They play basketball in the park on Sundays.

   _____

6 She listens to some podcasts every day.

   _____

9 Rewrite the sentences using the Simple Past.

1 The doctor calls the police when she notices something unusual.

_____

2 My father never agrees with me.

_____

3 The local community complains when factories close.

_____

4 My sister cries every time I stop talking to her.

_____

5 The guests rarely enjoy Julia's parties.

_____

6 The couple welcomes their new neighbors.

_____

10 Rewrite the sentences in the interrogative form.

1 The police stopped them on their way to the concert.
   Did the police stop them on their way to
   the concert?

2 The flood destroyed many houses in the city.

_____

3 The photographers started taking pictures when he opened the car door.

_____

4 Ralph wanted to study abroad at that time.

_____

5 The principal talked to the students in the morning.

_____

6 Marisa and Jim stretched before going for a run.

_____

11 Use the prompts to write sentences in the Simple Past.

1   my friend / work / as a DJ / last year / .
    My friend worked as a DJ last year.
    _____

2   What / you / study / last night / ?
    _____

3   Vicky / walk / to work / yesterday / .
    _____

4   Why / the baby / cry / five minutes ago / ?
    _____

12 Number the messages to put the conversation in order.

Job Corner 2

Cover Letter

A cover letter accompanies your résumé and introduces you to the employer. It explains why you are interested in the job and includes information on how you can be contacted.

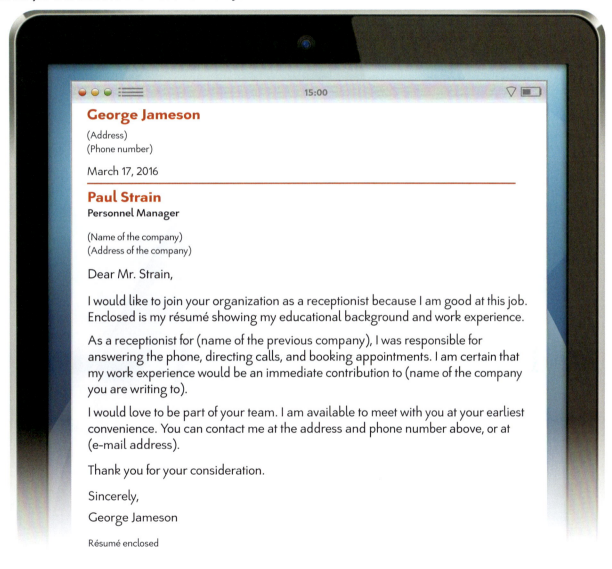

George Jameson
(Address)
(Phone number)

March 17, 2016

Paul Strain
Personnel Manager

(Name of the company)
(Address of the company)

Dear Mr. Strain,

I would like to join your organization as a receptionist because I am good at this job. Enclosed is my résumé showing my educational background and work experience.

As a receptionist for (name of the previous company), I was responsible for answering the phone, directing calls, and booking appointments. I am certain that my work experience would be an immediate contribution to (name of the company you are writing to).

I would love to be part of your team. I am available to meet with you at your earliest convenience. You can contact me at the address and phone number above, or at (e-mail address).

Thank you for your consideration.

Sincerely,

George Jameson

Résumé enclosed

Based on <http://jobsearch.about.com/od/coverlettersamples/a/covertemplate.htm>; <www.theguardian.com/careers/covering-letter-examples>.
Accessed on September 2, 2015.

Vocabulary

accompany: acompanhar
appointment: compromisso
available: disponível
background: formação

book: agendar
cover letter: carta de apresentação
direct calls: transferir ligações
employer: empregador(a)

enclosed: anexo(a)
introduce: apresentar
join: ingressar
personnel manager: gerente de recursos humanos

Look at the picture and answer orally.

1 What does the picture tell you about this unit?

2 What are the seven forms of fine arts?

3 Do you practice and/or like any form of art?

4 Is art important in our lives? Why?

Language in Context

1 Take a look at the dialogue.

🎧⟨10⟩

> **Gloria:** Hi, Carol! What's up?
>
> **Carol:** I got that job at the pet shop.
>
> **Gloria:** Great. When did you start?
>
> **Carol:** Last week. What about you, what's going on?
>
> **Gloria:** I got that job as a salad assistant.
>
> **Carol:** Cool! How is it going?
>
> **Gloria:** I cut my finger two days ago. But it's nice.
>
> **Carol:** I lost a dog yesterday, but I found it later.
>
> **Gloria:** Phew! Do the dogs like you?
>
> **Carol:** Yeah. The only problem is… there are too many of them!

Vocabulary

How is it going?: Como está indo?
Phew!: Ufa!
What's up?: E aí?

2 Give your opinion about the dialogue.

1 What are the girls talking about?

2 Do they know each other?

3 Are they happy with their new jobs?

3 Read, think, and answer orally.

A	B
She missed classes last week. They failed Math last month.	I cut my finger two days ago. I lost a dog yesterday.

1 What do the sentences have in common?

2 What is the difference between the verbs in group A and the ones in group B?

Language Practice

Simple Past – Irregular Verbs (ver página 382)

To go	
I You He She It We You They	**went**.

Afirmativa: He **went** to the barbecue yesterday.

Interrogativa: Did he **go** to the barbecue yesterday?

Negativa: He **did not go** to the barbecue yesterday.

Forma abreviada: didn't (did not)

Nota

Nas formas em que se usa o auxiliar *did*, o verbo principal fica no infinitivo sem *to*.
They **didn't** have much time to make a decision.
Did she get lost on her way to the stadium?
O auxiliar *did* não tem tradução em português.

Alguns verbos irregulares

Infinitive	Simple Past
to be	was/were
to become	became
to break	broke
to buy	bought
to come	came
to cut	cut
to do	did
to go	went

Infinitive	Simple Past
to have	had
to know	knew
to make	made
to meet	met
to see	saw
to take	took
to think	thought
to write	wrote

Nota

O verbo *to be* faz suas próprias formas interrogativas e negativas, sem utilizar o *did*.
He **was not/wasn't** home last Monday.   We **were not/weren't** hungry last night.
Was she late for class yesterday?   **Were** you in Chicago a week ago?

---

1   Circle all the irregular verbs in the Simple Past.

Todd was my best friend when I was ten. We went to school together. Sometimes we walked. Sometimes Mom took us by car. We did our homework and watched TV. We met our friends at the club to play soccer. On weekends, we ate popcorn and played video games. Then my best friend moved to another country. Today I am fifteen and I have new friends, but Todd is still my best friend.

2 **Complete the sentences using the verbs in parentheses in the Simple Past.**

1   We _____ (enjoy) the show last night.

2   Grandpa _____ (be) a salesperson when he _____ (be) young.

3   Later, he _____ (become) a businessman.

4   I _____ (try) to talk to her, but she _____ (ignore) me.

5   The car _____ (stop) near the mall.

6   I _____ (think) about you last week.

3 **Rewrite the sentences in the interrogative form.**

1   She broke her foot.
    Did she break her foot?
    _____

2   He wrote a letter last night.

    _____

3   They met him at the theater.

    _____

4   She saw her Biology teacher at the mall.

    _____

5   You took a lot of pictures at the concert.

    _____

4 **Complete the sentences.**

1   **A:** What did you buy last week?

    B: _____ I bought _____ a new T-shirt.

2   **A:** How did you come to school today?

    B: _____ by car.

3   **A:** When did you do your homework?

    B: _____ it yesterday.

4   **A:** Where did you go last Sunday?

    B: _____ to the movies.

5   **A:** Why did you write him an e-mail yesterday?

    B: Because _____ to me two days ago.

Possessive Adjectives and Pronouns

Possessive Adjectives	Possessive Pronouns
my	mine
your	yours
his	his
her	hers
its	its
our	ours
your	yours
their	theirs
This is **my** book.	This book is **mine**. (**my** book)

Nota

Antecedido por *of*, o *possessive pronoun* denota "um dos", "uma das".

She is a friend **of mine**. (= She is one of my friends.)
Quando o possuidor é indicado por um pronome indefinido, o *possessive adjective* pode concordar com o singular ou com o plural.

Everyone must bring **his/her** slide projector.
Everyone must bring **their** slide projector.

Uso

Os *possessive adjectives* vêm antes de substantivos. Já os *possessive pronouns* substituem os substantivos. Ambos, no entanto, concordam com o possuidor.

We are doing **our** homework. Are you doing **yours**?

5 Circle all the possessive adjectives and possessive pronouns in the text.

I am mad at my friend Janice. I showed my composition to her and she simply copied it. Mr. Swanson, our teacher, thought that the composition was hers, not mine. I told him what had happened and he said that it was not his problem.

Some of my friends tried to help me and talked to Mr. Swanson, but he said that it was not their problem. Finally, Janice confessed that the composition was mine.

6 Complete the sentences using the appropriate possessives.

1   Sheila, I didn't bring _____ umbrella. Can I borrow _____?

2   The boys ate _____ sandwiches, but the girls didn't eat _____ this morning.

3   Glenda is going to take _____ kids to the park. Why don't you take _____ too?

4   Last year my parents lost _____ luggage at the airport.

5   Rick likes _____ new job, but Alan and David don't like _____.

6   I did _____ homework. Did you do _____?

Go to page 84 for Extra Practice.

Reading

Before Reading

1   Discuss the questions below in Portuguese.

1   How often do you listen to classical music?

2   Do you know any classical musicians?

3   Have you ever heard of João Carlos Martins, the Brazilian pianist and conductor?

4   How important are the hands for a pianist?

2   Refer to text A on page 71 and check the correct answer.

1   In this text, it is possible to find...

a   ☐ director's name, running time, short description, and personal opinion.

b   ☐ writer's name, number of pages, list of characters, and detailed description.

c   ☐ designer's name, number of levels, system requirements, and personal opinion.

2   The characteristics above are typical of a...

a   ☐ book review.

b   ☐ game description.

c   ☐ movie review.

> **Scanning**
>
> A estratégia de *scanning* corresponde a uma leitura seletiva, com o objetivo de encontrar algo, sem a necessidade de compreender todo o texto.

3   Scan the texts on page 71 and write the following information.

1   The year João Carlos Martins was born. _____

2   Original title of the documentary. _____

3   Country where the movie was produced. _____

4   Sport that João Carlos Martins practiced. _____

5   Name of the orchestra he founded. _____

Text A

MARTINS' PASSION
★ ★ ★ ★ ★

Any storyteller would be hard-pressed to invent a biography as incredible as the life of Brazil's celebrated star pianist João Carlos Martins. Success and personal tragedies, traumatic injuries, and triumphant comebacks mark his fate. In the early 1960s, this temperamental Brazilian is celebrated as the greatest interpreter of the music of Bach next to Glenn Gould. But a disastrous injury throws his life off balance. In the late 1990s, Martins' career seems finally over when he has to undergo surgery to sever the nerves of his right hand. The pianist decides to attempt a comeback with his left hand only. With fanatic fervor, he makes his left hand work for two.

The film accompanies João Carlos Martins during his darkest hours, traces the early triumphs and dramatic events of his life. Unique film sequences from his childhood and early years breathe life into this scintillating universe. Martins' encounters with his friend, the soccer genius Pelé, and the legendary jazz pianist Dave Brubeck provide moments of bliss. A film about a man who never gives up and remains true to his passion – music.

INTERNATIONAL TITLE
Martins' Passion
ORIGINAL TITLE
Die Martins-Passion
COUNTRY
Germany
YEAR OF PRODUCTION
2003
GENRE
Documentary
DIRECTOR
Irene Langemann
RUNNING TIME
90 minutes

Adapted from <www.globalscreen.de/television.documentary.human_interest/content/show/74091>.
Accessed on September 14, 2015.

Text B

1940	1965	1995	2002	2003	2004
João Carlos Martins, pianist and conductor, was born in São Paulo.	He severely hurt his right hand during a soccer game.	He lost part of the movements of his right hand due to injuries received when he was robbed in Bulgaria.	A disease was discovered in his left hand.	He started preparing to be a conductor.	He founded the Bachiana Chamber Orchestra and began social programs for young people in São Paulo. Since then, he has performed with the orchestra both in Brazil and abroad.

Based on <www.cremesp.org.br/?siteAcao=Revista&id=391>.
Accessed on September 10, 2015.

Vocabulary

balance: equilíbrio
comeback: retorno
conductor: maestro/maestrina
disease: doença
fate: destino
injury: lesão, ferimento
sever: cortar
undergo: submeter-se a, passar por

After Reading

1 **Based on both texts, it is possible to affirm that…**

a ☐ it would be easy for a writer to create a story similar to João Carlos Martins' life.

b ☐ Glenn Gould and João Carlos Martins played Bach together in Bulgaria.

c ☐ the pianist played soccer with his friend Pelé in the 1960s.

d ☐ the documentary shows scenes of the time when Martins was a child.

e ☐ Martins now plays the piano for the Bachiana Chamber Orchestra.

2 **Check the alternatives that complete the statement correctly.**

João Carlos Martins is…

a ☐ a man who never gives up.

b ☐ a celebrated pianist.

c ☐ a man who makes documentaries.

d ☐ a man who remains true to music.

e ☐ an interpreter of the music of Bach.

3 **Check the correct meaning of each sentence.**

1 *"Success and personal tragedies, traumatic injuries, and triumphant comebacks mark his fate"* (text A, lines 4-5).

a ☐ Martins' life story and career present several ups and downs.

b ☐ The artist was successful at first, but then had to give up his career.

2 *"In the late 1990s, Martins' career seems finally over […]"* (text A, lines 9-10).

a ☐ His career seemed to be at an end.

b ☐ Martins started his career in 1990.

3 *"The pianist decides to attempt a comeback with his left hand only"* (text A, line 11).

a ☐ He couldn't play the piano only with his left hand.

b ☐ He intended to play with just one hand.

4 **Discuss the following questions with your classmates.**

1 What is necessary for a person never to give up?

2 Can you think of other examples of people who have overcome difficulties?

Vocabulary Expansion

1 **Read the information in the box and write new words.**

1 race _____

2 dance _____

3 sing _____

4 write _____

5 paint _____

6 work _____

7 teach _____

8 swim _____

2 **Read the information in the box and make new words to complete the charts below.**

in-	
1	conceivable	
2	correct	
3	credible	
4	definite	

un-	
1	happy	
2	known	
3	important	
4	natural	

3 **Check the best alternative to complete the sentences.**

1 She said she is going _____ in that job.

a ☐ insolvable   b ☐ insane   c ☐ inoffensive

2 This song is so famous that many people consider it _____.

a ☐ unbelievable   b ☐ unforgettable   c ☐ unknown

3 I didn't buy that chair because it was very _____.

a ☐ unknown   b ☐ uncomfortable   c ☐ improbable

4 He is _____ to her suffering.

a ☐ indefinite   b ☐ incredible   c ☐ indifferent

5 Jack doesn't have a job. He is _____.

a ☐ unnatural   b ☐ uninteresting   c ☐ unemployed

6 Ted was _____ yesterday at the party because Ann didn't show up.

a ☐ unhappy   b ☐ unimportant   c ☐ unconscious

6

What Are You Doing with Your Life?

Look at the picture and answer orally.

1 What does the picture tell you about this unit?

2 Can we tell what the future of some people will be like by looking at them?

3 Why do some teens accomplish more than others?

Language in Context

1 Take a look at the cartoon.

12

2 Give your opinion about the cartoon.

1 Why isn't the boy going to the beach?

2 Do you agree with the girl's decision? Why?

Vocabulary

What about me?: E eu?
while: enquanto

3 Read, think, and answer orally.

A	B
What were you doing yesterday at 5 p.m.?	I was sleeping.

A	B
What did you do yesterday at 5 p.m.?	I went to bed.

1 What do the two groups of sentences have in common?

2 Is there a difference in meaning between the two groups?

Language Practice

Past Continuous

Passado do verbo **to be** + verbo terminado em **-ing**	
I **was** You **were** He **was** She **was** It **was** We **were** You **were** They **were** sleep**ing**.	**Afirmativa:** He **was** sleep**ing**. **Interrogativa: Was** he sleep**ing**? **Negativa:** He **was not** sleep**ing**. **Formas abreviadas: wasn't** (was not) **weren't** (were not)

Uso

Expressa ações em andamento em um determinado momento do passado.

It **was raining** heavily five minutes ago.

They **were writing** a report yesterday morning.

É frequentemente usado com **when** e **while**.

when (quando)	He **was sleeping** <u>when</u> she arrived.
while (enquanto)	He **was sleeping** <u>while</u> his sister was cleaning the garage.

---

1 **Rewrite the sentences in the Past Continuous.**

1 He slept in his bedroom.

_____

2 Your sister cleaned the garage.

_____

3 Your mother and I washed the car.

_____

4 I didn't talk to the teacher in the classroom.

_____

5 The kids didn't watch a funny movie yesterday afternoon.

_____

2 Complete the sentences using the verbs in parentheses in the Past Continuous.

1 Yesterday, Sally _____ (read) a book while I
_____ (take) a nap.

2 It _____ (rain – neg.) when I left this morning.

3 _____ you _____ (have) dinner
when I called you last night?

4 They said they _____ (shout – neg.).

5 While I was packing, my parents _____ (look for) our
passports.

Modal Verbs (I)

Os **verbos modais** são verbos auxiliares que dão um significado específico ao verbo principal.

You **should** go now. (conselho)   It **may** rain. (possibilidade)

She **must** arrive on time. (obrigação)   He **can** play the piano. (habilidade)

Características

Os verbos modais:

• não têm infinitivo;

• não têm conjugação regular;

• têm a mesma forma para todas as pessoas;

• são seguidos pelo verbo principal no infinitivo sem *to*;

• fazem as próprias formas interrogativas e negativas.

	Can	Could	Must
Afirmativa	I **can** read.	I **could** read.	I **must** read.
Interrogativa	**Can** he read?	**Could** he read?	**Must** he read?
Negativa	We **cannot** read.	We **could not** read.	We **must not** read.
Forma abreviada	**can't**	**couldn't**	**mustn't**

Can/Could (pode, podia, poderia)

Expressam:

• capacidade e habilidade

He **can** read fast.   I **could** swim well years ago.

• possibilidade, permissão, pedido

They **can** go now.   **Could** you open the door, please?

> **Nota**
> **Be able to** pode substituir *can/could*.
> I **am able to** swim.   He **was able to** read that letter.

Must (deve)

Expressa:

- obrigação, dedução

  We **must** visit her.   She **must** be sick.

Nota

Have to pode substituir *must*.

I **have to** go now.   He **had to** work yesterday.

- proibição (forma negativa)

  You **must not** use your cell phone in the classroom.   You **mustn't** smoke here.

---

3 **Read the sentences and match them to the corresponding meaning.**

1 We must study because we have a test next week.

2 You mustn't enter this room. It's for employees only.

3 Everybody is in the classroom. The teacher must be there.

a ☐ obligation

b ☐ deduction

c ☐ prohibition

4 **Complete the sentences using *can*, *could*, *can't*, or *couldn't*.**

1 _____ you help me with my homework?

2 I'm sorry but I _____ talk right now.

3 He's an excellent athlete. He _____ break the record.

4 We _____ see that he was very happy.

5 Picasso _____ paint when he was five. He started painting when he was seven.

5 **Look at the pictures and complete the sentences using modal verbs.**

You _____ turn left.

You _____ smoke here.

You _____ ride a bicycle here.

You _____ park here.

Go to page 84
for Extra Practice.

Before Reading

1 Discuss the questions below in Portuguese.

1 What do you want to do when you graduate from high school?

2 Do you think your actions now will affect your future? How?

3 What do you think your life will be like in ten years?

4 What about your classmates? Can you imagine what their lives will be like in ten years?

2 Write the meaning of the terms below. Use the words/expressions from the box.

| trancar | gratificante | perceber | verdade | reconhecer |

1 acknowledge _____

2 realize _____

3 rewarding _____

4 lock _____

5 truth _____

3 Scan the text on page 81 and find...

1 the name of the person who wrote it. _____

2 the number of people that are mentioned. _____

3 three phrasal verbs that are synonyms for "enter". _____

4 a phrasal verb that means "to become something else". _____

> ### Skimming
>
> Consiste em ler o texto rapidamente, tentando enfocar apenas sua ideia central, sem dar muita atenção aos detalhes. Enquanto faz o *skimming*, o leitor se pergunta: "De que trata este texto?".

4 Skim the text and answer: what is it about? Write only one sentence in Portuguese.

_____

_____

_____

What Are You Doing with Your Life?

When a teenager tried to break into her home, Joey Garcia asked him an unexpected question.

by JOEY GARCIA

I was working on a poem on my laptop when I realized that afternoon had turned into evening. When I walked into the kitchen, I could clearly see a young man breaking into my home through a window.

He was a teenager, 17 or 18 years old. I felt strangely calm, probably because of my two decades as a high school teacher and life coach for teens. So it didn't surprise me when a sincere question came into my mind: "What are you doing with your life?" He froze, speechless. He thought he had misheard me. I asked again: "What are you doing with your life?"

Watching me carefully for a moment, he seemed to ponder the question. Then he began to back out of the window and ran away. With shaky hands, I closed and locked my windows, then called the police.

When the police officer arrived, I explained what had happened. He asked if I knew the young man. "No," I said. The officer narrowed his eyes. "Then why did you ask what he was doing with his life?"

I don't remember what I told him. But the truth is I believe that we must all help teens to navigate a path into a rewarding life.

Looking back, I think that to be asked what you are doing with your life is to be acknowledged as if you matter, are loved, and are valued.

In the end, while he was trying to break into my house, I was trying to break into his consciousness.

Adapted from <www.kqed.org/a/perspectives/R201501060735>.
Accessed on September 15, 2015.

Vocabulary

consciousness: consciência
narrow: estreitar, apertar

path: caminho, via
ponder: refletir sobre, considerar

seem: parecer, aparentar
shaky: trêmulo(a)

After Reading

Identificar o propósito do texto

Cada texto responde a determinado propósito. Identificá-lo facilita o diálogo do leitor com o texto.

1 What is the main purpose of the text?

a ☐ To convince someone to do something.

b ☐ To instruct a person on how to do something.

c ☐ To provide definitions or explanations.

d ☐ To tell a story, focusing on a series of events in time.

2 Number the events in the order they happened in the text.

a ☐ Afternoon turned into evening.

b ☐ The woman asked the young man a question.

c ☐ The young man ran away.

d ☐ The police officer asked the woman a question.

e ☐ The woman saw a young man.

f ☐1 The woman was working on her computer.

3 Answer the questions according to the text.

1 What did Joey see when she entered the kitchen? <u>She saw a young man breaking into her home.</u>

2 How did she feel? _____

3 What did she do? _____

4 How did the young man react? _____

5 Why did she ask the teenager a question?

   a ☐ Because she wanted to get to know him.

   b ☐ Because she was trying to break into his consciousness.

   c ☐ Because she was trying to say that she loved him.

   d ☐ Because she was so afraid that she couldn't think of anything else.

4 Did the police officer understand Joey's question? Why? Discuss in Portuguese.

Vocabulary Expansion

1 **Read the information in the box and write which words are being defined below.**

1 place things in the wrong location _____misplace_____

2 not behave adequately _____

3 use things incorrectly _____

4 treat someone/something badly _____

5 pronounce words incorrectly _____

> **Prefix *mis-***
>
> O prefixo **mis-** indica "de forma ruim ou incorreta".
> understand – **mis**understand
> hear – **mis**hear

2 **Read the information in the box and circle the correct alternative.**

1 The accident was the cause of his **sadness / regardless**.

2 The shelter helps **careless / homeless** people.

3 This movie is too long. It seems **speechless / endless**.

4 I don't know what to say. I am **speechless / flavorless**.

5 The **loneliness / happiness** was too much: she really missed them.

6 His **dizziness / rudeness** to strangers was caused by **shyness / kindness**.

> **Suffixes *-ness* and *-less***
>
> O sufixo **-ness** forma substantivos; já o sufixo **-less** forma adjetivos e advérbios e indica "sem", "falta de".
> conscious – conscious**ness**
> care – care**less**

3 **Substitute the words in bold for synonyms. Use the box for help.**

> **False Cognates**
>
> Os falsos cognatos são palavras semelhantes na forma, mas diferentes no significado.
>
> **realize:** perceber, ter consciência de   **parents:** pais
> **accomplish:** realizar   **relatives:** parentes
>
> **actually:** de fato, realmente   **library:** biblioteca
> **nowadays:** atualmente, hoje em dia   **bookstore:** livraria

1 Ross **noticed** that the woman was **in fact** telling the truth. _____

2 Is there a **place that sells books** nearby? _____

3 I live in that house with my **father and my mother**. _____

4 The politician was not able to **achieve** his goals. _____

5 That school has a big **place where you can read books**. _____

6 Be careful. The streets are dangerous **at the present time**. _____

7 He had lunch with his **uncles, aunts, and cousins**. _____

Extra Practice 3

1 Read the information in the box. Then match the opposites.

1 hot   a ☐ nervous
2 nightmare   b ☐ married
3 calm   c ☐ cold
4 outside   d ☐ dream
5 single   e ☐ attic
6 big   f ☐ inside
7 basement   g ☐ small

> **basement:** porão
> **nightmare:** pesadelo
> **outside:** fora, do lado de fora
> **single:** solteiro(a)

2 Read the information in the box and complete the sentences.

1 She's going _____ school now.
2 My sister arrived _____ Japan yesterday.
3 This letter _____ England came last night.
4 The milk we drink comes _____ his farm.
5 I'm not traveling _____ Mexico this month.

> **from:** de (origem)
> **to:** para

3 Substitute the expressions in bold for possessive pronouns.

1 This is his book and the other one is **my book**.
   This is his book and the other one is ___mine___.
2 This is my favorite color. What is **your favorite color**?
   This is my favorite color. What is _____?
3 Paul brought his book. Did Sheila bring **her book**?
   Paul brought his book. Did Sheila bring _____?
4 Louise is writing her composition and Richard is writing **his composition**.
   Louise is writing her composition and Richard is writing _____.
5 I couldn't finish my homework. Could they finish **their homework**?
   I couldn't finish my homework. Could they finish _____?
6 They invited their friends. We can invite **our friends**.
   They invited their friends. We can invite _____.

4 **Choose the correct alternative to complete the sentences.**

1 In 1965, he severely _____ his right arm.

a ☐ saw b ☐ brought c ☐ hurt

2 João Carlos Martins _____ his left hand work for two.

a ☐ made b ☐ sees c ☐ make

3 He _____ the Bachiana Chamber Orchestra in 2004.

a ☐ learns b ☐ found c ☐ founded

5 **Answer the questions. Use the box for help.**

1 **A:** Did you bring the blue box? (the red box)

B: No, I didn't bring the blue box. I brought the red box _____.

2 **A:** Did the dogs destroy the vase? (the flowers)

B: No, _____.

3 **A:** Did you find your watch? (my keys)

B: No, _____.

4 **A:** Did he take the bus to school? (a taxi)

B: No, _____.

5 **A:** Did she try to play tennis? (soccer)

B: No, _____.

bring – brought
destroy – destroyed
find – found
take – took
try – tried

6 **Underline the verbs in the Past Continuous.**

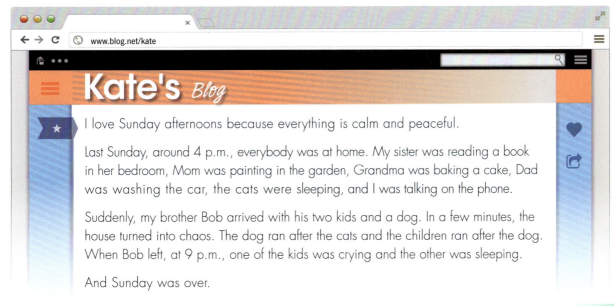

www.blog.net/kate

Kate's *Blog*

I love Sunday afternoons because everything is calm and peaceful.

Last Sunday, around 4 p.m., everybody was at home. My sister was reading a book in her bedroom, Mom was painting in the garden, Grandma was baking a cake, Dad was washing the car, the cats were sleeping, and I was talking on the phone.

Suddenly, my brother Bob arrived with his two kids and a dog. In a few minutes, the house turned into chaos. The dog ran after the cats and the children ran after the dog. When Bob left, at 9 p.m., one of the kids was crying and the other was sleeping.

And Sunday was over.

7 **Complete the sentences about the text on page 85.**

1 My sister was not reading a magazine. She <u>was reading a book</u>.

2 Mom wasn't cooking. She _____.

3 Dad wasn't fixing the car. He _____.

4 Grandma _____.

5 The cats _____.

6 I _____. I _____.

8 **Answer the questions according to the text.**

1 Who did Bob arrive with?

_____

2 What time did Bob arrive?

_____

3 What did the kids do in the house?

_____

4 What time did Bob leave?

_____

5 What were the kids doing when they left?

_____

9 **Make sentences with the prompts given. Use the Simple Past or the Past Continuous.**

1 My father / hurt / his foot / while / he / play / basketball /.

_____

2 I / have / a nightmare / when / the alarm clock / go off /.

_____

3 My family / see / amazing animals / when / they / travel / around Australia /.

_____

4 Carla / chat / on the computer / while / her parents / watch / TV /.

_____

5 It / rain / when / I / leave / the gym / .

_____

10 Ask questions using the words/expressions in parentheses.

1   They were running in the park at 5 o'clock.

(Where) Where were they running at 5 o'clock?

(What time) What time were they running in the park?

2   He was buying a magazine this morning.

(What) _____

(When) _____

3   Mom was sleeping because she was tired.

(What) _____

(Why) _____

4   The children were eating sandwiches in the kitchen five minutes ago.

(Who) _____

(What) _____

(Where) _____

11 Write sentences about your abilities. Use _can_ or _can't_ and the expressions in the box.

ride a bike	use the computer	swim	play the guitar	play volleyball	dance
drive a car	play soccer	run a marathon	sing in English		

I can play soccer.

I can't ride a bike.

12 Talk about the things you could or couldn't do when you were a child.

ride a bike

work in an office

read magazines

drive a car

play soccer

swim

watch TV all day

eat hot dogs

go to the park

Job Corner 3

JOB INTERVIEW TIPS

There are two key rules to make your job interview go well.

Be Prepared

Learn about the company you will be interviewed by — where they are from, what they do/offer, etc.

Practice the interview with a friend. You can try these questions:

• Why are you interested in this job?
• Why are you interested in this company?
• What are your strengths and weaknesses?

• Why are you leaving your current job?
• Where do you see yourself in five years?

Get ready for the interview ahead of time: decide what you're going to wear and how you're going to get to the location of the interview.

Get together anything you must bring with you. Wear comfortable clean clothes. Do not chew gum or smoke. Make a good first impression.

Be Relaxed

People don't believe you can be relaxed at an interview, but you can. Listen to the questions attentively and answer them thoughtfully. Speak in a normal conversational tone.

When you're done, thank the interviewer for taking the time to meet with you.

Based on <www.bls.gov/careeroutlook/2000/Summer/art02.pdf>; <http://jobsearch.about.com/cs/interviews/a/jobinterviewtip.htm>.
Accessed on September 17, 2015.

Vocabulary

ahead of time: com antecedência	**get ready:** arrumar-se	**strength:** ponto positivo/forte
attentively: atentamente	**get together:** juntar	**thoughtfully:** refletidamente
chew: mascar	**interview:** entrevista; entrevistar	**tone:** tom
current: atual	**rule:** regra	**weakness:** ponto negativo/fraco

Look at the picture and answer orally.

1 What does the picture tell you about this unit?

2 Have you ever heard of stem cells? What do you know about them?

3 What are the possible uses of stem cells in scientific research?

4 Can these studies generate ethical dilemmas? If so, how could they be handled or solved?

Language in Context

1 **Take a look at the dialogue.**

Mr. Stanley: How much did you spend at the mall, Josie?

Josie: Not much, Dad.

Mr. Stanley: Is that so? Those things look expensive!

Josie: Don't worry. I spent little money.

Billy: How much is "little" money, Dad?

Mr. Stanley: It depends on the person. For me, it's about 20 or 30 dollars.

Josie: Then I spent a few dollars, Dad.

Billy: How much is "a few" dollars, Dad?

Mr. Stanley: I think it's 40 to 50 dollars.

Josie: In that case, I spent many dollars, Dad.

> **Vocabulary**
>
> **look:** *parecer*
> **mall:** *shopping center*

2 **Give your opinion about the dialogue.**

1 Does Billy know much about money?

2 In your opinion, how much is "little" money? What about "a little" money?

3 **Read, observe the words in bold, and answer orally.**

1 I spent **few** dollars.   2 I spent **a few** dollars.   3 I spent **many** dollars.

a Which sentence indicates the greatest amount of money? _____

b Which sentence indicates the smallest amount of money? _____

Language Practice

Quantifiers

Substantivos

Os substantivos podem ser contáveis ou incontáveis.

Os **substantivos contáveis** (*countable nouns*) referem-se a coisas que podemos contar.

dollars, bottles, liters, kilos, packs, slices, apples, boys

Os **substantivos incontáveis** (*uncountable nouns*) referem-se a coisas que não podemos contar.

money, milk, sugar, bread, meat, liberty, happiness

Uso

Antes de **substantivos contáveis** usa-se:

- **many:** muitos(as)
  I bought **many** bottles of milk.

- **few:** poucos(as) / **a few:** alguns/algumas
  I have **few** cents; I can't take a bus.

  We have **a few** minutes to talk.

- **fewer:** menos
  You have **fewer** friends than I do.

Antes de **substantivos incontáveis** usa-se:

- **much:** muito(a)
  There wasn't **much** milk in the bottle.

- **little:** pouco(a) / **a little:** algum(a)
  He has **little** money; he can't buy a car.

  We have **a little** time to rest.

- **less:** menos
  I have **less** time than you do.

A lot of, **lots of** e **plenty of** podem substituir *much* e *many*.

I don't have **a lot of** things to do on the weekend.

Is there **lots of** meat for the barbecue?

They have **plenty of** money.

> **Nota**
>
> **Very** significa "muito" e é usado antes de adjetivos e advérbios com a função de enfatizá-los.
> She's **very** tired.
> The teacher is **very** proud of his students.
> My father speaks Spanish **very** well.

1 **Check what you need for a party.**

1 invitations
   a ☐ much   b ☐ many

2 balloons
   a ☐ little   b ☐ a few

3 sandwiches
   a ☐ a lot of   b ☐ a little

4 soda
   a ☐ many   b ☐ much

5 money
   a ☐ a little   b ☐ a few

6 friends
   a ☐ many   b ☐ much

2 **Complete the sentences using *few* or *little*.**

1 There is _____ money in the drawer.

2 There was _____ sugar in the sugar pot.

3 There are _____ children in the park.

4 There were _____ guests at the party yesterday.

5 She needs _____ time to get ready.

6 Only _____ people think they are right.

3 Complete the sentences using *much* or *many*.

1 There are _____ Brazilians in the United States.

2 There are _____ animals in the zoo.

3 There isn't _____ water in the refrigerator.

4 There is _____ work to be done today.

5 We don't need _____ time to finish this activity.

6 She invited _____ friends to her birthday party.

4 There are mistakes in some of the sentences below. Circle and correct them.

1 Give (fewer) food to the animals. _____ *less* _____

2 Take a little children to the game. _____

3 I have lots of friends to invite to the party. _____

4 She knows less pop songs than I do. _____

5 He has few money because he is unemployed. _____

6 She doesn't like me very much. _____

5 Check the correct alternative.

1 I received _____ presents on my 15th birthday.

a ☐ a little   b ☐ many   c ☐ much

2 My mother was _____ tired yesterday.

a ☐ very   b ☐ many   c ☐ few

3 We spent a _____ dollars at the mall; there was a big sale.

a ☐ much   b ☐ little   c ☐ few

4 He has _____ time; he's working a lot.

a ☐ little   b ☐ a few   c ☐ less

5 My brother has _____ friends now than he did when he was a teen.

a ☐ less   b ☐ a little   c ☐ fewer

6 They didn't get _____ love when they were children.

a ☐ many   b ☐ much   c ☐ very

Go to page 110 for Extra Practice.

Reading

Before Reading

1 **Discuss the questions below in Portuguese.**

1   Do you know what stem cells are?

2   What are they used for?

3   Why are some people against treatments and research involving stem cells?

2 **Find a synonym for each term below. Use the words/expressions in the box.**

consequently   origin   illnesses   presently   replace   restoration   gives   turn into

1   diseases (line 3) _____

2   root (line 5) _____

3   become (line 8) _____

4   replenish (line 10) _____

5   therefore (line 11) _____

6   repair (line 12) _____

7   provides (line 13) _____

8   currently (line 15) _____

What are you doing here, son?

I want you to take a stem cell from me.

What for?

To make me a new brother. He must be 15 and good at Math.

Stem Cells

Background Information on Stem Cells

Stem cells, which can transform themselves into many other tissue types, give rise to all the cells in the human body and hold the key to finding cures for many diseases, such as Parkinson's, Alzheimer's, heart disease, and diabetes. These master cells are found in the
5 body at any age, acting as the root of all the cells that make up the body's tissues.

When a stem cell divides, each new cell has the potential to either remain a stem cell or become a specialized cell, such as a muscle cell, a red blood cell, or a brain cell. Stem cells can
10 theoretically divide without limit to replenish other cells [...]. Scientists believe, therefore, that it should be possible to turn stem cells into a "repair kit" for the body.

Human fetal tissue provides the best source of stem cells (embryonic stem cells). Stem cells are also found within adult
15 organs (adult stem cells), but currently their potential to become other types of cells is limited.

[...]

Vocabulary

blood: sangue
brain: cérebro
heart: coração
muscle: músculo
stem cell: célula-tronco

Available at <http://newsroom.ucr.edu/1909>.
Accessed on August 3, 2015.

After Reading

Deduzir o significado de palavras por meio do contexto

Ao se deparar com uma palavra desconhecida, os leitores podem tentar inferir/deduzir seu significado a partir do contexto. Com base no entendimento do sentido geral da frase e no conhecimento de palavras vizinhas, é possível chegar a conclusões sobre o significado do termo desconhecido.

1 Check the meaning of the words in bold.

1 *"Stem cells [...] can transform themselves into many other* **tissue** *types [...]"* (lines 1-2).

a ☐ lenço　　　　b ☐ tecido　　　　c ☐ textura

2 *"[...]* **give rise** *to all the cells in the human body [...]"* (line 2).

a ☐ causar　　　　b ☐ crescer　　　　c ☐ dar origem

3 *"[...] each new cell has the potential to either* **remain** *a stem cell or become a specialized cell [...]"* (lines 7-8).

a ☐ permanecer　　　　b ☐ remanejar　　　　c ☐ favorecer

4 *"Human fetal tissue provides the best* **source** *of stem cells [...]"* (line 13).

a ☐ fonte　　　　b ☐ conteúdo　　　　c ☐ recurso

2 Check the correct alternative according to the text.

1 According to the first paragraph, what can be said about stem cells?

a ☐ They can become different types of cells in the body.

b ☐ They do not divide in human beings.

c ☐ They are special muscle cells.

2 What happens when stem cells divide?

a ☐ They can only generate other stem cells.

b ☐ They are always transformed into specialized cells.

c ☐ The new cells can be used to replenish other cells.

3 What is true about the different sources of stem cells?

a ☐ Embryonic cells are better than adult cells.

b ☐ Adult cells are better than embryonic cells.

c ☐ Embryonic cells are as good as adult cells.

Vocabulary Expansion

Suffix -ly

Acrescentado a adjetivos, o sufixo **-ly** forma advérbios, indicando circunstância de modo, tempo etc.
Jim works **slowly**.

1 Read the box and write new words.

1 current _____

2 present _____

3 theoretical _____

4 gradual _____

5 immediate _____

6 annual _____

2 Complete the sentences using the words in parentheses and the suffix -ly.

1 The boy arrived home _____ (extreme) sick.

2 Jessica makes the same mistake _____ (repeated).

3 Bob is not a careless boy, but today he is doing things _____ (careless).

4 Embarrassed, he smiled _____ (weak) and left the room.

3 Complete the sentences with the words/expressions from the box.

1 They need an answer from him. He must _____ call _____ send an e-mail.

2 She sings just _____ her mother.

3 I like colors _____ the ones you are wearing.

4 Frank can _____ remain here _____ go to another room.

either... or...: ou... ou...
like: como, do mesmo modo
such as: tal/tais como

4 Find synonyms and opposites using the words in the box.

| heal | separate | permitted | multiply | impossible | retain | continue | ordinary |

Synonyms

1 divide _____

2 cure _____

3 remain _____

4 hold _____

Opposites

5 special _____

6 divide _____

7 possible _____

8 prohibited _____

8

Physical Exercise

Look at the picture and answer orally.

1   What does the picture tell you about this unit?

2   Which physical activities do you do? How often?

3   Do you think you should exercise more?

4   What are the possible benefits of working out for our health?

Language in Context

1 **Take a look at the dialogue.**

Naomi: Hi, Kenny. What's up?
You look upset this morning!

Kenny: I am upset! I think I'm going
to play volleyball from now on.

Naomi: Are you going to quit tennis?

Kenny: Yeah, I guess I will.

Naomi: Why? You're a good
tennis player.

Kenny: I don't know, Naomi.
Volleyball is more exciting
than tennis.

Naomi: Well, if you want excitement,
you can practice kitesurfing.

Kenny: In fact, I want to work with sports in
the future. Maybe as a coach.

Naomi: Then choose a sport you like.
Do you like volleyball?

Kenny: Good point…

> *Vocabulary*
>
> **from now on:** daqui em diante
> **maybe:** talvez
> **quit:** abandonar

2 **Give your opinion about the dialogue.**

1 Why is the boy upset?

2 In your opinion, which sport should he play?

3 **Read, think, and answer orally.**

Volleyball is more exciting than tennis.
Kitesurfing is more dangerous than volleyball.

1 Which adjectives can you find in the sentences?

2 What do the sentences have in common?

Language Practice

Comparison (I)

Em inglês, a maioria dos adjetivos e alguns advérbios podem aparecer nos graus absoluto, comparativo e superlativo.

Absoluto

She is **pretty**.

He speaks **slowly**.

Comparativo

É usado quando é feita uma comparação entre dois itens.

as... as (tão... quanto)

I run **as fast as** you.

not as... as (não tão... quanto)

Ann is **not as smart as** Paul.

less... than (menos... que/do que)

Today is **less cold than** it was yesterday.

more... than (mais... que/do que)

Jane is **more beautiful than** Sally.

Superlativo

É usado quando é feita uma comparação entre mais de dois itens.

the least... (o/a menos...)

He is **the least strong** of the boys.

the most... (o/a mais...)

She is **the most intelligent** writer that I know.

> **Nota**
>
> **More** e **most** são usados com adjetivos com duas sílabas ou mais (exceto no caso de adjetivos de duas sílabas que terminam em **y**), como *comfortable, expensive, intelligent, dangerous* etc.
>
> These black shoes are **more** <u>comfortable</u> than the brown ones.
> This is the **most** <u>expensive</u> item in the store.

---

1 Read the sentences and answer the questions.

1 Julian is not as successful as Charles, but Gill is.

   Who is as successful as Gill? _____

2 Tom is as tall as Barry, but neither of them is as tall as Helen.

   Is Tom as tall as Helen? _____

3 **Eve:** I'm going to buy this motorbike.

   Carol: Why? It's uncomfortable!

   Eve: Cars are too expensive. I only have enough money to buy a motorbike.

   Carol: That red car is as cheap as the motorbike.

   Eve: Really?

   Can Eve afford the red car? _____

4 If Math is as difficult as Physics and Physics is as difficult as Biology, is Math as difficult as Biology? _____

2 Complete the sentences using the words in parentheses and *more… than* or *the most…*

1 Brenda is _____ (energetic) her brother.

2 You are _____ (nervous) person that I know.

3 Physics is _____ (complicated) subject that I study.

4 In my opinion, cars are _____ (comfortable) buses.

5 Skydiving is _____ (dangerous) sport that I know.

3 There are mistakes in some of the sentences below. Rewrite the sentences correcting them.

1 Mary and I are less curious than my cousin.

_____

2 My car is the least expensive than yours.

_____

3 These activities are the least difficult in the whole book.

_____

4 The new dictionary is less complete in our library.

_____

Verb Tense Review

Simple Present	**Forma**	Infinitivo sem *to* 3ª pessoa do singular + *-s/-es* Auxiliar: ***do/does***
	Advérbios	*often, always, every day, sometimes, never* etc.
	Exemplos	I often **drink** tea. He **likes** tea.
	Indica	hábitos, verdades universais
Present Continuous	**Forma**	***To be*** (*Simple Present*) + verbo + ***-ing***
	Advérbios	*now, at present, at this moment* etc.
	Exemplo	The kids **are sleeping** now.
	Indica	ações em andamento no presente
Future with *Going to*	**Forma**	***To be*** (*Simple Present*) + ***going to*** + verbo
	Advérbios	*tomorrow, next…, in…* etc.
	Exemplo	I **am going to visit** you next month.
	Indica	ações futuras planejadas

	Forma	Infinitivo sem *to*	
Imperative	Advérbios	*now, right now*	
	Exemplos	**Get out** now!	**Don't come back** here!
	Indica	ordens, pedidos	
Simple Past	Forma	Regulares: verbo + ***-ed/-d***	
		Irregulares: ver página 382	
		Auxiliar: ***did***	
	Advérbios	*yesterday, last…, in…* etc.	
	Exemplos	I **danced** last night.	He **swam** last week.
	Indica	ações ocorridas em determinado momento no passado	
Past Continuous	Forma	***To be*** (*Simple Past*) + verbo + ***-ing***	
	Advérbios	*yesterday, last…, in…, when, while* etc.	
	Exemplo	She **was sleeping** two minutes ago.	
	Indica	ações em andamento no passado	

4 Circle the verbs in the text. Then write these verbs in the categories below.

Street dance is a category that encompasses different dance styles, the most famous of which is hip-hop. It started in the 1970s in the U.S. and its name comes from the fact that amateurs who were constantly dancing on the streets, schools, and nightclubs were the ones who created it. Street dance involves improvisation and interaction with the audience. It is popular in many countries and there are lots of competitions all over the world. If you are looking for an opportunity to have fun, meet new people, and exercise, look for competitions in your neighborhood: you are certainly going to find plenty of interesting events.

Based on <www.need2know.co.uk/health/keeping_fit/article1079>.
Accessed on August 20, 2015.

1 Simple Present _____

2 Present Continuous _____

3 Future with *Going to* _____

4 Imperative _____

5 Simple Past _____

6 Past Continuous _____

Go to page 110 for Extra Practice.

Reading

Before Reading

1 **Discuss the questions below in Portuguese.**

   1   What is intelligence?

   2   Do you think there are different kinds of intelligence? Which ones?

   3   Do you think exercising has any effect on intelligence over time?

2 **Write synonyms for the terms below. Use the words/expressions from the box.**

> can   in the same way   to mend   to adjust   to handle   to maintain

   1   to fix _____

   2   to keep _____

   3   to adapt _____

   4   like _____

   5   be able to _____

   6   to deal with _____

3 **Fill in the blanks with words from the text on page 107. The first letter is given to you.**

   1   Sunbathing **i**_____ the risk of skin cancer.

   2   His eyes were **u**_____ for that job.

   3   The doctor needs to **s**_____ him before he can go home.

   4   She had a very **a**_____ lifestyle.

   5   The police officer made an **e**_____ to check all the cars.

   6   Because of the economic crisis, sales continue to **d**_____.

4 **Take a look at page 107. Then identify the type of text on it.**

   a ☐ anúncio   c ☐ texto informativo

   b ☐ crônica   d ☐ conto

Physical Exercise and Intelligence

Intelligence is not a simple quality. It involves abilities such as learning, solving problems, and thinking and responding quickly.

Different people use these skills in different ways
5 when interpreting abstract ideas, solving practical problems (being good at fixing computers, for example), and relating to other people.

One of the most effective ways to stay mentally sharp is to keep the mind active – especially as
10 we grow older. Intelligence increases until the age of 26, stabilizes until the age of 40, and then declines slowly.

A well-exercised mind uses less energy than an untrained one when dealing with a complex
15 situation. One of the reasons is that the brain adapts to mental training similar to the way that muscles respond to physical training. A trained brain uses fewer neurons, just like fit muscles use fewer fibers to perform a task. Consequently, less
20 fuel (carbohydrates) is consumed, resulting in more efficiency. Similarly to the body, the mind is able to do more with less effort.

Moreover, studies show that exercising increases the release of "growth hormones", which help improve brain health. Physical activities have also 25 been associated with the growth of new neurons.

To sum up, although the combination of physical and mental activity is not the fountain of youth, it certainly is the best thing we can do to keep our intelligence sharp. 30

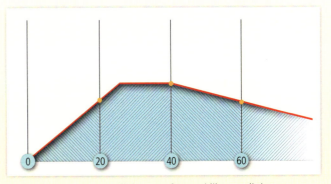

Intelligence increases until the age of 26, stabilizes until the age of 40, and then declines slowly.

Based on <www.psychologytoday.com/blog/the-athletes-way/201312/can-physical-activities-improve-fluid-intelligence>; <https://news.google.com/newspapers?nid=1356&dat=19930302&id=ptFPAAAAIBAJ&sjid=1AcEAAAAIBAJ&pg=6326,1006703&hl=en>. Accessed on August 5, 2015.

▶ Vocabulary

| **deal with:** lidar com | **fit muscle:** músculo exercitado | **grow older:** envelhecer | **like:** como | **perform:** executar |

After Reading

 Identificar conectivos e associá-los à organização do texto

Palavras de ligação, ou conectivos, são usadas para articular as ideias do texto. Elas podem indicar causa e efeito, contraste, sequência cronológica, ênfase, ordem de importância, exemplificação, conclusão etc.

1 Complete the sentences with the connectives from the box.

> consequently   moreover   then   to sum up

1 _____, it is possible to affirm that the test was successful.

2 First, enter the website. _____, type your username and password.

3 The woman changed her eating habits; _____, her health improved.

4 The new movie has more action scenes; _____, the dialogues are better.

2 Now look at the sentences in activity 1 and match the connectives to the ideas they express.

1 consequently   a ☐ sequence of events

2 moreover   b ☐ result

3 then   c ☐ additional information

4 to sum up   d ☐ summary

3 Find out what the words in bold refer to.

1 "*Intelligence is not a simple quality. **It** involves abilities such as learning […]*" (lines 1-2).

_____

2 "*A well-exercised mind uses less energy than an untrained **one** […]*" (lines 13-14).

_____

4 Answer the questions about the text.

1 What does intelligence involve? _____

_____

2 What is one of the most effective ways to stay mentally sharp? _____

_____

3 Which uses more energy: an untrained mind or a trained one? _____

_____

4 What fuel do our body and our mind use? _____

Vocabulary Expansion

1 **Complete the sentences using the appropriate form of the verbs given.**

| eat | donate | finish | work | pay | leave |

> **Preposition + verb + -ing**
>
> Após preposições, os verbos devem ser usados com a terminação **-ing**.
> She is interested **in studying** History.
> He is good **at playing** the guitar.

1   The kids can play after _____eating_____ something.

2   You can't leave without _____ your debts.

3   I'd like to thank you for _____ a lot of money to our charity.

4   Please call me before _____ for school.

5   I'm tired of _____ for him.

6   He left the office after _____ all his tasks.

2 **Match the words to their meaning.**

> **Well + adjective**
>
> **well-exercised:** bem exercitado

1   well-defined   a ☐ bem conhecido

2   well-done   b ☐ bem-intencionado

3   well-known   c ☐ bem passado; bem feito

4   well-intentioned   d ☐ bem definido

3 **Complete the sentences using the words from activity 2.**

1   Cielo is a _____ swimmer. Everybody knows him.

2   Tom called the waiter and asked for a _____ steak.

3   Mary is the most _____ girl at school. She helps everyone.

4   John's projects are all _____. His instructions are very precise.

4 **Write the correct meaning of the word "as". Use the box for help.**

1   My uncle's friend worked **as** a personal trainer. _____

2   Last week I talked to Mary **as** we were jogging. _____

3   My father is **as** intelligent **as** my mother. _____

4   **As** a child, Pelé lived in Bauru. _____

5   **As** you aren't reading the book, I will give it back to Peter. _____

> **As**
>
> enquanto
> quando
> tão… quanto
> uma vez que
> como (na função de)

Extra Practice 4

1 Check the meaning of the words and expressions in bold.

1 **Few people** are aware that children are harvesting cocoa.

a ☐ Muitas pessoas

b ☐ Várias pessoas

c ☐ Poucas pessoas

2 The man promised to help the boy **get** to the Ivory Coast.

a ☐ chegar

b ☐ voltar

c ☐ ficar

3 Waves **beat** against the cliffs for hours this morning.

a ☐ presentearam

b ☐ bateram

c ☐ lembraram

4 The traffickers tried **to avoid** the official border checks.

a ☐ evitar

b ☐ encontrar

c ☐ enganar

2 Remove the suffixes and find the original words.

1 production _____

2 dangerous _____

3 immediately _____

4 trafficker _____

5 owner _____

6 doer _____

7 honorary _____

8 repeatedly _____

9 Malian _____

10 consulate _____

11 extremely _____

12 slowly _____

13 comfortable _____

14 monthly _____

3 **Check the correct alternative to complete the sentences.**

1 I don't have _____ time to talk to you because I am _____ late.

  a ☐ very – very   **c** ☐ much – very

  b ☐ many – very   **d** ☐ much – many

2 _____ people know that there are _____ children working in sweatshops.

  a ☐ Many – less   **c** ☐ Less – little

  b ☐ Few – many   **d** ☐ Fewer – much

3 There isn't _____ bread in the house. Could you buy _____ loaves, please?

  a ☐ many – less   **c** ☐ much – a few

  b ☐ little – much   **d** ☐ much – much

4 I ordered _____ gallons of lemonade this month because the children aren't home.

  a ☐ fewer   **c** ☐ less

  b ☐ very   **d** ☐ much

5 I want to ask you _____ questions. It won't take _____ time.

  a ☐ a lot of – many   **c** ☐ many – very

  b ☐ a few – much   **d** ☐ much – many

6 Nowadays we spend _____ money to buy _____ things.

  a ☐ less – less   **c** ☐ few – few

  b ☐ much – less   **d** ☐ more – fewer

7 My brother is a _____ curious person.

  a ☐ many   **c** ☐ few

  b ☐ fewer   **d** ☐ very

8 She drinks _____ coffee because she is always _____ tired.

  a ☐ many – much   **c** ☐ a lot of – very

  b ☐ few – little   **d** ☐ very – a little

4 Complete the sentences using the words in parentheses and *less... than* or *the least...*

1 Douglas is _____ (popular) Charles.

2 Harold is _____ (intelligent) boy in my class.

3 A bicycle is _____ (expensive) a car.

4 This is _____ (important) aspect of the problem.

5 You are sitting on _____ (comfortable) chair in the room.

5 Complete the sentences using the words in parentheses and *more... than* or *the most...*

1 My project was _____ (successful) in the Science fair.

2 Our experiment is _____ (difficult) theirs.

3 Your car is _____ (economical) mine.

4 This dictionary is _____ (complete) in the library.

5 Apple pies are _____ (delicious) strawberry pies.

6 I think English is _____ (interesting) Geography.

6 Complete the sentences using *as... as* and the words given.

1 The red blouse is _____ (cheap/skirt).

2 I am _____ (hungry/the children).

3 Grace is _____ (beautiful/Sally).

4 Your apartment is _____ (big/my house).

5 Aren't you going to help me? I am _____ (tired/you).

7 Ask questions using the Simple Present.

1 We like coffee.

What _____?

2 She goes to school in the afternoon.

When _____?

3 He lives nearby.

Where _____?

4 They study English in the morning.

What _____?

8 Complete the sentences using the verbs in parentheses.

1 Many rivers _____ (flow) into the sea.

2 Jimmie never _____ (worry) about taking tests.

3 That cat always _____ (destroy) the flowers in my garden.

4 The kids never _____ (help) me when I need something.

5 Does your brother _____ (study) in the morning?

9 Answer the questions using the Present Continuous and the words given.

1 What is she doing now? (read a magazine)

_____

_____

2 Where are the boys swimming? (lake)

_____

_____

3 What are the kids doing? (watch TV)

_____

4 What is Sally eating? (a sandwich)

_____

5 Where are the girls studying? (their room)

_____

6 What is he doing? (fix the car)

_____

10 Complete the sentences using the verbs in parentheses.

1 She isn't swimming now. She _____ (dance).

2 They aren't working at the moment. They _____ (play) the guitar.

3 I _____ (read – neg.) now. I am writing some e-mails.

4 We _____ (leave – neg.) now. We are just talking.

5 They _____ (help – neg.) me. They are doing their homework.

11 Rewrite the sentences using *going to* and the words/expressions given. Make the necessary changes.

1 She types her boss's e-mails every day. (tomorrow)

_____

2 I eat fish every week. (next week)

_____

3 They tell stories to the children every day. (in the afternoon)

_____

4 The weather is fine today. (the day after tomorrow)

_____

5 I take the subway to work every day. (next year)

_____

6 We have tennis lessons this semester. (next semester)

_____

12 Underline the correct alternative.

1 There aren't **much** / **many** things to do in this city.

2 We can't go out tonight. I have **little** / **few** money.

3 Best friends **doesn't** / **don't** lie to each other.

4 When I **was coming** / **came** to school yesterday I **see** / **saw** an accident.

5 We **destroy** / **are destroying** our forests faster and faster.

6 My mom **started** / **is going to start** a new course next week. She **is going to learn** / **learns** Mandarin.

13 Complete the sentences using the verbs in parentheses in the Simple Past or in the Past Continuous.

1 It _____ (rain) this morning when I got up.

2 When you called, she _____ (take) a shower.

3 I _____ (cut) my finger while I was making some bread.

4 You _____ (cross) the street when I saw you.

5 The light went out while we _____ (have) dinner.

6 He was talking to his friend when he _____ (hear) a strange noise.

Job Corner 4

Things Never to Do during a Job Interview

There are many things that you should NEVER do during a job interview. Some of them are listed below.

Ask what the company works with. Instead, research the company before going to the interview.

Lie about your qualifications.

Use very informal language or slangs.

Emphasize your weaknesses. If asked questions like "What is your greatest weakness?", say you don't like to waste time on small talk and are working on being more friendly where you work. This is a positive "weakness".

Ask how much the job pays.

Criticize a former employer.

Say "No" when asked if you have any questions. Instead, ask questions about the company's plans for the future, for example.

Tell them your life story. If asked to talk about yourself, tell them where you went to school or where you have worked.

Based on <http://pattyinglishms.hubpages.com/hub/5_things_you_should_NEVER_say>; <www.businessinsider.com/worst-things-say-job-interview-career-2015-7>. Accessed on August 11, 2015.

Vocabulary

criticize: criticar　　**employer:** empregador(a)　　**friendly:** amigável　　**slang:** gíria

emphasize: enfatizar　　**former:** anterior　　**should:** deveria　　**waste:** desperdiçar

9 Cyberbullying

Look at the picture and answer orally.

1 What does the picture tell you about this unit?

2 How would you define "cyberbullying"?

3 Have you ever received intimidating or offensive messages online?

4 Can you name some of the possible effects of cyberbullying?

Language in Context

1 **Take a look at the text.**

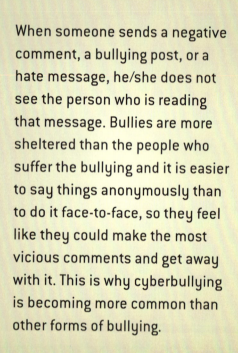
When someone sends a negative comment, a bullying post, or a hate message, he/she does not see the person who is reading that message. Bullies are more sheltered than the people who suffer the bullying and it is easier to say things anonymously than to do it face-to-face, so they feel like they could make the most vicious comments and get away with it. This is why cyberbullying is becoming more common than other forms of bullying.

Based on <http://nobullying.com/sad-bullying-stories>. Accessed on March 3, 2016.

2 **Give your opinion about the text.**

1 Do you think the identity of an anonymous bully is never going to be revealed?

2 What other forms of bullying besides cyberbullying are there?

3 **Read, think, and answer orally.**

Cyberbullying is becoming more common than other forms of bullying.
They feel like they could make the most vicious comments and get away with it.

1 What do the sentences have in common?

2 What is being compared in each one of them?

Vocabulary

bully: pessoa que pratica *bullying*
bullying: intimidação, assédio moral
get away with: escapar, ficar impune
hate: ódio
sheltered: protegido(a), escondido(a)
vicious: cruel, maldoso(a)

Language Practice

Comparison (II)

Ortografia

Geralmente formam-se o comparativo e o superlativo de **adjetivos e advérbios de uma sílaba** acrescentando-se **-er/-est** a eles:

strong – strong**er** – strong**est**   young – young**er** – young**est**

Roy is strong**er** than me.   James is the young**est** person in my family.

Observe as alterações de grafia:

- adjetivo de uma sílaba terminado em **e**: larg**e** – larg**er** – larg**est**
- adjetivo de uma sílaba terminado em **consoante + vogal + consoante**: hot – hot**ter** – hot**test**
- adjetivo de duas sílabas terminado em **y**: happ**y** – happ**ier** – happ**iest**

This room is larg**er** than the kitchen.

The weather today is hot**ter** than yesterday.

She is the happ**iest** girl in our group.

Adjetivos com **duas ou mais sílabas** recebem **more/most**:

more charming   **more** obscure   **more** hopeful

most curious   **most** surprised   **most** comfortable

She is **more** <u>charming</u> than her sister.

He is the **most** <u>curious</u> boy I know.

Formas irregulares:

good – better – best   bad – worse – worst

far – farther/further – farthest/furthest   much/many – more – most

Yesterday was the **best** day of my life.

You threw the ball far but I threw it **farther**.

That was the **worst** idea that came up.

Uso

Construções especiais:

It is getting colder and colder. (Está ficando cada vez mais frio.)

She is getting more and more beautiful. (Ela está ficando cada vez mais bonita.)

The hotter the soup, the better. (Quanto mais quente a sopa, melhor.)

The more difficult, the more fascinating. (Quanto mais difícil, mais fascinante.)

1 Write the comparative and superlative forms of the adjectives below.

		Comparative	Superlative
1	lucky	_____	_____
2	fat	_____	_____
3	good	_____	_____
4	furious	_____	_____
5	sweet	_____	_____
6	bad	_____	_____

2 Complete the sentences using the adjectives in parentheses in the comparative form.

1 This street is _____ (safe) during the day than at night.

2 Your brother is probably _____ (thin) than mine.

3 My backpack is _____ (light) than yours today.

4 This book is _____ (bad) than the one I read last week.

5 I'm not sure, but I think that my son is _____ (tall) than yours.

6 Airplanes are definitely _____ (fast) than cars.

3 Complete the sentences using the adjectives in parentheses in the superlative form.

1 My dad is _____ (strong) man in my family.

2 Your grandpa is _____ (old) man in the neighborhood.

3 Our uncle is _____ (lucky) person in the world.

4 This is _____ (large) river in Brazil.

5 Gloria is _____ (short) girl among my friends.

6 English is _____ (easy) subject at school.

4 Write the sentences in English.

1 Quanto mais fácil, melhor.

_____

2 Quanto mais misterioso, mais interessante.

_____

3 Eu estou ficando cada vez mais curioso.

_____

5 **Read the sentences below and answer the questions.**

1   I am 17, Joan is 19, and Fred is 21 years old.

Who is the oldest of the three?
Fred is the oldest of the three.

2   My mother was born in 1961. Dave's mother was born in 1957. Lionel's mother was born in 1974.

Who is the youngest of the three?

_____

3   Your teacher is 170 cm tall. Your brother's teacher is 180 cm tall.

Who is the tallest of them?

_____

4   The blue book costs $10, the red book costs $15, and the white one costs $50.

Which is the least expensive of the three?

_____

5   The temperature in São Paulo is 25° C, the temperature in Rio de Janeiro is 31° C, and the temperature in Florianópolis is 28° C.

Which city is the hottest of the three?

_____

6 **Answer the questions. Write complete sentences.**

1   Which vacation plan do you think is nicer: going to the beach or going to the countryside?

_____

2   Which city do you think is more expensive: São Paulo or New York?

_____

3   Who is the funniest person you know?

_____

4   Who is your most intelligent friend?

_____

5   What is the best movie you have ever seen?

_____

Go to page 136 for Extra Practice.

Before Reading

1 **Discuss the questions below in Portuguese.**

1 Do you know anyone who has received a bullying message?

2 Do you know anyone who has sent a bullying message?

3 How would you react if you received a bullying message?

>
>
> **Identificar e reconhecer a organização textual**
>
> Observar como o texto é organizado ajuda o leitor a entender seu contexto de circulação e seus objetivos comunicativos.

2 👓 **Look at the text on page 123 and check the correct alternative.**

1 The text is organized...

a ☐ evidencing cause and effect.   c ☐ in questions and answers.

b ☐ in chronological order.   d ☐ focusing on comparison and contrast.

2 A text with this characteristic can be considered...

a ☐ a scientific report.   c ☐ a tutorial.

b ☐ an interview.   d ☐ a fable.

3 👓 **Which elements in the text helped you in activity 2? Answer in Portuguese.**

_____

4 **Infer the meaning of the words/expressions in bold based on the context.**

1 *"She was going to **attend** a school that would be good for her"* (lines 13-14).

a ☐ atender   b ☐ ajudar   c ☐ frequentar

2 *"They **exchanged** messages all summer"* (line 19).

a ☐ apagaram   b ☐ mudaram   c ☐ trocaram

3 *"[...] whose daughter had had a **brawl** with Tina at school"* (lines 28-29).

a ☐ briga   b ☐ encontro   c ☐ amizade

How Cyberbullying Changed Ms. Cashter's Life

The story told in the interview below is true; however, the interview itself never took place and the names of the people involved were changed. This situation is the reality in our days, and many other mothers around the world have
5 similar stories to tell. Perhaps there is a Tina close to you.

Reporter: What was Tina like?
Daisy Cashter: My daughter was a normal 13-year-old girl.

R: In what aspects?
DC: Well, you know: crazy about her friends, crazier about games and films in her cell phone, and a bit insecure
10 about her body. Sometimes she was a little depressed, especially when kids at school made fun of her. But she usually enjoyed spending time with her family and also with her friends.

R: Can you tell us what happened to Tina?
DC: When she got to eighth grade, we transferred her to a private school. She was going to attend a school that would be good for her: uniform, no makeup, stricter discipline. About that time, she started using social
15 media, under my supervision. She made an online friend, Timothy Legger. Tina was the happiest girl in the world because she was friends with a handsome boy.

R: She didn't have any boy friends?
DC: Just classmates, not a special friend. She had problems with her weight and low self-esteem. But then this boy came up and he was nicer to her than most kids at school. They exchanged messages all summer. But then
20 right before school started, it happened.

R: What happened?
DC: His messages became mean and hateful. Tina was very upset and I told her to stop using the social networks, but she didn't. She kept talking to Timothy. He finally told her that everybody at school knew that she was fat and ugly and that they thought the world would be a better place without her.

25 **R: And how did she react to that?**
DC: She got desperate and hanged herself in the closet. We took her to the hospital, but she died the next day.

R: Did you go after Timothy or anything like that?
DC: The police found out that there was no Timothy. The bully was a 45-year-old woman whose daughter had had a brawl with Tina at school.

Based on <http://nobullying.com/sad-bullying-stories>. Accessed on March 3, 2016.

Vocabulary

come up: surgir	**handsome:** bonito(a)	**makeup:** maquiagem	**self-esteem:** autoestima
enjoy: gostar	**hang:** enforcar	**mean:** maldoso(a)	**take place:** acontecer
especially: principalmente	**make fun:** ridicularizar	**perhaps:** talvez	**weight:** peso

After Reading

1 Why was Daisy Cashter interviewed?

a ☐ To defend a person who was accused of cyberbullying.

b ☐ To inform about the dangers of cyberbullying.

c ☐ To help Tina's mother find her daughter's bully.

2 What was the true nature of Timothy Legger?

a ☐ He was a handsome boy that was nice to Tina.

b ☐ He was someone who wanted to help Tina with her depression.

c ☐ He was the false identity created by an older woman online.

> **Ler nas entrelinhas**
>
> A capacidade de fazer inferências permite ao leitor buscar o significado mais profundo do texto, apreendendo aquilo que não está explicitamente dito.

3 Check all the correct statements about Tina.

a ☐ She had communication issues with her family.

b ☐ She had quite a few boy friends at her old school.

c ☐ She thought Timothy was a very handsome boy.

d ☐ She was happier after she became friends with Timothy.

e ☐ She never found out who Timothy really was.

4 What did Ms. Cashter mean when she said "But then this boy came up and he was nicer to her than most kids at school" (lines 18-19)?

a ☐ Tina was not accepted by most of her classmates at school.

b ☐ Tina was treated nicely by her classmates at school.

c ☐ Timothy made their classmates be nicer to Tina.

5 Discuss with your classmates.

1 Do you think the issue presented in the interview is common in your community?

2 What could Tina have done in order to deal with her problem?

3 Do you think the police should be involved in cases of cyberbullying?

Vocabulary Expansion

> **Suffix -ity**
>
> O sufixo **-ity** forma substantivos e indica o estado ou a qualidade descritos por determinado adjetivo.
> real – real**ity**
> able – abi**lity**

1 Read the information in the box. Then write new words based on the ones in parentheses to complete the sentences.

1 Where are you from? What's your _____ (national)?

2 What I admire in him is his strong _____ (personal).

3 These boys are my _____ (responsible).

4 There is a high _____ (probable) of rain tonight.

5 The students complained about the _____ (complex) of the test.

6 They were shocked by the _____ (absurd) of the situation.

2 Complete the sentences below based on the information in the box.

> **Adverbs**
>
> **also** (também): Chris is **also** going to London.
> **too** (também, em frases afirmativas): Chris is going to London **too**.
> **either** (também, em frases negativas): Chris isn't going to London **either**.

1 Carla plays the piano very well and she sings _____.

2 I didn't know the answer to the question and he didn't know it _____.

3 Frank was _____ in the room and saw everything.

4 Harry is not living in Canada; Susan is not living there _____.

5 We are studying for the test; they are _____ studying.

3 Read the information in the box and circle the best alternative.

> **False Cognates**
>
> **attend:** frequentar, comparecer
> **answer:** atender (ao telefone, à porta)
> **pretend:** fingir
> **intend:** pretender
> **policy:** política
> **police:** polícia

1 She never **answers** / **attends** the phone when she is having dinner.

2 My friend is a medical student. He **pretends** / **intends** to be a doctor.

3 The party was so noisy last night that my neighbor called the **policy** / **police**.

4 My father **attended** / **answered** high school in London.

5 The thief **intended** / **pretended** to be innocent.

6 The Brazilian president is expected to implement an environmental **policy** / **police**.

10 Relationships

Look at the picture and answer orally.

1   What does the picture tell you about this unit?

2   Can you list different kinds of relationships?

3   Are all relationships positive? Can you name some examples of harmful relationships?

Language in Context

1 **Take a look at the cartoon.**

2 Give your opinion about the cartoon.

Vocabulary

too far: longe demais

1 Why is the boy speaking so cautiously with his father?

2 Have you ever done anything like that? What happened?

3 Read, think, and answer orally.

Dad, you love me, don't you?

It's not my problem, is it?

1 Are the sentences in the affirmative, negative, or interrogative form?

2 What is the purpose of "don't you?" and "is it?" in these sentences?

Language Practice

Tag Questions

Verbo auxiliar/modal + pronome	
Oração afirmativa	*tag question* negativa (verbo na forma contraída)
Oração negativa	*tag question* afirmativa

Uso

As *tag questions* são usadas para pedir uma confirmação do que foi dito.

- Oração afirmativa:

  Cindy <u>works</u> hard, **doesn't she**?

  The girls <u>ate</u> the cake, **didn't they**?

  You <u>can</u> read, **can't you**?

- Oração negativa:

  That man <u>doesn't work</u>, **does he**?

  Your mom <u>wasn't</u> happy, **was she**?

  The babies <u>won't cry</u>, **will they**?

- Exceções:

  I <u>am</u> late, **aren't I**?

  <u>Let's</u> dance, **shall we**?

  <u>Open</u> the door, **will you**?

  <u>Don't open</u> the door, **will you**?

  She <u>never came</u>, **did she**?

1 **Complete the sentences using the tag questions from the box.**

will you	hasn't she	will he	shall we	doesn't she	must we

1 Your sister has seen the accident, _____?

2 Your brother won't come for dinner, _____?

3 That girl plays the piano, _____?

4 Let's talk for a moment, _____?

5 We mustn't stay here, _____?

6 Don't step on the grass, _____?

2 Complete the sentences with the appropriate tag question.

1 I am crazy, _____?

2 Mary doesn't like hot coffee, _____?

3 The boys are walking to school, _____?

4 You ate my sandwich last night, _____?

5 Paul didn't work yesterday, _____?

Simple Future

Will + verbo principal

I You He She It We You They	will work.	**Afirmativa:** He **will work** on Sunday. **Interrogativa: Will** he **work** on Sunday? **Negativa:** He **will not work** on Sunday. **Formas abreviadas:** '**ll** (will) **won't** (will not)

Uso

Expressa ações futuras ou previsões para o futuro.

I think I **will go** with you.   The fortune-teller said he **will meet** someone.

Geralmente usado com expressões que indicam futuro: *tomorrow*, *next year*, *in July*, *on Monday* etc.

We **will study** hard <u>next year</u>.

Pode ser usado também para fazer um pedido.

Will you **open** the door, please?

> **Nota**
> Com *I* e *we*, é possível substituir *will* por **shall**, mas esse uso é considerado formal, sendo mais comum em perguntas ou quando se faz uma oferta, uma sugestão ou um convite.
> **Shall** <u>I</u> help you?   **Shall** <u>we</u> go?

Future Continuous

Will be + verbo terminado em **-ing**

Afirmativa: He **will be** work**ing** tonight.
Interrogativa: Will he **be** work**ing** tonight?
Negativa: He **will not be** work**ing** tonight.

Uso

Expressa uma ação que estará em progresso em um determinado momento no futuro.

Tomorrow at 4 o'clock I'**ll be talking** to him.

3 Write the following sentences in the negative and interrogative forms.

1 They will study Math tomorrow.
   They will not/won't study Math tomorrow.
   _____
   Will they study Math tomorrow?
   _____

2 She will come home after 10 o'clock.
   _____
   _____

3 We will meet them in the cafeteria.
   _____
   _____

4 My brother will play basketball in the park after school.
   _____
   _____

4 Complete the sentences using the Future Continuous and the information in parentheses.

1 At 4 o'clock tomorrow they _____ will be leaving for London _____ (leave for London).

2 In July next year I _____ (paint my house).

3 At this time on Saturday we _____ (swim in the ocean).

4 Tomorrow evening Grandma _____ (arrive from Canada).

5 Unscramble the words to make sentences.

1 people – be – salad – will – a few – at – lunchtime – eating
   _____

2 be – bus – his – tonight – we – for – waiting – him – will – arrives – when
   _____

3 tomorrow – come – will – she – probably – back
   _____

4 meet – won't – next – my – weekend – friends
   _____

Go to page 136 for Extra Practice.

Before Reading

1 Discuss the questions below in Portuguese.

  1 What do you understand by "abusive relationship"?

  2 Do you think this is a problem in your community?

> **Relacionar o suporte do texto à sua finalidade**
>
> Identificar o suporte em que o texto está sendo veiculado ajuda o leitor a entender com qual finalidade ele foi escrito.

2 **Skim the text and answer the questions.**

  1 What type of text is it?

  a ☐ An online scientific report.   b ☐ An informative leaflet.

  2 What is its main objective?

  a ☐ To provide statistic data on dating violence around the world.

  b ☐ To narrate events in the lives of teens that are victims of dating violence.

  c ☐ To provide information about a possible problem in the lives of teenagers.

3 Check the correct meaning of the words in bold.

  1 "*Dating violence is a type of intimate **partner** violence*" (lines 1-2).

  a ☐ entre parceiros   b ☐ partida

  2 "*This means forcing a partner to **engage** in a sex act [...]*" (lines 13-14).

  a ☐ envolver-se em   b ☐ evitar

  3 "*[...] when he/she does not or cannot **consent***" (lines 14-15).

  a ☐ conseguir   b ☐ consentir

4 Look up these words in the glossary.

  1 name-calling _____   3 harass _____

  2 embarrass _____   4 tease _____

DATING VIOLENCE

(21)

Dating violence is a type of intimate partner violence. It occurs between two people in a close relationship. The nature of dating violence can be physical, emotional, or sexual.

- **Physical** – This occurs when a partner is hit, shoved, slapped, or kicked.

- **Psychological/Emotional** – This means threatening a partner or harming his/her self-esteem. Examples include name-calling, bullying, embarrassing on purpose, or keeping him/her away from friends and family.

- **Sexual** – This means forcing a partner to engage in a sex act when he/she does not or cannot consent. This can be physical or nonphysical, like threatening to spread rumors if a partner refuses to have sex.

- **Stalking** – This refers to harassing or threatening tactics that cause fear in the victim.

Dating violence can occur in person or electronically, as repeated texting or posting sexual pictures of a partner online.

Unhealthy relationships can start early and last long. Teens often think some behaviors, like teasing and name-calling, are a "normal" part of a relationship. However, these behaviors can become abusive and develop into more serious forms of violence.

WHO IS AT RISK FOR DATING VIOLENCE?

Factors that increase risk for dating violence include:

- belief that dating violence is acceptable;
- depression, anxiety, and other trauma symptoms;
- aggression towards peers and other aggressive behavior;
- drug and alcohol use;
- having a friend involved in dating violence;
- witnessing or experiencing violence at home.

Dating violence is an issue that has serious effects. Many teens will not report it because they are too afraid to tell friends and family. However, many prevention strategies can stop or reduce dating violence, such as school-based programs that promote changes to the school environment or training adults (like parents and teachers) to work with youth. Therefore, it is essential to discuss this issue at schools and at home, isn't it?

Adapted from <www.cdc.gov/violenceprevention/pdf/teen-dating-violence-factsheet-a.pdf>.
Accessed on October 2, 2015.

Vocabulary

harm: prejudicar, causar dano a
peer: colega
refuse: recusar

shove: empurrar
slap: estapear
spread: espalhar

stalk: perseguir
threaten: ameaçar
witness: testemunhar

After Reading

1 Check the items that are mentioned in the text.

a ☐ List of effects of dating violence.

b ☐ Elements that increase the risk of dating violence.

c ☐ Possible environments in which dating violence happens.

d ☐ Types of dating violence.

2 Write T (true) or F (false) according to the text. Then correct the false statements.

1 ☐ Dating violence can occur between people who don't know each other.

_____

2 ☐ Calling a person names is a type of psychological/emotional violence.

_____

3 ☐ If a boyfriend harasses his girlfriend, he may be stalking her.

_____

4 ☐ Dating violence can only happen in person, when partners are together.

_____

5 ☐ Sometimes teens are suffering dating violence but they think this behavior is normal.

_____

6 ☐ All teens who experience dating violence talk about it.

_____

Reagir ao texto

Uma estratégia para a apropriação do conteúdo de um texto é reagir a ele de alguma forma, por exemplo, perguntando-se "O que o texto não disse?" ou "O que posso fazer com as informações que obtive?".

3 Discuss the following questions in Portuguese.

1 Who do you think are the most common victims of dating violence? Why?

2 Why do you think victims of dating violence are afraid to talk to others about the problem? What do they think could happen to them?

3 In your opinion, what can be done to help people deal with this issue?

Vocabulary Expansion

1 **Read the box and write new words. Then translate these new words.**

> **Suffix *-ship***
>
> O sufixo *-ship* forma substantivos e indica condição, *status* ou habilidade (de).
> relation – relation**ship**   member – member**ship**

1	friend	friendship	amizade
2	author		
3	leader		
4	champion		
5	citizen		
6	partner		

2 **Match the words below to their meaning.**

1	readership	a	☐	propriedade
2	dictatorship	b	☐	bolsa de estudos
3	ownership	c	☐	público leitor
4	scholarship	d	☐	companheirismo
5	companionship	e	☐	ditadura
6	sponsorship	f	☐	patrocínio

3 **Complete the sentences using the words in the box.**

> **Too**
>
> Além de "também", a palavra *too* significa "demais", quando usada antes de adjetivos.
> They were **too** afraid to say anything.

> against   enough   too (2x)   always   only

1   I'm not going to the game today. I'm _____ tired.

2   _____ teachers can come into this room.

3   He is a terrible candidate. Everybody is _____ his ideas.

4   Jack never goes out on Sundays. He is _____ at home.

5   She will not buy that house because it is _____ expensive.

6   My brother can't go to the movies with us: he's not old _____.

1 Choose the correct alternative.

1 The man said, "_____".

    a ☐ The more interesting, the better.   **c** ☐ The interesting, the better.

    b ☐ The most interesting, the best.   **d** ☐ The more interesting, the good.

2 His financial situation was getting _____.

    a ☐ worse and worst   **c** ☐ worse and worse

    b ☐ worser and worser   **d** ☐ bad and badder

3 This dog is _____ dangerous _____ a lion.

    a ☐ more – as   **c** ☐ as – most

    b ☐ as – as   **d** ☐ as – more

4 Sandra is thin. Josie is _____ Sandra. Anne is _____.

    a ☐ as thin – the most thin of all   **c** ☐ thinner than – the thinnest of all

    b ☐ thinner than – the thin of all   **d** ☐ thinner as – the thinnest of all

5 Which was the _____ day of your life?

    a ☐ bad   **c** ☐ worse

    b ☐ baddest   **d** ☐ worst

6 I think I have _____ car in town.

    a ☐ the slow   **c** ☐ the more slow

    b ☐ the slower   **d** ☐ the slowest

2 **There are mistakes in some of the sentences below. Circle these mistakes and rewrite the sentences correcting them.**

1 Their car is more new than ours: they bought it last week.

_____

2 I bought the cheapest skateboard I could find in the store.

_____

3 Small cities are usually most safest than big cities.

_____

4 Apples are sweeter than lemons, but I like both.

_____

5 Metal is heaviest than cotton.

_____

6 Sports cars are more fast than trucks.

_____

3 **Complete the sentences using the adjectives in parentheses in the correct form.**

1 Giraffes are _____ (thin) than elephants.

2 John looks _____ (young) than his brother Peter.

3 My brother is the _____ (lucky) person in our family.

4 This is the _____ (recent) file I could find for the report.

5 Pamela is _____ (excited) about the party than I am.

6 India is the _____ (hot) country I have ever visited.

4 **Use the adjectives from the box in the correct form to complete the sentences below.**

| easy | soon | pretty | hot | large | good | intelligent |

1 Russia is _____ country in the world.

2 The coffee is _____ the tea.

3 She is _____ person I know. I learn a lot from her.

4 Which dress do you think is _____: the black one or the purple one?

5 I think the English test was _____ the Chemistry one.

6 Don't forget to give me an answer: the _____, the _____!

5 Check the appropriate tag question.

1 You will travel next month, _____?

   a ☐ will you   c ☐ won't you

   b ☐ are you   d ☐ won't I

2 Drink your milk, _____?

   a ☐ shall we   c ☐ do you

   b ☐ won't you   d ☐ will you

3 Kate can sleep here tonight, _____?

   a ☐ can't she   c ☐ doesn't she

   b ☐ can she   d ☐ can't I

4 Those men work hard, _____?

   a ☐ don't he   c ☐ doesn't he

   b ☐ don't they   d ☐ do they

5 Your friend Marcus couldn't come today, _____?

   a ☐ did he   c ☐ could she

   b ☐ couldn't he   d ☐ could he

6 I told you we would win this game, _____?

   a ☐ did you   c ☐ did I

   b ☐ didn't I   d ☐ didn't we

6 **Complete the sentences using the correct tag questions.**

1 I am late for my Spanish class again, _____?

2 You weren't in the park yesterday, _____?

3 The dogs won't run away, _____?

4 Let's talk for a minute about what happened, _____?

5 It's so cold in here! Don't open the door, _____?

6 Your parents are upset this morning, _____?

7 **Complete the sentences using the verbs in parentheses in the Simple Future.**

1 I _____ (arrive – neg.) at the airport before 2 o'clock.

2 _____ Paul _____ (work) on this new project next weekend?

3 The Browns _____ (move) to a house in London in November. They're very excited about it.

4 They _____ (catch – neg.) the midnight train to Amsterdam, so they have to find a place to stay.

5 _____ the recording of her new album _____ (begin) in February or in March?

6 Dad _____ (make) dinner for us next Monday.

8 **Rewrite the sentences in the Future Continuous.**

1 At 7 o'clock tomorrow I will play tennis.

_____

2 They will fly to Japan at this time tomorrow.

_____

3 She will study when I get home.

_____

4 In half an hour I will watch a movie.

_____

5 We will eat pizza soon.

_____

6 He will travel to Recife tomorrow afternoon.

_____

9 Unscramble the words to make sentences.

1 meet – will – I – Janet – cafeteria – in – week – the – next

_____

2 at – in – to – London – February – she – this – be – time – flying – will

_____

3 they – will – us – to – visit – when – come – they – São Paulo – ?

_____

4 travel – to – because – they – holiday – need – won't – no – , – the – on – they – study

_____

5 call – him – he – sleeping – will – when – be – you

_____

6 train – the – be – raining – station – will – it – probably – we – get – when – to

_____

10 You went to the fortune-teller yesterday. Write four things she predicted for your future.

Social Media

The explosive growth of networks such as Facebook, LinkedIn, Twitter, Pinterest, Instagram, and Snapchat (plus international networks such as China's Weibo or Russia's VKontakte) has given rise to a social media industry which directly employs hundreds of thousands, if not millions, of people worldwide in a wide variety of specialist roles. Different careers are available in this area.

Software/UX Developers

Social platforms, apps, and games require software developers to put them together in the first place and to continuously redevelop them according to users' expectations. The vital importance of a good User Experience (UX) to the success of such developments means that UX specialists will continue to be in high demand.

Community Managers

After attracting an audience on social media, it's important to ensure that users feel part of a community. A social media community manager encourages active involvement, measures performance using various social media analytic tools, and recommends content according to user demand.

Personal Customer Service Managers

Social media gives companies the opportunity to create and maintain a genuine one-to-one relationship with their customers. Expect demand for customer service professionals skilled in nurturing relationships via social channels to grow rapidly over the next few years.

Digital Marketers

Advertising is the largest component of revenue growth in social media. The flexibility, cost-efficiency, and effectiveness of social media ads mean that digital marketing agencies will continue to require a high volume of digitally-savvy marketing consultants.

Corporate Games Master

With companies trying to have the type of success created by social games such as Candy Crush and Angry Birds, the "gamification" of business processes will require in-house talent.

Content Creators

It is now understood that a steady stream of fresh, engaging, timely, and relevant content is the lifeblood of social media success, which is great news for creative professionals of all kinds: writers, designers, artists, musicians, and video makers.

Social Media Personal Trainer

Whether your end goal is a new job or a new romance, are your social media profiles fit for purpose? The age of the social media personal trainer is coming soon!

Adapted from <www.socialbro.com/social-media-career>.
Accessed on December 9, 2015.

Vocabulary

demand: demanda, procura
ensure: garantir, assegurar
fit for purpose: adequado(a), pertinente
give rise to: causar, originar
goal: objetivo, meta
growth: crescimento
in-house: interno(a)
lifeblood: força vital
nurture: cultivar, promover
revenue: receita, rendimento
savvy: especialista
stream: fluxo, corrente

11 Animal Farm

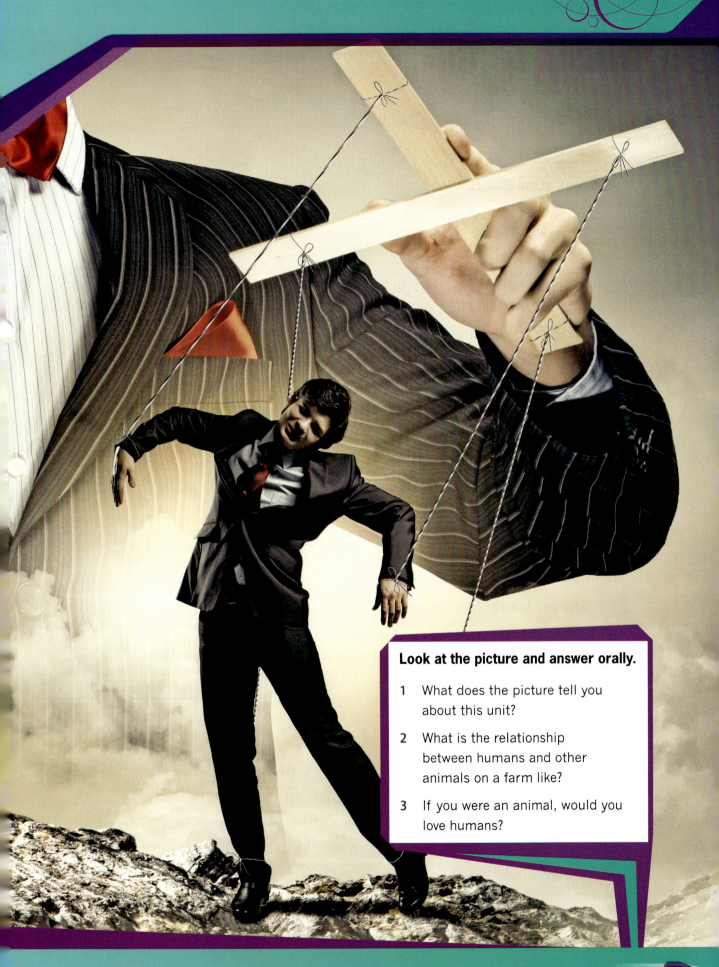

Look at the picture and answer orally.

1   What does the picture tell you about this unit?

2   What is the relationship between humans and other animals on a farm like?

3   If you were an animal, would you love humans?

Language in Context

1 **Take a look at the dialogue.**

Dr. Costello: Dr. Costello speaking.

Sophie: Dad? Where did you put the first-aid kit?

Dr. Costello: Second drawer of the desk in my bedroom. What's the matter, Sophie?

Sophie: I need a bandage. Josie cut herself with a piece of broken glass. Her finger is bleeding a lot.

Dr. Costello: Wash it in running water.

Sophie: I did, but it is still bleeding. It's a bad cut.

Dr. Costello: Bring her to the hospital.

Sophie: I can't. Mom is out with the car.

Dr. Costello: Wait, then. I'm coming home. I want to see that finger myself.

Vocabulary

bleed: sangrar
drawer: gaveta
first-aid kit: *kit* de primeiros socorros
running water: água corrente

2 **Give your opinion about the dialogue.**

1   How do you think Sophie is feeling about the situation?

2   What would you do if you had an emergency like that?

3 **Read, think, and answer orally.**

1   Josie cut the apple in three pieces.

    a   Who did the action?

    _____

    b   Who/What received the action?

    _____

2   Josie cut herself with a piece of broken glass.

    a   Who did the action?

    _____

    b   Who/What received the action?

    _____

Language Practice

Reflexive Pronouns

Personal Pronouns	Reflexive Pronouns
I	my**self**
you	your**self**
he	him**self**
she	her**self**
it	it**self**
we	our**selves**
you	your**selves**
they	them**selves**

Uso

Reflexivo – Indica que o sujeito pratica e recebe o efeito da ação do verbo. Nesse caso, o pronome vem logo após o verbo e concorda com o sujeito.

I hurt **myself** while playing basketball.

John sent **himself** a copy of the e-mail.

Enfático – Enfatiza o sujeito ou o objeto da oração. Não é parte essencial da oração e sua posição pode variar.

She talked to the king.

She **herself** talked to the king. / She talked to the king **herself**. (ênfase no sujeito)

She talked to the king **himself**. (ênfase no objeto)

Idiomático – O pronome vem precedido de *by*, formando uma expressão que significa "sozinho(a)", "sem ajuda".

He lives <u>by</u> **himself**.

I did my homework <u>by</u> **myself**.

1 **Complete the sentences with the appropriate reflexive pronoun.**

1 The reader lost _____ in the book. He found it very interesting.

2 The old lady _____ helped the firemen rescue the little girl.

3 They usually go to school by _____.

4 I made _____ a cup of tea before going to sleep.

5 Ask _____ what you can do to improve your grades.

6 We painted the school wall _____.

2 Rewrite the sentences. Insert reflexive pronouns according to the instructions in parentheses.

1 She looked in the mirror. (reflexive)

   She looked at herself in the mirror.

2 Karen and Tom walked in the park. (idiomatic)

   _____

3 Marion is singing in the shower. (reflexive)

   _____

4 I painted my room. (emphatic – subject)

   _____

5 My little brother can tie his shoes. (idiomatic)

   _____

6 I talked to Emma Watson. (emphatic – object)

   _____

Genitive Case (possuidor + 's/')

Uso

O caso genitivo expressa posse. Geralmente é usado para pessoas e animais em lugar da construção com *of*.

Mary's room (the room of Mary)   the dog's eyes (the eyes of the dog)

Particularidades

Substantivos não terminados em **s** recebem **'s**.

Alan's car   the man's shirt   the women's dresses

Substantivos no singular terminados em **s** recebem **'s**.

my boss's car   the albatross's wings

Substantivos no plural terminados em **s** recebem apenas **'**.

the boys' shoes   the ladies' room

Nomes próprios terminados em **s** recebem **'s**, porém, se forem nomes clássicos ou bíblicos, recebem apenas **'**.

Denis's car   Moses' laws   Jesus' disciples

Substantivos compostos são tratados como substantivos simples.

my mother-in-law's house

O caso genitivo também é usado:

- para se referir a lugares
  We're going to the barber's. (the barber's shop)

- com expressões de tempo
  my two weeks' vacation   a month's salary

- para indicar posse conjunta
  John and Mary's house (os dois possuem a mesma casa)

- para indicar posse individual
  John's and Mary's houses (cada um possui a sua casa)

3 Complete with 's or '.

1 My father _____ friends will arrive tomorrow from Germany.

2 The kids _____ toys are in the garage.

3 The ladies _____ hats were very expensive; they came from Paris.

4 Those men _____ cars aren't very economical.

5 Your neighbor _____ cat is in my kitchen. What should I do?

6 Where's Mr. Andersen _____ book? He is looking for it.

4 Check the correct alternative.

1 My stepsister _____ phone is old. She needs to buy a new one.

a ▢ '   b ▢ 's   c ▢ X

2 I am going to take a four days _____ holiday.

a ▢ '   b ▢ 's   c ▢ X

3 Giulia _____ and Fred _____ apartments are on sale.

a ▢ ' – 's   b ▢ 's – X   c ▢ 's – 's

4 The teacher is going to correct the students _____ tests at home.

a ▢ '   b ▢ 's   c ▢ X

5 My sisters _____ boyfriends are playing soccer.

a ▢ X   b ▢ '   c ▢ 's

Go to page 162 for Extra Practice.

Before Reading

1 Discuss the questions below in Portuguese.

   1 Do you believe human beings respect other forms of life?

   2 Have you ever heard of George Orwell? What do you know about him?

   3 What do you expect a book entitled *Animal Farm* to be about?

2 Read the box below to learn about the author.

George Orwell

Pen name of Eric Arthur Blair [1903-1950]. He was an English novelist, essayist, and journalist. Orwell's novels presented social and political themes and the most famous ones are *Animal Farm* [published in 1945] and *1984* [published in 1949].

Based on <www.george-orwell.org/l_biography.html>. Accessed on September 30, 2015.

 Skimming para situar a leitura

Em trechos de textos literários, pode ser bastante útil realizar um *skimming* como uma estratégia de pré-leitura, com o objetivo de identificar o que está sendo descrito ou narrado. Isso situará melhor o leitor para uma leitura mais aprofundada do trecho.

3 Skim the text on page 149 and check the correct alternative.

   a ☐ A group of animals is talking about the terrible conditions they live in.

   b ☐ One of the animals is trying to convince the others about something.

   c ☐ The animals are debating how to stop working for men because they are enemies.

4 The text is...

   a ☐ basically descriptive.

   b ☐ mainly narrative.

   c ☐ mostly argumentative.

Animal Farm

Comrades, consider this: we live in misery, work like hell, and die young. After we are born, we receive just enough to keep us alive. Then we have to work until we have no more strength to keep standing. We live like slaves – that is the real truth.

5 Why are we in this miserable condition? Because human beings steal nearly all products of our labor. That, comrades, is the cause of our problems: man. Man is the only real enemy we have.

Man is the only creature that consumes without producing. He does not give milk, he does not lay eggs, he is too weak to plow by himself.
10 He cannot run fast enough to catch rabbits. Yet he is the lord of all animals. He puts other animals to work and gives back to them the bare minimum to prevent starvation. The rest, he keeps for himself.

For myself, I do not grumble. I am a 12-year-old pig. I will soon die. But I warn you: whatever goes upon two legs is your enemy.
15 Whatever goes upon four legs, or has wings, is a friend.

Adapted from ORWELL, G. *Animal Farm*. Harlow: Addison Wesley Longman Ltd., 1996.

Vocabulary

comrade: companheiro(a), camarada	**lay eggs:** botar ovos	**steal:** roubar
grumble: resmungar, lamentar	**plow:** arar	**warn:** avisar, alertar
labor: trabalho	**starvation:** inanição	**whatever:** qualquer coisa que

After Reading

1 Check what man <u>can't</u> do, according to the text.

☐ lay eggs   ☐ control animals   ☐ consume

☐ work   ☐ plow by himself   ☐ catch rabbits

☐ steal   ☐ grumble   ☐ give milk

> Scan this QR code to watch a video about the environmental impacts caused by human action.

2 Check what the words in bold refer to.

1 *"Because human beings steal nearly all products of **our** labor"* (lines 5-6).

   a ☐ products   b ☐ animals   c ☐ human beings

2 *"Man is the only creature that consumes without producing. **He** does not give milk [...]"* (lines 8-9).

   a ☐ man   b ☐ creature   c ☐ milk

3 *"He puts other animals to work and gives back to **them** the bare minimum to prevent starvation"* (lines 11-12).

   a ☐ the bare minimum   b ☐ man   c ☐ other animals

4 *"For **myself**, I do not grumble"* (line 13).

   a ☐ the enemy   b ☐ the pig   c ☐ the reader

3 Check the alternative that best summarizes the pig's arguments.

a ☐ I am a 12-year-old pig that will soon die, but I know that we live like slaves.

b ☐ Man is too weak to plow and too slow to run, but he is the lord of all animals.

c ☐ Man, the animals' enemy, is responsible for their miserable living conditions.

d ☐ Every man treats both animals and other human beings like slaves.

4 Discuss the following questions in Portuguese.

1 "All animals are equal, but some animals are more equal than others." This sentence is said by one of the animals at the end of the book. Why do you think it was said? In your opinion, what does it mean?

2 The text on page 149 is at the beginning of the book. The sentence in item 1 is at the end of it. What do you think happens between these two moments?

3 In your opinion, is it possible to say that all men are born equal, but some men are more equal than others? Why?

Vocabulary Expansion

1 Complete the sentences using the words in the box.

1 You can call me _____ you need a friend.

2 Her dog follows her _____ she goes.

3 _____ you have to do before your vacation, do it quickly.

4 _____ asks me for help, I try to help immediately.

5 Choose _____ you want, as long as you're careful.

2 Read the box and complete the sentences.

Special Difficulties

to lie	lied	lied	mentir
to lie	lay	lain	deitar-se, jazer, encontrar-se (situar-se)
to lay	laid	laid	pôr, colocar

1 Jonathan _____ to me about his age: he told me he was 18.

2 Dogs, cats, cows, and horses don't _____ eggs.

3 Lake Titicaca _____ between Bolivia and Peru.

4 Yesterday I _____ under a tree in the park to read a book.

5 Don't _____ to children. They will notice if you're not telling the truth.

3 Rewrite the sentences.

1 My brother is sixteen years old.
   My brother is a sixteen-year-old boy. _____

2 Sally is twelve years old.
   _____

3 This house is fifty years old.
   _____

4 Ross is seven years old.
   _____

5 This chair is ten years old.
   _____

12 Water

Look at the picture and answer orally.

1 What does the picture tell you about this unit?

2 Why is it important to save water? Who should do it?

1 Take a look at the cartoon.

I can't believe we have run out of water again!

Vocabulary

run out of: ficar sem

2 Give your opinion about the cartoon.

1 What is the cartoon about?

2 What would you change in the scene?

3 Read, think, and answer orally.

We have run out of water again!

We ran out of water yesterday.

1 Are the sentences talking about the present, the past, or the future?

2 Is it possible to know when the actions happened?

Language Practice

Present Perfect (I)

Have/Has + verbo no *Past Participle*

I **have**	
You **have**	
He **has**	**Afirmativa:** He **has worked** hard.
She **has**	**Interrogativa: Has** he **worked** hard?
It **has**	**worked.**
We **have**	**Negativa:** He **has not worked** hard.
You **have**	**Formas abreviadas: 's** (has) **hasn't** (has not)
They **have**	**'ve** (have) **haven't** (have not)

Past Participle (ver lista na página 382)

Regular verbs: to work – worked – **worked**	to dance – danced – **danced**
Irregular verbs: to see – saw – **seen**	to tell – told – **told**

Uso

O *Present Perfect* expressa ações que ocorreram em um tempo indefinido no passado; elas podem ter terminado ou ainda estar ocorrendo.

> I **have worked** hard. (Trabalhei/Tenho trabalhado muito.)

> He **has written** a paper on sustainability. (Ele escreveu um trabalho sobre sustentabilidade.)

> Ben and Karen **have** never **been** to China. (Ben e Karen nunca estiveram na China.)

Porém, se o tempo for mencionado ou sugerido, usa-se o *Simple Past*.

> I **worked** hard <u>yesterday</u>. (Trabalhei muito ontem.)

> I **worked** hard <u>when I was young</u>. (Trabalhei muito quando era jovem.)

---

1 Complete the sentences using the verbs in parentheses in the Present Perfect.

1 Richard _____ (text) his friends to ask for a favor.

2 My parents _____ (decide – neg.) what to do on Christmas Eve.

3 They _____ (arrive – neg.) on time because of the rain.

4 We _____ (be) very busy this week organizing the convention.

5 The students _____ (bring) many items to donate to the campaign.

6 Lily _____ (watch) twenty movies this year.

2 Complete the sentences using the Simple Past or the Present Perfect.

1 They _____ (be) in the restaurant an hour ago.

2 I _____ (write) many books for children.

3 My parents _____ (be) to Lençóis Maranhenses many times.

4 Jennifer _____ (send) me a postcard from Rio de Janeiro in January.

5 My grandparents _____ (sell) their apartment at the beach last year.

6 Many people in our city _____ (help) fight pollution.

3 Complete Lara's report on the children she works with. Use the verbs in parentheses in the Simple Past or in the Present Perfect.

Lara Elliott
Reading class volunteer

Daily Report

Today was a special day because we _____ (have) three birthdays in the group. Kamal and Bob _____ (be) absent for two days. I hope they come next class. Sheila _____ (be – neg.) feeling well when she _____ (arrive) this morning, but she _____ (take) some medicine and was soon feeling OK. Jennifer _____ finally _____ (decide) to participate in the group projects. We _____ (read) three books so far this week and the kids _____ (enjoy) them very much.

Present Perfect (II)

O *Present Perfect* pode ser usado com:

• *since* (desde): I **have worked** here since June. (Trabalho aqui desde junho.)

• *for* (por; há): She **has worked** here for five months. (Ela trabalha aqui há cinco meses.)

• *just* (ação recente): They **have** just **arrived**. (Eles acabaram de chegar.)

• *ever* (já, alguma vez): **Have** you ever **seen** that movie? (Você já viu aquele filme?)

• *never* (nunca): I **have** never **seen** her. (Eu nunca a vi.)

• *already* (já): They **have** already **arrived**. (Eles já chegaram.)

• *yet* (já – em perguntas; ainda – em negativas): **Has** he **arrived** yet? (Ele já chegou?)
  He **has not arrived** yet. (Ele ainda não chegou.)

• *lately* (ultimamente): We **have not seen** you lately. (Não temos visto você ultimamente.)

Present Perfect Continuous

> **Have/Has been** + verbo + **-ing**
>
> **Afirmativa:** He **has been** travel**ing**.
> **Interrogativa:** **Has** he **been** travel**ing**?
> **Negativa:** He **has not been** travel**ing**.

Uso

O *Present Perfect Continuous* enfatiza a continuidade de uma ação que começou no passado e que se prolonga até o presente.

It **has been raining** hard. (Tem chovido muito.)

4 **Check the appropriate word to complete the sentences below.**

1 I haven't finished my homework _____.

   a ☐ yet   b ☐ just   c ☐ already

2 He has _____ sent his postcards.

   a ☐ yet   b ☐ already   c ☐ ever

3 She has _____ made a cake.

   a ☐ just   b ☐ lately   c ☐ since

4 We have been waiting for you _____ an hour.

   a ☐ since   b ☐ ever   c ☐ for

5 They have lived in Miami _____ 2001.

   a ☐ for   b ☐ since   c ☐ ever

5 **Complete the sentences using the verbs in parentheses in the Present Perfect Continuous.**

1 They _____ (wait) for half an hour.

2 We _____ (try) to call the doctor all day.

3 Natalie _____ (feel) sick.

4 I _____ (do – neg.) much lately.

5 My coworkers _____ (raise) money for charity.

6 Fred _____ (go – neg.) to the gym lately.

Go to page 162 for Extra Practice.

Reading

Before Reading

1 **Discuss the questions below in Portuguese.**

1   What do you use water for in your everyday life?

2   Can you guess how much water you use in a day?

3   Which do you think uses more water: producing 1 kg of rice or producing 1 kg of beef?

4   Do you know who the largest users of water in the world are?

2 **Write the meaning of the words below. Use the glossary.**

1   resource _____

2   sustainability _____

3   improvement _____

4   withdrawal _____

5   rate _____

6   crop _____

3 **Write the words from activity 2 after the corresponding definition.**

1   The action of removing something or taking it away. _____

2   Something used to achieve an objective. _____

3   Plants that are cultivated by farmers. _____

4   The quantity/frequency of something compared to something else. _____

5   Ecological balance that can be maintained. _____

6   What makes something better or more valuable. _____

4 **Complete the expressions using words from the text on page 159.**

1   ____developing____ countries

2   _____ habitats

3   _____ production

4   _____ of water

5   economic _____

6   sustainable _____

5 **Write the meaning in Portuguese of the expressions from activity 4. Use the glossary.**

1   _____

2   _____

3   _____

4   _____

5   _____

6   _____

Humanity
Needs Water

A drop of water is powerful.
A drop of water is in demand.

Water is at the core of sustainable development. Water resources, and the services they provide, are the base for poverty reduction, economic growth, and environmental sustainability. From food and energy security to human and environmental health, water contributes to improvements in social well-being and inclusive growth, affecting the lives of billions.

Water Is Food

Each American uses 7,500 liters of water per day – mostly for food. One liter of water is needed to irrigate one calorie of food. If resources are not used in a proper manner, 100 liters of water can be wasted in the production of one calorie of food. Globally, agriculture is the largest user of water, accounting for 70% of total withdrawal. By 2050, agriculture will need to produce 60% more food globally, and 100% more in developing countries.

Economic growth is causing diets to shift from predominantly starch-based to meat and dairy, which require more water. Producing 1 kg of rice, for example, requires about 3,500 liters of water, while 1 kg of beef uses about 15,000 liters.

The current growth rates of agricultural demands on the world's freshwater resources are unsustainable. The overuse of water in food production reduces river flows, degrades wildlife habitats, and has caused salinization of 20% of the irrigated land area in the world. In order to increase efficiency in the use of water, agriculture can reduce water losses and, most importantly, increase crop productivity with respect to water.

Adapted from <www.unwater.org/WORLDWATERDAY/LEARN/EN>.
Accessed on October 13, 2015.

Vocabulary

account for: corresponder a, responder por
core: núcleo, centro
dairy: laticínio
loss: perda
require: requerer, necessitar
shift: mudar
starch: amido
waste: desperdiçar

After Reading

1 **Look at the text on page 159 and check all the correct alternatives.**

1 Who is the target audience?

a ☐ Adults.   b ☐ Children.   c ☐ Teens.

2 The objective of the text is to _____ something.

a ☐ denounce   b ☐ inform about   c ☐ present data on

3 Its general tone is...

a ☐ satirical.   b ☐ critical.   c ☐ informative.

2 **Check the topics that are not mentioned in the text.**

a ☐ Figures about food production.   c ☐ Industrial uses of water.

b ☐ How to save water at home.   d ☐ Use of water in agriculture.

Resumir (*summarizing*)

Elaborar um pequeno resumo é uma estratégia muito útil para verificar a compreensão do sentido geral do texto. Para resumir, o leitor precisa organizar as ideias apresentadas pelo texto (e as relações entre elas) de forma clara e sucinta.

---

3 **Summarize the text in two parts. Write in Portuguese.**

1 Write one sentence summarizing the first part of the text (paragraph 1).

_____

2 Write one sentence summarizing the second part of the text (paragraphs 2, 3, and 4).

_____

4 **Do the activities that follow based on the text.**

1 How are dietary changes affecting the use of water?

_____

2 List the problems caused by the overuse of water in food production.

_____

3 List two measures to increase water use efficiency.

_____

Vocabulary Expansion

1 Answer the questions below.

1 What's a science-based method?
It's a method based on science.

2 What's computer-based education?

_____

3 What's an evidence-based investigation?

_____

4 What's a content-based course?

_____

2 Read the information in the box and complete the sentences.

False Cognates

divert: mudar o curso ou destino, desviar	**proper:** adequado(a)	**push:** empurrar
have fun: divertir-se	**own:** próprio(a)	**pull:** puxar

1 You must have your _____ pen and pencil to take the test.

2 The boy was _____ the girl's hair.

3 The farmers want to _____ water from the river to the field.

4 Don't _____! There are a lot of people entering the subway.

5 A craftsman needs the _____ tools to do a good job.

6 They always _____ when they travel by plane.

3 Match the words in bold to their meaning.

over: demais; excessivo(a)

1 Some addicts die of drug **overdose**.

2 He was **overdressed** for the wedding.

3 The hotel where we stayed was good, but **overpriced**.

4 Sometimes she **overreacts** to difficult situations.

5 She is **overcareful** with her children.

6 I don't know why you love this band: it's so **overrated**.

a ☐ cuidadoso(a) demais

b ☐ caro(a) demais

c ☐ superestimado(a)

d ☐ arrumado(a) demais

e ☐ reagir exageradamente

f ☐ quantidade exagerada

Extra Practice 6

1 Circle the correct alternative to complete the sentences.

1 Do you consider **yourself** / **myself** funny?

2 My mom never gives **ourselves** / **herself** a day off.

3 What do you teens see when you look at **themselves** / **yourselves**?

4 I cut **myself** / **itself** yesterday while I was making lunch.

5 Our cat saw **yourself** / **itself** in the mirror and was very surprised.

6 I can't believe you managed to write this all by **yourself** / **himself**.

2 Complete the sentences using the appropriate reflexive pronoun.

1 We have to congratulate the students for creating this NGO by _____.

2 Julia looked at _____ in the mirror before leaving for work.

3 My brother is extremely selfish. He only thinks of _____.

4 We were frightened last night because the door opened by _____.

5 You look very tired. You should give _____ a holiday.

6 We went to the cafeteria to buy _____ some lunch.

3 Rewrite the sentences using reflexive pronouns. Follow the instructions in parentheses.

1 Virginia planned this whole trip. (idiomatic)

_____

2 They looked in the mirror before leaving for the party. (reflexive)

_____

3 Philip came up with the idea for the ad. (emphatic – subject)

_____

4 I went for a walk and saw Luan Santana in the street! (emphatic – object)

_____

5 Sarah found out what was wrong with the laptop. (idiomatic)

_____

6 We sent a copy of the e-mail. (reflexive)

_____

4   **Check the correct alternative.**

1   **A:** Frances doesn't know how to fix my smartphone.

    B: Don't worry! I'll do it _____.

   a ☐ himself

   b ☐ itself

   c ☐ myself

2   **A:** Did the kids give any of the chocolate bars to Carla?

    B: No, they ate it all _____.

   a ☐ themselves

   b ☐ herself

   c ☐ itself

3   I want you to do the job _____.

   a ☐ myself

   b ☐ himself

   c ☐ yourself

4   The players _____ cleaned the field after the game.

   a ☐ itself

   b ☐ themselves

   c ☐ himself

5   **A:** Sandra doesn't believe Roy is telling the truth.

    B: I _____ believe he is.

   a ☐ myself

   b ☐ himself

   c ☐ herself

5   **Discuss the questions below with your classmates.**

1   Do you like to spend some time by yourself? What do you like to do?

2   Have you ever taught yourself how to do anything? What?

3   Do you think teens like what they see when they look at themselves in the mirror? Why?

6 Complete the sentences using 's or ' and the words in parentheses.

1 Joe gave _____ (Sally) Geography book to Amanda.

2 My _____ (parents) car is at the _____ (mechanic) now. They don't know what's wrong with it.

3 The _____ (women) dresses are very expensive in this store!

4 Let's go to _____ (grandma) next Saturday. It's her birthday.

5 Those _____ (sailors) ship is leaving the country tomorrow.

6 My _____ (friends) children always misbehave in class, so the principal called them for a meeting.

7 Rewrite the sentences inserting 's or ' where necessary.

1 That man feet were hurt in the accident.

_____

2 The presidents wives are having tea in the garden.

_____

3 Dan, Carla, and Tom shoes were behind the couch.

_____

4 Bob and Julia daughter is very beautiful.

_____

5 I intend to have my two weeks holiday next month.

_____

6 My father-in-law shoe shop is right around the corner.

_____

8 Complete the sentences using the verbs in parentheses in the correct verb tense.

1 We _____ (study) English at the moment.

2 They _____ (watch) TV in their room five minutes ago.

3 She never _____ (read) the newspaper in the morning.

4 I _____ (see) many plays with my friends.

5 My brother _____ (send) me an e-mail yesterday morning.

6 He _____ (invite) many people to our wedding.

9 **Rewrite the sentences below in the negative and interrogative forms.**

1 Carol has brought sandwiches for the kids.

_____

_____

2 You have arrived very late for our meetings.

_____

_____

3 She has been to the museum lately.

_____

_____

4 Frank has helped me a lot.

_____

_____

5 Josie has worked at the mall for two years.

_____

_____

6 The boys have been to the amusement park.

_____

_____

10 Decide if the interrogative sentences are right (R) or wrong (W). Then write the correct form of the wrong ones.

1 The students have been to the library.

    Do the students been to the library? ☐

    _____

2 You have tried really hard.

    Have you tried really hard? ☐

    _____

3 She has done her best.

    Does she do her best? ☐

    _____

4 We have been to the game.

    Have we been to the game? ☐

    _____

5 My father has decided to take a vacation next month.

    Did my father decide to take a vacation next month? ☐

    _____

11 Rewrite the sentences below in the Present Perfect Continuous.

1 I have worked hard.

    _____

2 They have traveled abroad.

    _____

3 I have lived here for about three years.

    _____

4 He has spoken too much in class.

    _____

5 We have worked for him since 2015.

    _____

6 You have written a lot of poems.

    _____

Job Corner 6

Exploring Different Career Paths in the Gaming Industry

When most people imagine careers in the video game industry, they immediately think of developers. As the medium grows more popular, more jobs are opening up in the field. Tons of careers are available, and there's something for just about everyone.

COMPOSER

A lot of people, composers included, don't think about creating music for video games. [...] A great way to get started is to compose music for a friend who is making a small indie game.

DEVELOPER

This one is the most obvious: if you want to work in the game industry, make video games. While going to school to become a triple-A developer is an option, it is becoming increasingly easier to become an independent developer. [...] Steam Greenlight is one way to get your game out there.

MARKETING

With so many new titles coming out every month, marketing is very important. If you don't promote your game enough, even if it's good, it will fall in the shadows of the big games that have a lot of PR behind them. [...]

JOURNALIST

The term is "games journalist," and for those who know nothing about the industry, this sounds like a made-up job. It is, in fact, very real, and it's becoming an increasingly competitive field. Getting into games journalism is all about who you know. [...] I would advise anyone who is interested in games journalism to [...] start a personal blog, where you can display your work, and most importantly, read articles written by professional journalists. Reading other people's work will help you understand what you need to do to improve and possibly give you inspiration for a new article.

TESTER

A lot of people see this as a dream job: "I can play video games for a living! Sign me up!" However, in order to be a video game tester, you must be very good at playing all kinds of games, demonstrate an outstanding attention to detail, and have lots and lots of patience. Many forget that testers don't just play the good games; they also have to play the really, really bad ones. They must be able to find the flaws in order for developers to fix them before a title releases. This job isn't easygoing, but it can be a great fit for some. [...]

Available at <http://venturebeat.com/community/2013/08/10/careers-in-the-video-game-industry>.
Accessed on October 19, 2015.

Vocabulary

display: expor, mostrar
easygoing: tranquilo(a)
field: campo, área

flaw: falha, defeito
indie: independente
made-up: inventado(a)

outstanding: excepcional
PR: relações públicas
release: ser lançado(a)

shadow: sombra
Sign me up!: Contratem-me!
triple-A: de ponta, um(a) dos(as) melhores

13

The Origin of the World

Look at the picture and answer orally.

1   What does the picture tell you about this unit?

2   According to scientists, how was the world created?

3   Are there any religions or cultures that have different theories for the origin of the world?

4   What do these theories have in common? How are they different?

Language in Context

1 **Take a look at the text.**

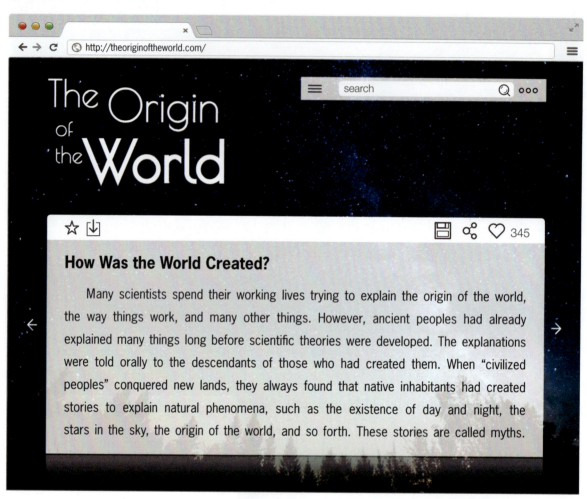

The Origin of the World

search

How Was the World Created?

Many scientists spend their working lives trying to explain the origin of the world, the way things work, and many other things. However, ancient peoples had already explained many things long before scientific theories were developed. The explanations were told orally to the descendants of those who had created them. When "civilized peoples" conquered new lands, they always found that native inhabitants had created stories to explain natural phenomena, such as the existence of day and night, the stars in the sky, the origin of the world, and so forth. These stories are called myths.

2 **Give your opinion about the text.**

1 How does the text describe a myth?

2 Why are myths created? What do they explain?

3 Why are quotation marks used in the expression "civilized peoples"?

3 **Read, think, and answer orally.**

Ancient peoples had explained many things long before scientific theories were developed.

1 What are the verbs in the sentence?

2 Which of these actions happened first?

> **Vocabulary**
>
> **and so forth:** e assim por diante
> **conquer:** conquistar
> **land:** terra, território

Language Practice

Past Perfect

Had + verbo no *Past Participle*	
I You He She It We You They	**had left**.

Na segunda coluna:
- **Afirmativa:** He **had left**.
- **Interrogativa: Had** he **left**?
- **Negativa:** He **had not left**.
- **Formas abreviadas:** **'d** (had)
- **hadn't** (had not)

Uso

O *Past Perfect* expressa uma ação que aconteceu no passado antes de outra ação que também aconteceu no passado. Geralmente é usado com *after*, *before*, *when* etc.

The kids **had slept** <u>before</u> we arrived.

He **had left** <u>when</u> you called him.

Clara **had lived** in Spain <u>before</u> she moved to Paris.

Past Perfect Continuous

Had been + verbo + *-ing*	
I You He She It We You They	**had been** work**ing**.

Na segunda coluna:
- **Afirmativa:** He **had been** work**ing**.
- **Interrogativa: Had** he **been** work**ing**?
- **Negativa:** He **had not been** work**ing**.
- **Formas abreviadas:** **'d** (had)
- **hadn't** (had not)

Uso

O *Past Perfect Continuous* expressa uma ação que estava acontecendo no passado antes de outra ação também no passado.

I **had been working** before you called.

John failed the final exam because he **hadn't been attending** class.

We **had been waiting** for more than an hour when he finally arrived.

1 Complete the sentences using the verbs in parentheses in the Past Perfect.

1 She told me she _____ (fall) from a tree.

2 The kids _____ (leave) before I arrived.

3 She lost the book Paul _____ (give) her.

4 I washed the dishes after they _____ (have) dinner.

5 He didn't have any money because he _____ (lose) his wallet.

6 Justin knew Orlando because he _____ (be) there before.

2 Complete the e-mail using the verbs in parentheses in the Past Perfect or in the Past Perfect Continuous.

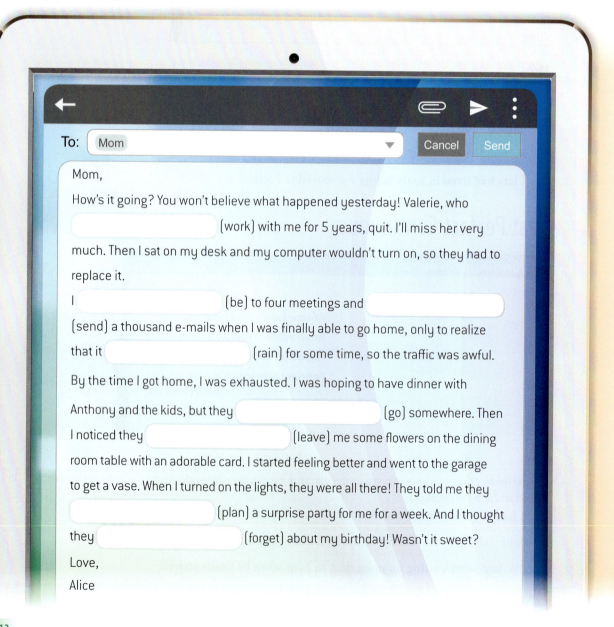

To: Mom   Cancel Send

Mom,

How's it going? You won't believe what happened yesterday! Valerie, who
_____ (work) with me for 5 years, quit. I'll miss her very
much. Then I sat on my desk and my computer wouldn't turn on, so they had to
replace it.

I _____ (be) to four meetings and _____
(send) a thousand e-mails when I was finally able to go home, only to realize
that it _____ (rain) for some time, so the traffic was awful.
By the time I got home, I was exhausted. I was hoping to have dinner with
Anthony and the kids, but they _____ (go) somewhere. Then
I noticed they _____ (leave) me some flowers on the dining
room table with an adorable card. I started feeling better and went to the garage
to get a vase. When I turned on the lights, they were all there! They told me they
_____ (plan) a surprise party for me for a week. And I thought
they _____ (forget) about my birthday! Wasn't it sweet?

Love,

Alice

3 **Make questions and answer them using the Past Perfect.**

1   We arrived at work. Before that we ate breakfast.
Had we eaten breakfast before we arrived at work?

Yes, we had eaten breakfast before we arrived at work.

2   They left the house. Before that they turned off the lights.

_____

_____

3   Carol arrived. Before that my brother left.

_____

_____

4   He got to his house. Before that the game didn't start.

_____

_____

5   She had a test. Before that she reviewed all her notes.

_____

_____

4 **Complete the sentences with your own ideas. Use the Past Perfect or the Past Perfect Continuous.**

1   _____ before I arrived.

2   She told me her name after _____.

3   When I interrupted him, _____.

4   _____ before they came to Australia.

5   They started dinner after _____.

5 **Explain the difference between these two sentences. Answer in Portuguese.**

1   The bomb exploded when the bomb squad arrived.

2   The bomb had exploded when the bomb squad arrived.

_____

_____

Go to page 188 for Extra Practice.

Before Reading

1 Discuss the questions below in Portuguese.

1 Have you ever heard of the Yoruba people?

2 What do you know about them?

3 Where do they live?

4 Do you know other African peoples or cultures?

2 Skim the text. What concept can you associate with it?

a ☐ A prediction of what will happen in the future made by a prophet who is inspired by God or some other divine being.

b ☐ A traditional, ancient story in which supernatural or extraordinary beings are involved in a natural phenomenon.

c ☐ A current narrative concerning actual facts that explain or describe a social phenomenon and its impacts on real life.

d ☐ A fictional story for children presenting fantastic beings and magic elements, which usually has a happy ending.

3 Which type of text usually presents the characteristics you checked in the previous activity?

a ☐ A piece of news.

b ☐ A prophecy.

c ☐ A myth.

d ☐ A fairy tale.

4 Match the words to their synonyms.

1 task   ☐ banquet

2 feast   ☐ mental confusion

3 journey   ☐ trip

4 haze   ☐ free

5 release   ☐ job

The Yoruba people, from West Africa, have different stories about the origin of the world. According to one of them, there were two realms: the invisible one, inhabited by the gods, and the physical one. This physical realm was filled with water until God decided to transform it into the world as we know it. He looked for someone who could do it and sent Obatala, his messenger, to perform this task. And what a hard task it was! So Obatala brought along his helper, Oduduwa, as well as a bag full of earth and a chicken.

Along the way, they stopped over at a feast, where Obatala got drunk from drinking too much palm wine. Having found his master drunk, Oduduwa picked up the bag and the chicken and continued the journey by himself.

After Oduduwa arrived, he dumped the earth from the bag on the water and released the chicken. The chicken then ran, spreading the earth all around. After it ran over the earth in every direction, there was land. Oduduwa had created the world from what used to be water.

Later, when Obatala got out of his drunken haze, he discovered that Oduduwa had already performed his task, which made him very upset. But God gave him another task to perform: to create the noble people that would populate the planet. ■

Adapted from <www.allfolktales.com/wafrica/yoruba_creation.php>. Accessed on October 28, 2015.

Vocabulary

dump: despejar

earth: terra

inhabit: habitar, morar em

palm wine: vinho de palma

realm: reino, mundo

spread: espalhar

After Reading

1 How is the text organized?

a ☐ In the form of a list.

b ☐ In a structure based on comparison and contrast.

c ☐ In chronological order.

> **Entender a sequência de eventos**
>
> Em textos narrativos, factuais ou ficcionais, entender o sequenciamento e as relações de temporalidade dos eventos ajuda a compreender o desenrolar da narrativa e também a estabelecer relações de causa e efeito entre os acontecimentos.

2 Number the events in the correct time order, according to the text.

a ☐ God sent Obatala to create the world.

b ☐ Obatala received the mission of creating people.

c ☐ The chicken spread the earth all around.

d ☐ Obatala drank too much wine at a feast.

e ☐ Obatala left bringing Oduduwa, a bag full of earth, and a chicken.

f ☐ 1 There was only water in the physical realm.

g ☐ Oduduwa dumped the earth on the water and released the chicken.

3 Based on this sequence of events, answer the questions below.

1 Why did Obatala bring Oduduwa along with him?

_____

2 Why did Oduduwa continue the journey by himself?

_____

3 Why did Obatala become upset?

_____

4 Choose the best title for the text.

a ☐ My Friend Obatala Has a Drinking Problem

b ☐ The Creation of the World: A Yoruba Myth

c ☐ The Danger of Myths and Legends in Today's Society

Scan this QR code to learn more about folklore and myths with the example of some Brazilian celebrations.

Vocabulary Expansion

1 **Complete the sentences with the phrasal verbs from the box.**

Phrasal Verbs

look: olhar; parecer
look after: cuidar, tomar conta
look at: olhar para
look for: procurar
look into: investigar
look up: consultar (uma lista, um dicionário)

1 Investigators are _____ the incident to find out who was responsible for it.

2 Everyone was _____ the pictures of his trip to Egypt.

3 She can't go with us because she has to _____ the kids.

4 Can you _____ these words in the dictionary, please?

5 Phoebe _____ old and tired after the accident.

6 The teacher is _____ a book to read.

2 **Read the information in the box and check the correct alternative.**

1 I don't like tomatoes **but** the doctor told me I have to eat them.

a ☐ mas   b ☐ exceto

2 We can help many people but we can't **save** the world.

a ☐ economizar   b ☐ salvar

3 Everybody **but** me is going to the concert.

a ☐ mas   b ☐ exceto

4 Delia had **saved** only $1.87 to buy Jim a present.

a ☐ economizado   b ☐ salvo

Words with Two Meanings

but: mas; exceto
save: salvar; economizar

3 **Complete the sentences using the words in the box.**

1 Look at the sky _____ us.

2 The cat was hidden _____ the sofa.

3 In Finland the temperature in winter is usually _____ zero.

4 The horse jumped _____ the fence.

5 From the top of the building we can see the streets _____ .

6 It's hard to see things _____ water.

above: acima
below: abaixo
over: por cima
under: embaixo

14

Displacement

Look at the picture and answer orally.

1   What does the picture tell you about this unit?

2   What is a refugee?

3   How are they different from immigrants?

4   Which problems might immigrants and refugees face in their home countries?

1 Take a look at the text.

We should know that an immigrant is someone who decides to try a new life in another country, and that refugees are forced to leave their home countries because of war, environmental disasters, political persecution, and/or religious or ethnic intolerance.

However, immigrants and refugees have a lot in common. They left the countries where they used to live and have to experience new cultures and languages. They are often ethnic minorities who might face discrimination or other kinds of hostility, regardless of the cause of their displacement.

Vocabulary

displacement: deslocamento
face: enfrentar
regardless of: independentemente de

2 Give your opinion about the text.

1 What is the difference between immigrants and refugees?

2 What do they have in common?

3 Which problems might they face in the countries to which they move?

3 Read, think, and answer orally.

A	B
They are often ethnic minorities who face discrimination.	They are often ethnic minorities who might face discrimination.
Immigrants and refugees have difficulty adapting to a new country.	Immigrants and refugees might have difficulty adapting to a new country.

1 What does "might" mean in the sentences in column B?

2 What's the difference in meaning between the two groups of sentences?

Language Practice

Modal Verbs (II)

May/Might, Should/Ought to

Os verbos modais dão um significado específico ao verbo principal.

Formas	May/Might	Should/Ought to
Afirmativa	He **may** stay here. He **might** stay here.	We **should** go now. We **ought to** go now.
Interrogativa	**May** he stay here? **Might** he stay here?	**Should** we go now? **Ought** we **to** go now?
Negativa	He **may not** stay here. He **might not** stay here.	We **should not** go now. We **ought not to** go now.
Formas abreviadas	**mightn't**	**shouldn't** **oughtn't**

Uso

May/Might (pode, podia, poderia) – expressam possibilidade, dedução.

> It **might** rain.

> He **may** be sick.

> I **might not** have time to do it.

> They **may not** travel with us after all.

May também pode ser usado para expressar pedido ou permissão. Nesses casos, ele pode ser substituído por ***be allowed to***, que é conjugado em todos os tempos.

> **May** I go?

> You **may** leave now.

> He **was allowed to** call her.

> We **are allowed to** play cards on the bus.

Nota
may – mais informal
might – mais formal

Should/Ought to (deveria) – expressam necessidade, dever, conselho.

> We **should** study hard.

> I **ought to** help her with her shopping.

> They **ought to** respect the law.

> You **should** talk to her.

> They **shouldn't** get angry.

1 Match the ideas to the sentences below.

1 possibility

2 advice

3 permission

a ☐ May I open the windows?

b ☐ She should travel in the morning; it's safer.

c ☐ We may help you if we have some time left.

d ☐ You ought to talk to Mary about her grades.

e ☐ They might be trying to call us right now.

f ☐ Tell Ted that he may leave now.

2 Circle the correct alternative.

1 They **may / are allowed to** get there on time if they hurry.

2 He doesn't exercise much, but he really **ought to / might**.

3 **Ought to / May** I use your phone?

4 Parents **should / might** spend more time with their children.

5 Nobody knows what **might / ought to** happen in the future.

6 The students **ought to / aren't allowed to** enter class after it starts.

3 Check the correct alternative.

1 She is crying because her mother said she _____ go to the mall with her friends.

  a ☐ is allowed to   b ☐ ought to   c ☐ may not

2 You look pale. You _____ see your doctor.

  a ☐ should   b ☐ oughtn't to   c ☐ mightn't

3 My team _____ win this championship, but I don't think it will.

  a ☐ may not   b ☐ shouldn't   c ☐ might

4 The teacher _____ to give us an easier test next time.

  a ☐ might   b ☐ ought   c ☐ should

5 We _____ arrive late at the concert if we want to get good seats.

  a ☐ should   b ☐ shouldn't   c ☐ are allowed to

Language Practice

Used to vs. Be Used to

Uso

Used to + **infinitivo:** expressa uma situação passada que não ocorre mais.

> I **used to play** soccer, but I don't anymore. (Eu jogava futebol, mas não jogo mais.)

> He **used to study** hard, but he doesn't anymore. (Ele estudava muito, mas não estuda mais.)

Be used to + **verbo +** *-ing* **ou objeto direto:** expressa costume (presente, passado ou futuro).

> I **am used to working** here. (Estou acostumado a trabalhar aqui.)

> We **were used to playing** in the same team. (Estávamos acostumados a jogar no mesmo time.)

> I **will be used to the noise** by tomorrow. (Estarei acostumado com o barulho até amanhã.)

4 Circle the correct alternative.

1   Don't worry about the kids: they are used to **get up** / **getting up** early.

2   My cousin lives in Toronto and she is used **to going** / **to go** to Niagara Falls.

3   There used to **being** / **be** a grocery store in the neighborhood in those days.

4   My family used to **travel** / **traveling** to the beach when I was a kid.

5 Complete the sentences with the correct form of the verbs in parentheses.

1   He used to _____ (go out) a lot, but now he usually stays at home.

2   My father used to _____ (play) soccer when he was young.

3   She is used to _____ (ride) her bike to school.

4   They aren't used to _____ (drink) a lot of coffee.

6 Answer the questions about yourself.

1   What ought you to do in case there's a fire?

_____

2   What did you use to do when you were 10?

_____

3   What are you used to doing every day?

_____

Go to page 188 for Extra Practice.

Reading

Before Reading

1 **Discuss the questions below in Portuguese.**

1 Do you know any immigrants or refugees?

2 Why did they leave their home countries?

3 Look at page 185: what kind of text is it?

4 What in the text helped you answer the previous question?

2 **Check the meaning of the words in bold.**

1 "[...] the **tears** in her eyes, her clenched and shaking fists [...]" (line 4).

   a ☐ alegrias   b ☐ lágrimas   c ☐ reflexos

2 "In that moment, her **soul** was in my arms" (line 8).

   a ☐ alma   b ☐ determinação   c ☐ peculiaridade

3 "[...] spoke the only words I could **fathom** [...]" (lines 20-21).

   a ☐ inventar   b ☐ fantasiar   c ☐ compreender

4 "Two strangers [...] knowing nothing of each other's **suffering** [...]" (lines 31-32).

   a ☐ alegria   b ☐ paixão   c ☐ sofrimento

5 "[...] and yet we **shared** the weight [...]" (line 33).

   a ☐ pesamos   b ☐ dividimos   c ☐ enchemos

6 "[...] the **barrier** of language was broken" (line 35).

   a ☐ barreira   b ☐ estrutura   c ☐ vantagem

3 **Scan the poem to find the following information.**

1 The number of people involved in the story. _____

2 What the lyric self compares the woman's emotions to. _____

3 The location where the scene takes place. _____

4 What the weather was like when the characters met. _____

5 Languages that are mentioned or spoken. _____

We are used to reading poems about romantic themes, such as love and heroes. But we may also find poetry that might make us think about social problems. Read the poem below and enjoy.

Language Barrier

By James Kelley

I couldn't understand the language she spoke,
at least not all of it,
but the emotion pouring past her lips,
the tears in her eyes, her clenched and shaking fists
5 enunciated more clearly,
than any piece of English Poetry I had ever read,
and grabbed me, held me still.
            …In that moment, her soul was in my arms.
In that finite, tender breath of our lives,
10 she was my mother, my best friend…
but I could not console her.
I didn't have the words;
and my heart sank into the
concrete between us,
15 wet with the pain of God's rain
and her tears.
                          …Were my tears

So, I simply opened my palms
toward her crouched form and

20 spoke the only words I could
fathom, that would be accepted
by a stranger on a dangerous street.
"I am sorry, It will be okay. God will bless you."
I knew she did not understand…
25 "Lo siento"
                "que va a estar bien"
                          "Dios te bendecirá"
the words were as messy as the overturned
duffle bag at her feet…and fumbled, slowly
30 from my lips, as my knees hit the street.
Two strangers, cried in the rain,
knowing nothing of each other's suffering,
and yet we shared the weight,
together, for those few moments;
35 the barrier of language was broken.
Love spoke for us.
    …Love transcends any language

Available at <www.poetrysoup.com/poem/language_barrier_563383>.
Accessed on October 30, 2015.

Vocabulary

at least: pelo menos	**breath:** respiração; sopro	**crouched:** agachado(a), encolhido(a)	**pour:** derramar, transbordar
bless: abençoar	**clenched:** fechado(a), cerrado(a)	**fumble:** sair de forma desajeitada	**sink:** afundar

After Reading

1 At the beginning of the poem, what called the attention of the lyric self?

a ☐ The language the woman spoke.

b ☐ The woman's emotions, tears, and gestures.

c ☐ All the English poetry the narrator had read.

2 What was the attitude of the lyric self towards the woman?

a ☐ He/She tried to comfort the woman using words and gestures.

b ☐ He/She tried to grab the woman and arrest her on a dangerous street.

c ☐ He/She couldn't do anything because they didn't speak the same language.

3 How did the lyric self and the woman connect?

a ☐ Through language.

b ☐ Through love.

c ☐ Through politics.

> **Recontar a história**
>
> Textos literários, em prosa ou verso, muitas vezes contam histórias, as quais envolvem personagens, locais e situações. Para recontar essa história, é preciso compreender tanto o sentido geral do texto quanto seus detalhes, sendo necessário estabelecer relações causais e cronológicas entre os fatos narrados.

4 Retell the story of the poem. Answer in Portuguese using your own words.

5 Write a paragraph about the poem. Use the questions below as a guide.

1 How do you interpret the context of the poem?

2 Why do you think the woman was carrying a bag?

3 Where might she come from?

4 Why is she suffering?

_____

_____

_____

_____

Vocabulary Expansion

1 Find eight words in the poem on page 185 to complete the spidergram.

2 Complete the idioms using the words from activity 1. They can be used in the singular or plural.

> **Idioms**
>
> Expressões idiomáticas (*idioms*) são conjuntos de palavras cujo significado não é formado pelo sentido literal de cada uma das palavras que as compõem.
> It's **raining cats and dogs**, so don't forget your umbrella.
> Of course I'm nervous, our first date is tomorrow! I **have butterflies in my stomach**!

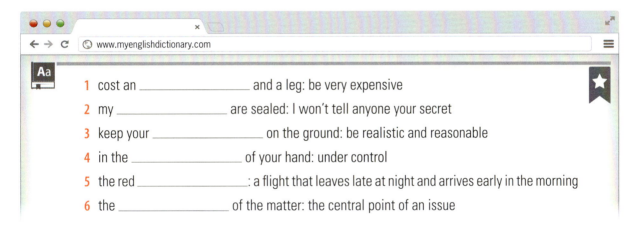

www.myenglishdictionary.com

1 cost an _____ and a leg: be very expensive

2 my _____ are sealed: I won't tell anyone your secret

3 keep your _____ on the ground: be realistic and reasonable

4 in the _____ of your hand: under control

5 the red _____: a flight that leaves late at night and arrives early in the morning

6 the _____ of the matter: the central point of an issue

3 Complete the sentences using the idioms from activity 2.

1 He got _____ and arrived in New York at 6 a.m.

2 I can't buy this video game. It _____.

3 The audience was fascinated by your speech! You had them _____.

4 After this long debate, I think we've finally found _____.

5 _____: you can trust me with your secret.

6 You probably won't win the lottery, so _____ and don't spend too much.

Extra Practice 7

1 Write the verbs below in the Past Perfect. See the irregular verbs list on page 382.

1 to be _____

2 to calculate _____

3 to plan _____

4 to see _____

5 to have _____

6 to go _____

2 Complete the sentences using the verbs in parentheses in the Past Perfect.

1 When you arrived yesterday, I _____ already _____ (leave).

2 She _____ already _____ (go) to bed when they called her.

3 By the time he asked for a piece of cake, the kids _____ already _____ (eat) all of it.

4 I wrote him a letter, but when it arrived there, he _____ already _____ (move) to San Francisco.

5 We went to her place for dinner but to our great surprise she _____ already _____ (eat).

3 There are mistakes in some of the sentences below. Circle these mistakes and rewrite the sentences correcting them.

1 We had finish the activities when the teacher called us.

_____

2 You told me you had saved some money.

_____

3 Roy said he had fallen from a tree.

_____

4 I had already asked her to close the window when she saw her notebook was wet because of the rain.

_____

5 She told me that the children has eat all the chocolates in the box.

_____

6 We had not been work when she arrived at the office.

_____

4 Complete the text using the verbs in parentheses in the Past Perfect.

When I arrived home yesterday Dad _____ (cook)

dinner, Mom _____ (bake) a cake, Tim, my younger

brother, _____ (clean) the garage, Theresa, my aunt,

_____ (water) the flowers, and Ted, my older brother,

_____ (walk) the dog. I was in shock, because everyone is

usually still doing their household chores when I get home! What happened to them?

5 Complete the sentences using the words in the box.

| above (2x)   under   below   over |

1   The president is working hard to keep the unemployment rate _____ 10% this year. He doesn't want it to go any higher than that.

2   High inflation rates impact society as a whole, but _____ all they deeply affect the working class.

3   I remember that my secretary put my report on foreign investments _____ this book, but it is not here anymore.

4   Mr. Smith is planning to fly _____ the English Channel with his experimental airplane. Some people say he won't succeed.

5   The reason why they think he won't succeed is that his airplane flies too low. It cannot fly _____ 400 feet.

6 Rewrite the sentences using *be allowed to* in the correct form.

1   You may leave now.
    You are allowed to leave now.

2   Her mother says she may walk around the park.

    _____

3   The principal told us we may enter this room.

    _____

4   The kids may play in the living room.

    _____

5   You may talk to him if you arrive early.

    _____

7 **Rewrite the sentences using the form indicated in parentheses.**

1 He might work in the morning.

   (interrogative) _____

2 You should call your friends today.

   (negative) _____

3 I might help them.

   (negative) _____

4 You ought not to pay her this week.

   (affirmative) _____

5 The children may play outside after class.

   (interrogative) _____

6 We shouldn't call our parents to see what they think.

   (affirmative) _____

8 **Decide if the following statements are pieces of advice (A) or deductions (D).**

1 ☐ Look at Mary. I think she may be happy with the news.

2 ☐ He doesn't exercise much, but he really ought to.

3 ☐ You should let them help you; you already have too much to do.

4 ☐ They look angry. They might have argued.

5 ☐ The children ought not to go out now. They have to finish their homework first.

6 ☐ He hasn't arrived yet. He must be late.

9 **Complete the sentences with the modal verbs given in the correct form.**

| may | might | should | ought to |

1 Your eyes are red. You _____ have a fever.

2 I need a pencil. _____ I use yours for a minute?

3 Mom is not sure, but she said she _____ arrive a little late today.

4 I _____ pass the examination, but I don't think I will.

5 She _____ travel with her friends because she is feeling sick.

6 In order to achieve their goals, athletes _____ have a lot of discipline and willpower.

10 Check the correct alternative.

1 The students _____ to study our history a bit more.

    a ☐ ought   **b** ☐ should

2 You _____ give her a present. It's her birthday.

    a ☐ ought not   **b** ☐ should

3 There's a special class tomorrow. You _____ arrive late.

    a ☐ should not   **b** ☐ ought to

4 She _____ pay the bill, but she knows she _____.

    a ☐ may not – ought to   **b** ☐ might – should

5 It _____ rain, but I don't think it will.

    a ☐ might   **b** ☐ ought

6 _____ I repeat the story?

    a ☐ Might not   **b** ☐ Should

11 Check the correct alternative to complete the sentences.

1 He was _____ every day.

   a ☐ used to swim   **b** ☐ used to swimming   **c** ☐ used swimming

2 My cousins _____ to the beach every summer.

   a ☐ used to go   **b** ☐ use to go   **c** ☐ used to going

3 I _____ early.

   a ☐ am not used to getting up   **b** ☐ used to getting up   **c** ☐ didn't use to getting up

4 Customers _____ from home.

   a ☐ didn't using shopping   **b** ☐ didn't used to shopping   **c** ☐ didn't use to shop

5 She _____ him, but now they are friends.

   a ☐ didn't used liked   **b** ☐ didn't used to like   **c** ☐ didn't use to like

6 My parents _____ in Porto Alegre when they were young.

   a ☐ used to living   **b** ☐ used to live   **c** ☐ use to live

12 Complete the sentences with *used to* or *be used to* and personal information so that they are true for you.

1 I _____ when I was five years old.

2 When I was ten years old, I _____.

3 My grandparents _____ when they were young.

4 I am _____ every day.

5 My parents are _____.

6 I am not _____ on weekends.

Job Corner 7

Design

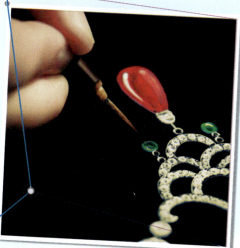

A design professional may choose to work in different segments: the best-known areas involve creating and developing graphic design or visual communication projects.

This work comprises creating logos, designing the pages of a publication (choosing the font type and size and placing text and images on a page), and developing interfaces for websites and apps.

Some prefer to work with industrial design, conceiving and creating objects or products, such as household appliances, furniture, apparel, jewelry, and even toys.

A designer may also work with machinery and equipment, developing parts that will be used in production processes at industrial plants.

Other possibilities include designing packaging, interior design, and preparing 2-D and 3-D animation projects for advertising and games.

In this area, companies seek professionals that are innovative and concerned with the sustainability of the materials used in the manufacturing of objects and products.

Based on <http://guiadoestudante.abril.com.br/profissoes/artes-design/design-684673.shtml>.
Accessed on December 2, 2015.

Vocabulary

advertising: publicidade

apparel: vestimenta

appliance: aparelho, utensílio, eletrodoméstico

comprise: englobar, incluir, abranger

conceive: imaginar, conceber

jewelry: joia

logo: logotipo

manufacturing: fabricação

packaging: embalagem

part: peça

plant: fábrica

seek: procurar, buscar

15

Multiple Intelligences

Look at the picture and answer orally.

1   What does the picture tell you about this unit?

2   In your opinion, what is intelligence?

3   Are all people born intelligent?

4   Can a person improve his/her intelligence? If so, how?

1 Take a look at the cartoon.

2 Give your opinion about the cartoon.

1 Why does the boy's mother think he is a genius?

2 Are kids now more intelligent than the kids in the past?

3 Read, think, and answer orally.

I don't need any cards now.

I still have some cards.

You can give me some more cards.

1 Which sentence has a negative meaning?

2 The word "some" expresses quantity. Is it possible to know what the quantity is?

▶ *Vocabulary*

darling: querido(a)
stay: ficar
still: ainda

Language Practice

Indefinite Adjectives and Pronouns

Some, **any** e **no** podem desempenhar a função de adjetivos ou de pronomes e indicam quantidade ou número indefinido.

I need **some** money. (adjetivo)

There is **no** bread in the cupboard. (adjetivo)

Do you need **any** money? (adjetivo)

No, I don't need **any**. (pronome)

Uso

Some [algum(ns), alguma(s), um pouco] é usado em frases afirmativas.

I want **some** coffee.

She wrote **some** letters.

Any [algum(ns), alguma(s), nenhum(a)] é usado em frases interrogativas e negativas.

Did she write **any** letters?

She didn't write **any** letters.

No e **none** [nenhum(a)] são usados com o verbo na forma afirmativa, mas dão sentido negativo à frase.

I have **no** money. (adjetivo)

I have **none** either. (pronome)

Indefinite Compounds

Compostos de **some**, **any** e **no**

Os compostos de **some**, **any** e **no** seguem as mesmas regras de uso apresentadas acima.

Some	someone/somebody
	something
	somewhere
Any	anyone/anybody
	anything
	anywhere
No	no one/nobody
	nothing
	nowhere

Nota

Some é usado em frases interrogativas para expressar um pedido, uma oferta ou quando se espera uma resposta positiva.
Would you like **some** coffee?
Do you need **some** money?
Any é usado em frases afirmativas:
- quando significa "qualquer/quaisquer".
  Call me at **any** time.
- após *if*.
  If you have **any** questions, ask me.
- com palavras de sentido negativo, como *seldom*, *rarely*, *never*, *without* etc.
  He <u>seldom</u> has **any** money.
  He <u>never</u> has **any** good ideas.

1 Circle the correct alternative.

1 Jerry hasn't eaten **any** / **no** cookies yet.

2 There are **any** / **no** cars in front of the bank.

3 They built **any** / **some** houses last year.

4 She bought a lot of books, but I bought **no** / **none**.

5 Are you going to write **any** / **no** e-mails tomorrow?

6 She rarely drinks **no** / **any** coffee in the afternoon.

2 Rewrite the sentences using the words in parentheses.

1 There is some sugar in the kitchen.

(any) There isn't any sugar in the kitchen. / Is there any sugar in the kitchen?

2 I have no doubts.

(any) _____

3 We can invite no friends for brunch tomorrow.

(some) _____

4 You didn't see any notebooks in the classroom.

(no) _____

5 I had seen some blue chairs in the living room.

(no) _____

6 She has planned to buy no expensive clothes.

(some) _____

3 Complete the sentences using *some*, *any*, or *no*.

1 We need to go to the supermarket: there's _____ milk in the fridge.

2 The reporter was curious, so she asked him _____ questions about the book.

3 If you have _____ questions, raise your hands.

4 They didn't have _____ problems getting to the hotel.

5 Would you like to have _____ tea?

6 I have _____ idea why she is so upset today. Maybe you should ask her.

4 Check the correct alternative.

1 Have you seen my glasses? I can't find them _____.

a ☐ nowhere   b ☐ anywhere   c ☐ somewhere

2 Is there _____ to eat in the kitchen?

a ☐ anything   b ☐ anytime   c ☐ nowhere

3 I know I've left my keys _____ around here.

a ☐ something   b ☐ somebody   c ☐ somewhere

4 There is _____ that I like in this store.

a ☐ anyone   b ☐ nothing   c ☐ anywhere

5 _____ knows what happened, it's a mystery!

a ☐ Nobody   b ☐ Someone   c ☐ Anything

6 _____ called you when you were out, I think it was John.

a ☐ Nothing   b ☐ Anyone   c ☐ Somebody

5 Complete the sentences using *some*, *any*, *no*, or the correct indefinite compound.

1 Don't put _____ on the table.

2 I asked him for _____ money, but he didn't have any.

3 _____ has taken my umbrella. I can't find it.

4 There are _____ students here. They must be _____ else.

5 _____ has arrived. Did you tell people the correct time?

6 Have you read _____ good books lately?

Go to page 214 for Extra Practice.

Reading

Before Reading

1 Discuss the questions below in Portuguese.

1 How many different kinds of intelligence are there?

2 In which situations can each kind be useful?

2 Write the meaning of the following words in Portuguese. Use the glossary.

1 grow _____

2 smart _____

3 belong _____

4 maze _____

3 In groups, discuss the following questions.

1 What are the easiest activities for you at school? And out of school?

2 What are the most difficult activities for you at school? And out of school?

3 Were the answers the same for all the classmates in your group? Why?

4 Read the box below to learn about the psychologist who developed the theory of multiple intelligences.

Howard Gardner

Howard Gardner (1943–) is both a psychologist and a professor of Cognition and Education at Harvard University. In 1983 he published his theory of multiple intelligences. He says that intelligence is multifaceted, so if you are good with words, for instance, you may not be good with something else, such as Math.

Based on <www.gse.harvard.edu/faculty/howard-gardner>. Accessed on March 22, 2016.

What Are Multiple Intelligences?

It has been claimed by some researchers that our intelligence or ability to understand the world around us is complex. Some people are better at understanding some things than others.

For some of us it is relatively easy to understand how a flower grows but it is
5 immensely difficult to understand and use a musical instrument. For others music might be easy but playing football is difficult.

Instead of having one intelligence, it is claimed that we have several different intelligences. What special intelligences do you have?

KINESTHETIC – BODY SMART

10 You may be body smart. You will enjoy sports and are good at swimming, athletics, gymnastics, and other sports. This is sometimes called being kinesthetic smart.

LINGUISTIC – WORD SMART

15 You may be word smart. You will enjoy reading, writing, and talking about things. This is sometimes called being linguistic smart.

LOGICAL – NUMBER SMART

You may be number smart. You will be good
20 at mathematics and other number activities; you are also good at solving problems. This is sometimes called being logical smart.

INTERPERSONAL – PEOPLE SMART

You may be people smart. You will like to mix
25 with other people and you will belong to lots of clubs. You like team games and are good at sharing. This is sometimes called being interpersonal smart.

INTRAPERSONAL – MYSELF SMART

30 You may be myself smart. You will know about yourself and your strengths and weaknesses. You will probably keep a diary. This is sometimes called being intrapersonal smart.

MUSICAL – MUSIC SMART

35 You may be music smart. You will enjoy music and can recognize sounds, and timbre, or the quality of a tone. This is sometimes called being musical smart.

VISUAL/SPATIAL – PICTURE SMART

40 You may be picture smart. You will be good at art and also good at other activities where you look at pictures, like map reading, finding your way out of mazes, and graphs. This is sometimes called being visual/spatial smart.

NATURALISTIC – NATURE SMART

45 You may be nature smart. You will like the world of plants and animals and enjoy learning about them. This is sometimes called being naturalistic smart.

Adapted from <www.bgfl.org/bgfl/custom/resources_ftp/client_ftp/ks3/ict/multiple_int/what.cfm>.
Accessed on November 23, 2015.

Vocabulary

instead of: em vez de

kinesthetic: cinestésico(a)

recognize: reconhecer

several: alguns/algumas; vários(as)

share: dividir, compartilhar

solve: resolver

After Reading

1 According to the text, are the following statements true (T) or false (F)?

1 ☐ The skills needed to play football and play a musical instrument are very similar.

2 ☐ There are two kinds of people: those with one type of intelligence and those with several types of intelligence.

3 ☐ People who have kinesthetic intelligence like practicing physical activities and sports.

4 ☐ Both interpersonal and intrapersonal skills are related to how a person deals with others.

5 ☐ People who have spatial intelligence can more easily find themselves if they are lost and have a map.

> **Reformular frases e expressões**
>
> A reformulação de frases e expressões que a princípio parecem difíceis leva o leitor a agir ativamente na compreensão do texto, fazendo proposições com base no seu entendimento do contexto.

2 Check the alternative that best restates the expressions in bold.

1 "*It has been claimed by some researchers* that our intelligence or ability to understand the world around us is complex" (lines 1-2).

   a ☐ Researchers have affirmed

   b ☐ People have claimed researchers

   c ☐ Claims have researched

2 "*Instead of having* one intelligence, it is claimed that we have several different intelligences" (line 7).

   a ☐ Because of having

   b ☐ Rather than having

   c ☐ Before having

3 Discuss the following questions with your classmates.

1 Which types of intelligence have you developed?

2 Which types do you want to be stronger at?

3 Can you relate people you know to each type of intelligence?

4 Can you think of occupations that people with each type of intelligence might be good at?

Vocabulary Expansion

1 **Read the information in the box and match the words to the definitions.**

| multicolored   multiracial   multiform |

Prefix _multi-_

O prefixo **_multi-_** significa "numeroso(a), em grande quantidade", geralmente enfatizando variedade.
multicultural   **multi**faceted

1 Region with people of different races. _____

2 Something that has many forms or shapes. _____

3 Something that has many different colors. _____

2 **Check the correct alternative to complete the sentences.**

1 Ms. Smith is a very competent _____.

   a ☐ teaches   **b** ☐ teacher

2 Monica _____ different subjects at university.

   a ☐ teaches   **b** ☐ teacher

3 They went to the party, but they didn't _____.

   a ☐ dance   **b** ☐ dancer

4 Richard is an honest _____.

   a ☐ politics   **b** ☐ politician

5 He is a good _____ teacher, the best one we've ever had.

   a ☐ mathematician   **b** ☐ Mathematics

6 Mr. Johnson is the _____ in charge of this research.

   a ☐ mathematician   **b** ☐ Mathematics

3 **Complete the sentences using _both_ or _together_.**

1 Sally and Kelly are going to travel to Europe _____.

2 _____ of us have already done our homework.

3 Don't worry. Let's do it _____. We'll help each other.

4 Sarah and Ernie always come to the meeting _____.

5 Eddie bought _____ books he needed.

both: ambos(as),
     os dois/as duas
together: juntos(as)

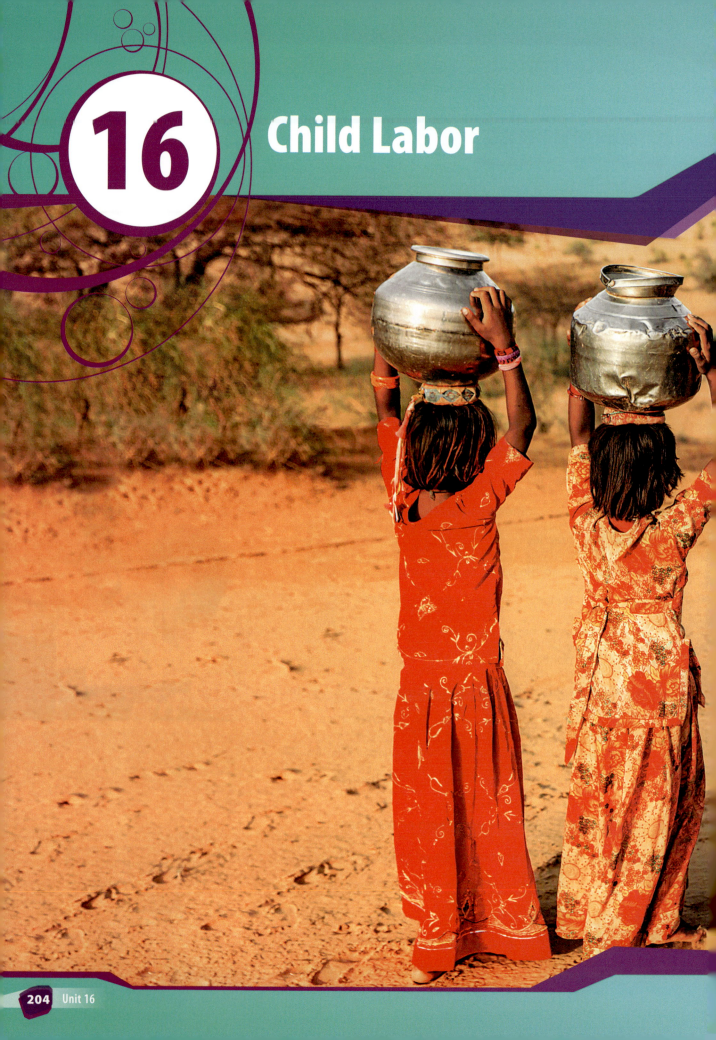

16 Child Labor

Look at the picture and answer orally.

1 What does the picture tell you about this unit?

2 How would you define child labor?

3 What are some possible causes of child labor?

4 And what are some possible consequences of it?

Language in Context

1 Take a look at the dialogue.

Derek: Wow, Lara! There are lots of kids here.

Lara: Yeah, Derek. And more and more come each day.

Derek: Are there instructors for everybody?

Celine: Yup. We have a lot of students who are volunteers. Look. The boy who is wearing a yellow T-shirt is our capoeira instructor.

Lara: And the girl in the fairy costume is our theater director.

Derek: What kind of youngsters come here?

Celine: All kinds. Kids who have nothing to do in the afternoon or on weekends. Everything is planned by them and we haven't had any kind of problem.

Derek: Which activities do they choose?

Lara: Capoeira, hip-hop, guitar lessons, and theater are their favorite.

Celine: We intend to have volleyball and choir singing, which many students have asked us about.

Derek: I'm a good hip-hop dancer and I'm free on weekends. Is there a place for me?

Vocabulary

choir: coral
costume: fantasia
guitar: violão
youngster: jovem
yup: sim (informal)

2 Give your opinion about the dialogue.

1 Do you think Celine is a volunteer at the community center? Why?

2 What does Derek want to do there?

3 Do you think volunteer work can help a community? How?

3 Read, think, and answer orally.

We have a lot of students who are volunteers.

The boy who is wearing a yellow T-shirt is our capoeira instructor.

They chose theater, which is their favorite activity.

1 All the sentences above have two clauses: a main clause and a subordinate clause. Identify them.

2 Which word introduces each subordinate clause?

3 Why is the subordinate clause in the last sentence introduced by a different word?

Language Practice

Relative Pronouns (I)

Os **pronomes relativos** introduzem orações subordinadas adjetivas. Essas orações definem, limitam ou acrescentam alguma informação ao substantivo da oração principal.

Uso

Who/That [que, quem] – Usados quando o antecedente do pronome relativo é uma pessoa.

The man [**who**/**that** arrived] is a pilot.

The woman [**who**/**that** just came in] is a lawyer.

Which/That [que, o(a) qual, os(as) quais] – Usados quando o antecedente não é uma pessoa.

The book [**which**/**that** is on the bed] is mine.

The dog [**which**/**that** I saw] was hurt.

Sujeito/Objeto – O pronome relativo pode ser sujeito ou objeto da oração subordinada.

The man [**who**/**that** arrived] is a pilot. (sujeito)

The man [**who**/**that** I saw] is a pilot. (objeto)

I saw a dog [**which**/**that** was hurt]. (sujeito)

The dog [**which**/**that** I saw] was hurt. (objeto)

Objeto – Quando o pronome relativo é objeto, ele pode ser omitido.

The man [**who**/**that**/**X** I saw] is a pilot.

The dog [**which**/**that**/**X** I saw] was hurt.

Whom [que, quem] – Pode substituir *who* quando este é objeto da oração subordinada. Entretanto, seu uso é obrigatório quando vier depois de preposição.

The man [**who**/**that**/**whom**/**X** I saw] is a pilot.

The man to **whom** you were talking is Mr. Taylor.

The woman [**who**/**that**/**whom**/**X** I interviewed for the position] is a lawyer.

She is the manager with **whom** I met about that job position.

---

1 **Complete the sentences using *who* or *which*.**

1 That is the person _____ sold me those rare books.

2 This is the house _____ I want to buy.

3 He is the mechanic _____ has fixed my car.

4 The dogs _____ you have at home are very dangerous.

5 The guests _____ have just arrived live in my neighborhood.

2 Join the sentences using relative pronouns.

1 The woman is wearing a white shirt. She is a physicist.
The woman who/that is wearing a white shirt is a physicist.

2 I bought a shirt. The shirt was very expensive.

_____

3 The girl plays the piano very well. She is thirteen years old.

_____

4 The boy is sick. He is my brother's friend.

_____

5 He has an apartment. His apartment was built in 2005.

_____

6 The man is the best soccer player in the world. He came here yesterday.

_____

3 Circle the correct alternative(s).

1 The woman **who / that / which** saved the baby was very brave.

2 The keys **that / who / which** were on the table are mine.

3 That is the boy about **who / whom / that** I was talking.

4 This is the book about **which / that / whom** she was talking.

5 The house **which / that / who** we bought has a very nice garden.

6 The girls **who / that / whom** you invited ate all the sandwiches.

4 Complete the sentences with relative pronouns. Write all the possibilities.

1 Is she the woman _____ you met yesterday, the one _____ helped you find the building you were looking for?

2 You are the professional _____ we are looking for.

3 Martin is the German boy _____ speaks Portuguese, so he is going to help you when you arrive in Berlin next week.

4 The car _____ you had sold me was stolen last weekend.

5 She is the girl to _____ I gave the book.

6 She is the dentist _____ talked about how to prevent tooth decay.

Relative Pronouns (II)

Uso

Where [onde] – Usado para se referir a lugares.
   The house **where** she lives is near the park.

Whose [cujo(s), cuja(s)] – Usado para indicar relação de posse.
   The girl **whose** mother is an astronaut wants to talk to you.

5 **Complete the sentences with *where* or *whose*.**

1   I went to a restaurant _____ the food was cheap and delicious.

2   I met a woman _____ son had studied at my school.

3   This is the park _____ I used to come when I was a child.

4   The man _____ cousin is a lawyer was arrested yesterday.

6 **Circle the relative pronouns in the sentences below. Some sentences have no relative pronouns.**

1   Is that the house that you like?

2   Which do you prefer, cinema or theater?

3   That is the school where I study.

4   Who is your English teacher?

5   She is the girl whose black shoes I loved.

7 **Check the correct alternative.**

1   The dress _____ you bought is amazing.

   a ☐ X   b ☐ that   c ☐ *a* and *b* are correct

2   The person _____ I most admire will be here tonight.

   a ☐ whom   b ☐ whose   c ☐ *a* and *b* are correct

3   The house in _____ she lives is very small.

   a ☐ where   b ☐ which   c ☐ *a* and *b* are correct

4   Sandy and John are the students _____ have passed the exam.

   a ☐ that   b ☐ who   c ☐ *a* and *b* are correct

Go to page 214 for Extra Practice.

Before Reading

1 **Discuss the questions below in Portuguese.**

1 How many people in your class work?

2 What kinds of jobs do they have?

3 How many hours do they work every day?

> 👓 **Fazer confrontações**
>
> Confrontar o conhecimento prévio do leitor sobre um assunto com informações novas trazidas pelo texto amplia o seu conhecimento sobre o tema e pode tanto reforçar suas concepções quanto fazê-lo questioná-las e repensá-las.

2 **Decide if the statements are true (T) or false (F) based on your personal knowledge about child labor.**

1 ☐ Any work done by children can be considered child labor.

2 ☐ Child soldiering, sexual exploitation, and drug trafficking are forms of child labor.

3 ☐ Most children who are responsible for doing household chores are girls.

4 ☐ Child labor is both a cause and a consequence of social injustice.

5 ☐ The majority of children engaged in child labor are older than 14.

3 **Skim the texts. In which one(s) does the following information appear?**

1 Figures concerning child labor around the world. _____

2 Definition of child labor. _____

3 Consequences of child labor. _____

4 **It is possible to state that the main objective of the texts is to...**

a ☐ criticize, based on opinions.

b ☐ criticize, based on facts.

c ☐ describe, based on facts.

d ☐ inform, based on facts.

e ☐ inform, based on opinions.

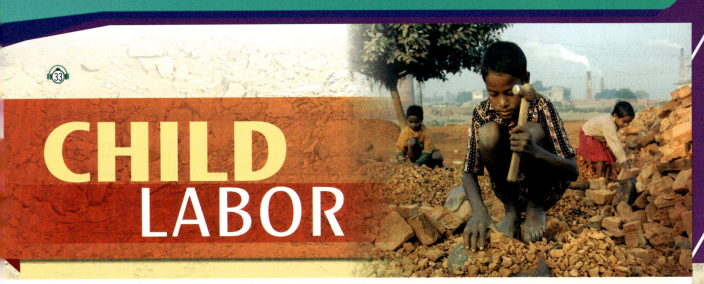

CHILD LABOR

Text A

Child labour is [...] work that children should not be doing because they are too young to work, or – if they are old enough to work – because it is dangerous or otherwise unsuitable for them. Not
5 all work done by children should be classified as child labour that is to be targeted for elimination.

[...] Whether or not particular forms of "work" can be called "child labour" depends on the child's age, the type and hours of work performed and the
10 conditions under which it is performed [...].

Available at <www.un.org/en/globalissues/briefingpapers/childlabour/index.shtml>.
Accessed on November 5, 2015.

Text B

Recent global estimates [...] indicate that 168 million children aged 5 to 17 are engaged in child labour. Some 120 million among them are below the age of 14, while a further 30 million children
5 in this age group – mostly girls – perform unpaid household chores within their own families. In addition, millions of children suffer in the other worst forms of child labour, including slavery and slavery-like practices such as forced [...] labour and
10 child soldiering, sexual exploitation, or are used by adults in illicit activities, including drug trafficking.

Despite a steady decline in child labour, progress is far too slow. At current rates, more than 100 million children will still be trapped in child labour by 2020.

15 The continuing persistence of child labour poses a threat to national economies and has severe negative short- and long-term consequences for the fulfillment of children's rights [...].

[...]

20 Child labour reinforces intergenerational cycles of poverty, undermines national economies and impedes achieving progress towards the Millennium Development Goals [...]. It is not only a cause, but also a consequence of social inequities reinforced
25 by discrimination. Children from indigenous groups or lower castes are more likely to drop out of school to work. Migrant children are also vulnerable to hidden and illicit labour.

Available at <www.unicef.org/protection/57929_child_labour.html>. Accessed on November 5, 2015.

Text C

"Child labor perpetuates poverty, unemployment, illiteracy, population growth and other social problems."
Kailash Satyarthi, Indian advocate of the rights of working children, winner of the Nobel Peace Prize of 2014

Available at <www.huffingtonpost.com/laura-n-henderson/kailash-satyarthi_b_6000782.html>. Accessed on November 5, 2015.

▶ *Vocabulary*

caste: casta, classe social	**drop out:** abandonar	**rate:** taxa, índice	**unpaid:** não remunerado(a)
despite: apesar de	**perform:** realizar, executar	**target:** ter como alvo/objetivo	**whether:** se

After Reading

1 📖 **After reading the texts, go back to your answers in activity 2 on page 210. Were they correct?**

2 **Find the following figures in the texts.**

1 The number of children engaged in child labor worldwide today.

_____

2 The number of children under 14 involved in child labor.

_____

3 The number of children under 14 performing unpaid housework within their own families.

_____

4 The number of children expected to be engaged in child labor by 2020.

_____

3 **Check the correct meaning of the sentences below.**

1 _"Not all work done by children should be classified as child labour that is to be targeted for elimination"_ (text A, lines 4-6).

a ☐ Any work done by children should be classified as a target for elimination.

b ☐ Only the work that could be classified as child labor needs to be eliminated.

2 _"Despite a steady decline in child labour, progress is far too slow"_ (text B, lines 12-13).

a ☐ Child labor is declining constantly, but very slowly.

b ☐ The number of children engaged in child labor is growing at a slow pace.

3 _"Children from indigenous groups or lower castes are more likely to drop out of school to work"_ (text B, lines 25-27).

a ☐ The probability of these children abandoning school is greater.

b ☐ These children prefer working to going to school.

4 **Discuss these questions with your classmates in Portuguese.**

1 Should unpaid household chores always be considered child labor? Why?

2 How does child labor perpetuate poverty? How about illiteracy?

3 Which other social problems can be caused by child labor?

Vocabulary Expansion

1 Rewrite the expressions.

1 a woman that screams _____ a screaming woman _____

2 children who labor _____

3 a child that sleeps _____

4 mothers who work _____

5 a dog that jumps _____

6 girls who smile _____

2 Complete the sentences using the expressions in the box.

> at an early age   for ages   underage   aged   aging   ageless

> **age:** idade; era, época; envelhecer

1 They have _____, but they are still a bit immature in some aspects. (envelheceram)

2 She looked beautiful and _____. (que não envelhece)

3 Rick and John can't enter the nightclub because they are _____. (menores de idade)

4 Since he was born in a poor family, he started working _____. (cedo na vida)

5 My family has lived in this town _____. (há muito tempo)

6 Lack of physical exercise contributes to the process of _____. (envelhecimento)

3 Find synonyms for the words below. Use the box for help.

> confined   inappropriate   concealed   injustice   continuous   weaken

1 unsuitable _____

2 steady _____

3 trapped _____

4 undermine _____

5 inequity _____

6 hidden _____

Extra Practice 8

1 **Write *some*, *any*, *no*, or *none*. In some cases, more than one answer may be possible.**

1 There were _____ children in the park this morning.

2 We wanted to eat _____ bananas before dinner, but Mom gave us _____.

3 I haven't had _____ chocolate for three days.

4 They were looking for _____ old books in the garage.

5 I need _____ more eggs to make the cake.

6 Do you have _____ tips for those who want to travel to Egypt?

2 **Rewrite the sentences using the word *no* without changing their meaning.**

1 He didn't have any money.
   He had no money.

2 He doesn't know any songs from this band.

3 You didn't make any mistakes.

4 She didn't hear any noise.

3 **In the sentences below the indefinite adjective or pronoun is not used correctly. Rewrite the sentences correcting them.**

1 Do you have none problems with the Chemistry homework?

2 I offered him any money.

3 I went to your house last night, but there was anybody at home.

4 They didn't want to cause no trouble, so they decided to leave.

4 Check the correct alternative to complete the sentences.

1 You can't sit down because there are _____ empty seats.

a ☐ no   b ☐ none   c ☐ some   d ☐ any

2 She asked me if he had _____ French books, but he has _____.

a ☐ any – none   b ☐ any – no   c ☐ some – any   d ☐ no – any

3 _____ students were playing the guitar yesterday: they sounded great!

a ☐ None   b ☐ Some   c ☐ Any   d ☐ No

4 _____ of my brothers speak English. They only speak French.

a ☐ Some   b ☐ Any   c ☐ No   d ☐ None

5 I couldn't go out yesterday. My car had _____ fuel.

a ☐ any   b ☐ none   c ☐ no   d ☐ some

6 Aren't there _____ doctors in the audience?

a ☐ some   b ☐ any   c ☐ none   d ☐ no

5 Check the correct alternative.

1 **A:** Is there _____ I can do for you?

B: No, _____.

a ☐ nothing – nothing   c ☐ anything – something

b ☐ anything – nothing   d ☐ something – anything

2 This bus can take you _____ near the museum.

a ☐ some   c ☐ somewhere

b ☐ someone   d ☐ nothing

3 Have you solved _____ mysterious cases?

a ☐ something   c ☐ nothing

b ☐ none   d ☐ any

4 **A:** Are you waiting for _____?

B: No, I'm waiting for _____.

a ☐ anyone – no one   c ☐ nobody – anyone

b ☐ anybody – somebody   d ☐ no one – someone

6 Combine the sentences using *who*.

1 The man abandoned the child. He was punished.
   The man who abandoned the child was punished.

2 The old lady bought some flowers. She was my teacher.

3 Mary and Helen were talking to a man. He was the director of that computer company.

4 The boy is standing near the bakery. He goes to my school.

5 The girl studied with my brother. She is my friend.

7 Complete the sentences using *which* and the information in the box.

It was later adopted by their family.   It looks like a castle.
It belonged to my grandfather.   Nobody knows them.

1 I have been playing the piano _____.

2 The kids have brought home a dog _____.

3 He likes talking about subjects _____.

4 He is going to live in a house _____.

8 There are mistakes in the sentences below. Circle these mistakes and rewrite the sentences correcting them.

1 That's the man whom was looking for you.

2 The car who Paul bought was made in Italy.

3 Millions of girls which work as unpaid domestic servants are under 18.

4 The information who was shown in the survey was not completely true.

9 When possible, substitute the words in bold.

1 She is the lady **that** you helped some days ago.

Other possibilities: _____ who/whom/X _____

2 The research **that** you've proposed is very important.

Other possibilities: _____

3 The doctor **that** was in the hospital is my father.

Other possibilities: _____

4 The girl **who** I met yesterday is Canadian.

Other possibilities: _____

5 The boy **whose** father is a judge was arrested yesterday.

Other possibilities: _____

6 He was the first person **that** I met when I arrived here.

Other possibilities: _____

10 Answer the questions using *whose* and the information in parentheses.

1 Who is Maria? (the girl/brother/rock singer)
Maria is the girl whose brother is a rock singer.

2 Who is Giovanna? (the girl/mother/my neighbor)

_____

3 Who is Kylie? (the woman/husband/a Brazilian engineer)

_____

4 Who is Pietro? (the boy/father/my Italian teacher)

_____

11 Answer the questions with information about you.

1 Who is the person that you admire the most?

_____

2 What is the book which you like the most?

_____

3 Who is your classmate whose jokes are the funniest?

_____

12 Check the correct alternative.

1 I don't like people _____ are against the idea of saving water.

a ☐ which b ☐ that c ☐ X d ☐ whom

2 The man _____ son is sick is very sad.

a ☐ whom b ☐ whose c ☐ where d ☐ X

3 I don't want to talk about the people and the things _____ I like.

a ☐ whose b ☐ who c ☐ that d ☐ where

4 The woman _____ is near the door is a physicist.

a ☐ which b ☐ who c ☐ where d ☐ whom

5 The man to _____ many students are talking was my teacher.

a ☐ who b ☐ that c ☐ whom d ☐ which

6 The player _____ won the competition is my brother Peter.

a ☐ who b ☐ X c ☐ which d ☐ when

13 Check the alternative that <u>cannot</u> complete the sentence correctly.

1 The book _____ she showed you is mine.

a ☐ which b ☐ X c ☐ whose d ☐ that

2 The letters from Gary _____ I have kept contain lovely poems.

a ☐ who b ☐ X c ☐ which d ☐ that

3 Peter is the flight attendant _____ I was telling you about.

a ☐ who b ☐ that c ☐ X d ☐ whose

4 The girl _____ I met yesterday wants to major in Cinema.

a ☐ that b ☐ which c ☐ whom d ☐ who

Gastronomy

Gastronomy professionals are involved in the production of foods and beverages and in the management of restaurants. Many of those who have an interest in this industry intend to have a career as a chef, specializing in confectionery, bakery, or in a specific kind of cooking, such as Japanese or French cuisine. However, there is a wide range of career possibilities for Gastronomy students.

A gastronomist is a specialist in food safety and can develop menus for several types of establishments, from restaurants and hotels to air companies and hospitals. He/She can also supervise the operation of a kitchen, hire and train employees, prepare price lists, and negotiate with suppliers. Gastronomists can also offer consulting services for opening a restaurant or changing the menu of an existing one. Another possibility is to work as a food critic, making restaurant reviews for websites or magazines. This professional can also work with the development of products, by creating and preparing dishes that use the food items supplied by a given company.

Based on <http://vestibular.brasilescola.uol.com.br/guia-de-profissoes/gastronomia.htm>; <http://guiadoestudante.abril.com.br/profissoes/administracao-negocios/gastronomia-686303.shtml>. Accessed on December 7, 2015.

Vocabulary

bakery: panificação **confectionery:** confeitaria **hire:** contratar **review:** resenha, crítica

beverage: bebida **cuisine:** culinária típica de determinado local **management:** administração **supplier:** fornecedor(a)

17 Language and Identity

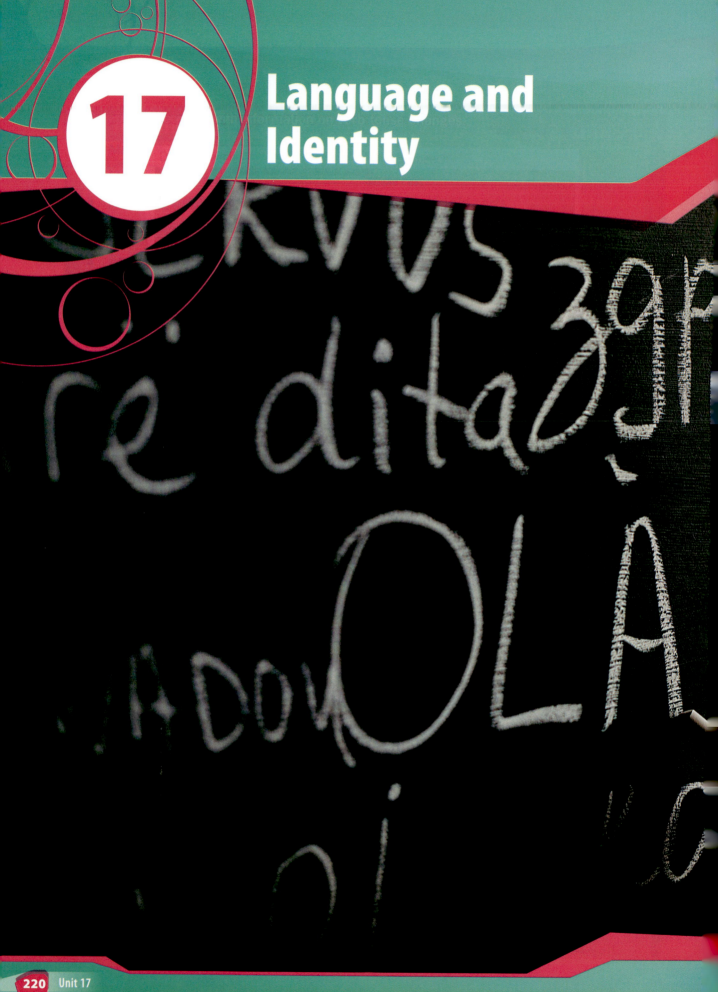

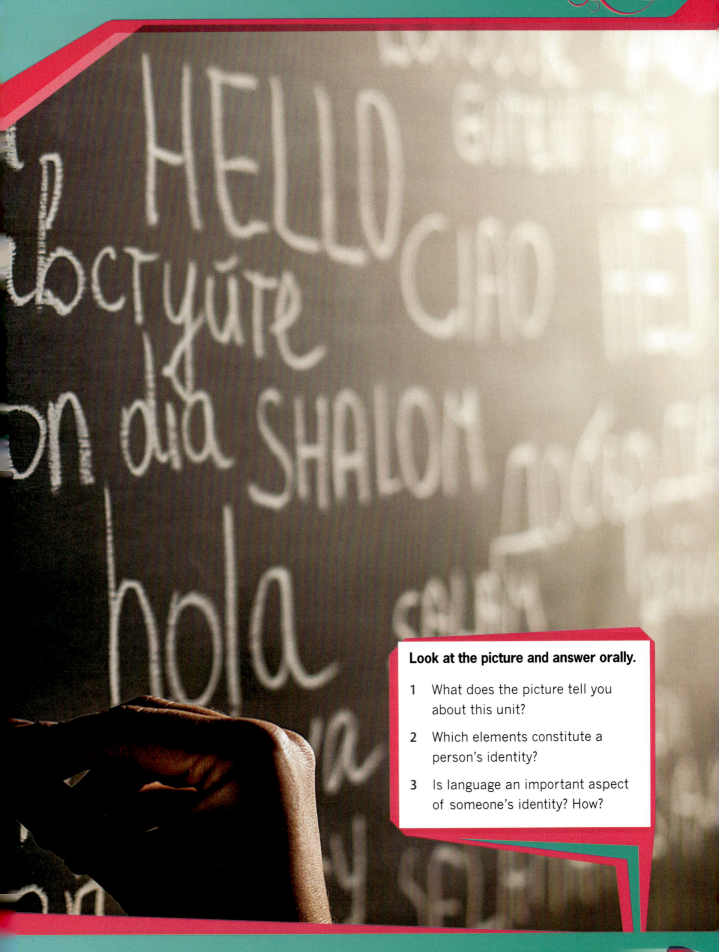

Look at the picture and answer orally.

1   What does the picture tell you about this unit?

2   Which elements constitute a person's identity?

3   Is language an important aspect of someone's identity? How?

Language in Context

1 **Take a look at the text.**

> People assumed English, like French and Portuguese, was the natural language of literary and political mediation between African people in the same nation, as well as between nations in Africa and other continents. In some cases people thought these European languages had the capacity to unite African peoples against the divisions that are typical of the multiplicity of languages in the continent. So in 1964, Chinua Achebe, who was a Nigerian novelist and had published several books in English, said:
>
> > Is it right that a man should abandon his mother tongue for someone else's? It looks like a betrayal and makes us feel guilty. But for me there is no other choice. I have been given the language and I intend to use it.
>
> However, he also stated:
>
> > I feel that the English language will be able to convey my African experience. But it will have to be a new English, still connected to its ancestral home but altered for new African contexts.

Adapted from THIONG'O, N. *Decolonising the Mind:* The Politics of Language in African Literature. Nairobi: East African Educational Publishers Ltd., 1986, p. 6-8.

Vocabulary

assume: supor, presumir
betrayal: traição
convey: comunicar, transmitir
guilty: culpado(a)
mother tongue: língua materna

2 **Give your opinion about the text.**

1 Does English help different nations communicate?

2 Does it help people from the same nation communicate? In which situations?

3 **Read, think, and answer orally.**

The novelist who wrote this book gave a wonderful speech at the local university.

Chinua Achebe, who was a Nigerian novelist and had published several books in English, gave his opinion on the issue.

1 How are the sentences different in terms of punctuation?

2 Identify the subordinate clauses in each sentence.

3 Which of the subordinate clauses is not essential to the meaning of the sentence?

Language Practice

Relative Pronouns (III)

Uso

Oração entre vírgulas (oração subordinada adjetiva explicativa) – Quando a oração subordinada adjetiva não é essencial para o significado da oração principal, ela vem entre vírgulas; o pronome relativo que a introduz não pode ser omitido e não se usa *that* para introduzi-la.

George Orwell, **[who wrote *Animal Farm*]**, was an English writer.

Mount Tambora, **[which is located in Indonesia]**, erupted in 1815.

Joseph Conrad, **[whose native language was Polish]**, wrote his books in English.

Paris, **[where the Eiffel Tower is located]**, is a beautiful city.

---

1 Check the correct alternative.

1 His grandpa, _____ was sick, looked very pale.

    a ☐ which   b ☐ X   c ☐ who

2 They were sitting in their living room, _____ was crowded.

    a ☐ which   b ☐ who   c ☐ X

3 He called her nurse, _____ lives nearby.

    a ☐ who   b ☐ whose   c ☐ X

4 That is the house _____ we bought.

    a ☐ who   b ☐ X   c ☐ whose

2 Complete the sentences with the appropriate relative pronoun.

1 Martin, _____ is German, is my friend.

2 Laura, _____ dog is barking, is my neighbor.

3 The attic, _____ I keep my French books, is full of old things.

4 My father, _____ is very tall, is a firefighter.

5 The Titanic, _____ was a very big ship, collided with an iceberg.

6 *Romeo and Juliet*, _____ is my favorite play, was written by Shakespeare.

Language Practice

Relative Pronouns (IV)

Uso – casos especiais

That – É o único pronome relativo usado:

• após *the first*, *the last* e superlativos

You are <u>the first</u> person [**that has said this to me**].   She is <u>the smartest</u> girl [**(that) I know**].

• após *all*, *every*, *some*, *any*, *no* e seus compostos

<u>All</u> [**that glitters**] is not gold.   <u>Nothing</u> [**(that) you say**] will convince her.

• quando há antecedentes diferentes

Tell me about the <u>people</u> and the <u>places</u> [**(that) you know**].

Preposições – Quando uma preposição antecede o pronome relativo:

• usa-se apenas ***whom*** ou ***which*** (para pessoa e não pessoa, respectivamente);

• não se pode omitir o pronome.

The man [**about whom we were talking**] is near the door.

The dog [**to which you gave food**] is better now.

> **Nota**
> ***That*** pode ser omitido quando exerce a função de objeto.
> He is the teacher [**(that) I told you about**].

---

3 **Match the columns to make complete sentences.**

1	This is the first time	a	☐	was presented in São Paulo.
2	I told him everything	b	☐	died in New York City.
3	John Lennon, who was a rock singer,	c	☐	I told you about.
4	*Les Misérables*, which is a famous play,	d	☐	(that) I have seen you crying.
5	She will talk about the places and food	e	☐	(that) she likes.
6	That is the man	f	☐	(that) I dislike about him.

4 **Underline all the correct alternatives.**

1 You can't believe anything **which / that / X** she says.

2 Alice, **that / who / X** is Canadian, is my new boss.

3 The mine from **X / which / whom** they extract gold belongs to the government.

4 She was the last person **that / which / X** I saw before going to sleep.

5 This is the most expensive car **that / which / X** I've ever bought.

6 Don't touch anything **which / that / X** is in that room.

5 Check the correct alternative to complete each sentence.

1 Joseph, to _____ I gave the flowers, is my gardener.

a ☐ whom   c ☐ whose

b ☐ who   d ☐ which

2 Joseph, _____ gave me the flowers, is my gardener.

a ☐ that   c ☐ who

b ☐ X   d ☐ whom

3 Escape Cruises, _____ is a nice ship, travels along the Brazilian coast in February.

a ☐ X   c ☐ which

b ☐ that   d ☐ where

4 My mother, _____ likes swimming, is afraid of the sea.

a ☐ whom   c ☐ X

b ☐ that   d ☐ who

5 The boy _____ was talking to you is my brother.

a ☐ X   c ☐ that

b ☐ which   d ☐ whose

6 Nobody _____ he invited went to his birthday party.

a ☐ X   c ☐ which

b ☐ whose   d ☐ where

Go to page 240 for Extra Practice.

Reading

Before Reading

1 **Discuss the questions below in Portuguese.**

1 What do you know about the division of the African territory and the establishment of some of its countries?

2 Do you know any countries where more than one language is spoken?

3 How would you feel if you were forbidden to speak your native language?

4 Can a language be an instrument of oppression? How?

2 **Match these words from the text on page 227 to their synonyms.**

1 recall

2 grown-up

3 riddle

4 deference

a ☐ respect

b ☐ puzzle

c ☐ adult

d ☐ remember

3 **How much do you know about the languages spoken in Kenya? Decide if the statements are true (T) or false (F) based on your personal knowledge.**

a ☐ Gikuyu is spoken in Kenya.

b ☐ Families in Kenya told stories at home in English.

c ☐ Speakers of Gikuyu believe that language is much more than words and structures.

d ☐ Students in Kenya were encouraged to speak both Gikuyu and English at school.

4 **Read the box below to learn about the author of the text on page 227.**

Ngugi wa Thiong'o, who is considered East Africa's leading novelist, was born in Kenya in 1938. He began writing novels, plays, and essays in English, but is now working in Gikuyu.

The novelist is currently also a theorist of post-colonial literature and Distinguished Professor of English and Comparative Literature at the University of California, Irvine.

Based on <www.ngugiwathiongo.com/bio/bio-home.htm>. Accessed on November 11, 2015.

Decolonising the Mind

[...]

We spoke Gikuyu in and outside the home. I can vividly recall those evenings of storytelling around the fireside. It was mostly the grown-
5 ups telling the children but everybody was interested and involved. We children would retell the stories the following day to other children who worked in the fields picking the pyrethrum flowers, tea leaves or coffee beans of our
10 European and African landlords.

[...]

There were good and bad storytellers. A good one could tell the same story over and over again, and it would always be fresh to us, the listeners. He or she could tell a story told by someone else and make it more alive and dramatic. The differences really were in the use of words and images and the
15 inflexion of voices to effect different tones.

We therefore learnt to value words for their meaning and nuances. Language was not a mere string of words. It had a suggestive power well beyond the immediate and lexical meaning. Our appreciation of the suggestive magical power of language was reinforced by the games we played with words through riddles, proverbs, transpositions of syllables, or through nonsensical but
20 musically arranged words. [...]

And then I went to school, a colonial school, and this harmony was broken. The language of my education was no longer the language of my culture. [...]

In Kenya, English became more than a language: it was *the* language, and all the others had to bow before it in deference.

25 Thus one of the most humiliating experiences was to be caught speaking Gikuyu in the vicinity of the school. The culprit was given corporal punishment – three to five strokes of the cane on bare buttocks – or was made to carry a metal plate around the neck with inscriptions such as I AM STUPID or I AM A DONKEY. [...]

The attitude to English was the exact opposite: any achievement in spoken or written English was
30 highly rewarded; prizes, prestige, applause; the ticket to higher realms. English became the measure of intelligence and ability in the arts, the sciences, and all the other branches of learning. [...]

Available at THIONG'O, N. *Decolonising the Mind:* The Politics of Language in African Literature. Nairobi: East African Educational Publishers Ltd., 1986, p. 10-12.

Vocabulary

bare: descoberto(a), desnudo(a)
be caught: ser pego(a)
bow: curvar-se; fazer reverência

buttock: nádega
cane: vara
culprit: culpado(a)

effect: causar, provocar
inflexion: mudança do tom de voz
landlord: senhorio, proprietário

nonsensical: absurdo(a), sem sentido
reward: recompensar
stroke: pancada

After Reading

1 After reading the text, go back to your answers in activity 3 on page 226. Were they correct?

> 📖 **Observar relações de causa e efeito**
>
> Relações de causa e efeito são bastante comuns, tanto em narrativas quanto em descrições e textos argumentativos. Identificá-las e compreendê-las aprofunda o conhecimento que o leitor constrói a partir do texto.

2 👓 Which words from the text introduce a consequence of something mentioned before?

a ☐ and   b ☐ therefore   c ☐ but   d ☐ then   e ☐ thus

3 👓 What were the consequences of the following events?

1 *"The differences really were in the use of words and images and the inflexion of voices to effect different tones"* (lines 14-15).

a ☐ *"We therefore learnt to value words for their meaning and nuances"* (line 16).

b ☐ *"Thus one of the most humiliating experiences was to be caught speaking Gikuyu in the vicinity of the school"* (lines 25-26).

2 *"In Kenya, English became more than a language: it was* the *language, and all the others had to bow before it in deference"* (lines 23-24).

a ☐ *"We therefore learnt to value words for their meaning and nuances"* (line 16).

b ☐ *"Thus one of the most humiliating experiences was to be caught speaking Gikuyu in the vicinity of the school"* (lines 25-26).

4 Complete the summary of the text using the words from the box.

> inflexion   punished   Gikuyu   stories   Kenya   English   words   intelligent

_____ was spoken at home and among family members in _____.
_____ were told and retold in the language, and changes in the choice of _____
and in the _____ of voices always made them sound fresh. At school, however, children were
_____ for speaking it. On the other hand, the use of _____ was highly
motivated and praised. The students who spoke it were considered more _____.

5 Why do you think achievements in English were rewarded and the use of Gikuyu was punished in schools in Kenya? Discuss with your classmates in Portuguese.

Vocabulary Expansion

1 **Read the box and write new words. Then translate these new words.**

1 move _____ _____

2 develop _____ _____

3 improve _____ _____

4 arrange _____ _____

5 govern _____ _____

6 invest _____ _____

> **Suffix -ment**
>
> Acrescentado a alguns verbos, o sufixo **-ment** forma substantivos que se referem a ações, processos ou estados.
> punish – punish**ment**
> achieve – achieve**ment**

2 **Complete the sentences using the words in parentheses and the suffixes from the box.**

> -ion   -ation   -ness   -ity   -ment

1 During her campaign, the candidate promised to invest in _____ (educate).

2 Everyone could notice their _____ (happy); they couldn't stop smiling.

3 After hours of negotiation, they finally reached an _____ (agree).

4 Her _____ (instruct) was clear: we had to call her as soon as we got the package.

5 His _____ (able) to draw and paint was incredible; he was a true artist.

3 **Read the information in the box and complete the sentences.**

> **False Cognates**
>
> **college:** faculdade   **novel:** romance   **data:** dados, informações   **sort:** classificar; separar
> **school:** colégio, escola   **soap opera:** novela   **date:** data; encontro   **luck:** sorte

1 Our teacher has to _____ all these papers for a meeting because the _____ principal asked him to.

2 My sister's _____ professor asked her class to choose an African _____ they would like to read.

3 Phil and June have a _____ on Sunday.

4 The police officers still need some _____ to complete the investigation.

5 My family doesn't like to watch _____ in the evening; we prefer to read.

6 I wished him good _____ before he left for the interview.

18

Paralympic Games

Look at the picture and answer orally.

1   What does the picture tell you about this unit?

2   Do you know any person with disabilities?

3   What kind of difficulties do people with disabilities face in your community?

Language in Context

1 **Take a look at the dialogue.**

Jarred: Are the Paralympic Games something new? I've heard about them just recently.

Ricky: Not really. The Olympic Games for athletes with disabilities were officially organized for the first time in Rome, in 1960.

Matthew: You mean there were no games before 1960?

Ricky: Well, unofficially the games started in 1948. But they were only for some types of athletes.

Jarred: Were there many competitors in 1960?

Ricky: Yes, 400 athletes.

Matthew: Have the games grown since then?

Ricky: A lot! By 2020 more than 40,000 athletes will have competed in the games.

2 **Give your opinion about the dialogue.**

Vocabulary
athlete: atleta
disability: deficiência

1 Were you aware of the existence of the Paralympic Games?

2 What do you know about Brazilians participating in the Paralympic Games?

3 **Read, think, and answer orally.**

1 When the Paralympic Games were officially invented, many athletes **had** already **competed** unofficially.

2 In 1960, 400 athletes **competed** in the Paralympic Games.

3 In 2020, many athletes **will compete** in the Paralympic Games.

4 By 2020, more than 40,000 athletes **will have competed** in the Paralympic Games.

a What period of time does each sentence refer to: past, present, or future?

b Which happened first: the official invention of the Paralympic Games or the fact that many Paralympic athletes competed unofficially?

c What are the differences in form and meaning between sentences 3 and 4?

Language Practice

Future Perfect

Will have + verbo no **Past Participle**

Afirmativa: He **will have left** when you arrive there.
Interrogativa: Will he **have left** when you arrive there?
Negativa: He **will not have left** when you arrive there.
Forma abreviada: won't (will not)

Uso

O *Future Perfect* indica que uma ação terá ocorrido (ou não) antes de determinado momento no futuro.

By 5 o'clock, I **will have arrived** home.
(Até as 5 horas, (já) terei chegado em casa.)

By January, she **will have bought** her house.
(Até janeiro, ela (já) terá comprado a casa dela.)

They **won't have fixed** the TV by 7 o'clock.
(Eles (ainda) não terão consertado a TV até as 7 horas.)

He **won't have become** a professional athlete by the time he finishes high school.
(Ele (ainda) não terá se tornado um atleta profissional quando terminar o Ensino Médio.)

Will the game **have started** when we get home?
(O jogo (já) terá começado quando chegarmos em casa?)

---

1 **Complete the sentences using the verbs in parentheses in the Future Perfect.**

1 By the time you come back from his birthday party, they _____ (see) the movie.

2 I _____ (tell) her the good news by the time you meet her.

3 _____ you _____ (finish) the job by April? I have a proposal for you.

4 He _____ (arrive – neg.) by 4 p.m.

5 By this time tomorrow, she _____ (meet) Charles.

6 _____ the children _____ (have) lunch by the time Grandma arrives?

2 Combine the sentences using the Future Perfect.

1 We will talk to him at 2 o'clock. You will arrive at 3 o'clock.
   By the time you arrive, we will have talked to him.

2 They will make a cake at 3 o'clock. You will get here at 4 o'clock.

3 He will talk to her in the morning. We will meet him in the afternoon.

4 The show will start at 8 o'clock. You will arrive at 8:15.

5 The cameramen will get here in an hour. The competition will start in five minutes.

6 The magazine will be published next week. The winners will be announced tomorrow.

Language Practice

Verb Tense Review

Verb Tense	Example
Simple Present	He **swims** every morning.
Present Continuous	He **is swimming** now.
Simple Past	He **swam** yesterday.
Past Continuous	He **was swimming** five minutes ago.
Present Perfect	He **has swum** in the English Channel.
Present Perfect Continuous	He **has been swimming** for 2 hours.
Past Perfect	He **had** already **swum** when I talked to him.
Past Perfect Continuous	He **had been swimming** before we arrived.
Simple Future	I think he **will swim** tomorrow.
Future Continuous	He **will be swimming** at 5 o'clock.
Future with *Going to*	He **is going to swim** next week.
Future Perfect	He **will have swum** by 6 o'clock.
Imperative	Don't **swim** now!

3 Check the correct alternative to complete the sentences.

1 They _____ the news when I called them.

   a ☐ watched   **b** ☐ were watching   **c** ☐ have watched

2 My friends _____ me some tips about the city before I arrived there.

   a ☐ had given   **b** ☐ were giving   **c** ☐ give

3 Marcia _____ the baby by the end of the month.

   a ☐ has   **b** ☐ has had   **c** ☐ will have had

4 _____ to answer her e-mail; she said it's urgent.

   a ☐ You forget   **b** ☐ Will you forget   **c** ☐ Don't forget

4 Complete the sentences using the verbs in parentheses in the correct verb tense.

1 They _____ (get) married three months ago.

2 Karl _____ (live) in Italy since last year.

3 Ted usually _____ (take) his children to school in the morning.

4 The kids _____ (play) in the garden now.

5 Mom _____ (make) lunch when I arrived yesterday, so I helped her finish it.

6 She _____ (finish) her French homework by the time the class starts.

5 Match the sentence halves.

1 They are going to the movies   **a** ☐ when I arrived.

2 They have gone to the museum   **b** ☐ several times this year.

3 She will be riding a horse   **c** ☐ by 6 o'clock.

4 They will have finished the project   **d** ☐ now.

5 He was cooking dinner   **e** ☐ in the evening.

6 Complete the sentences with information about yourself.

1 _____ since February.

2 _____ before I woke up.

3 _____ by the end of the month.

4 _____ next year.

Go to page 240 for Extra Practice.

Reading

Before Reading

1 **Discuss the questions below in Portuguese.**

  1   What are the Olympic Games?

  2   What are the Paralympic Games?

  3   Why are the Paralympic Games important?

2 **Match the words from the text to the corresponding definition.**

  1   disability   **a** ☐ A place or piece of equipment that serves a particular function.

  2   venue   **b** ☐ A condition that limits a person's movements or senses.

  3   facility   **c** ☐ A chair with wheels used as a means of transportation by people with physical disabilities.

  4   wheelchair   **d** ☐ The place where an organized event happens.

3 **Label the pictures with the names of the sports from the box.**

athletics   archery   wheelchair curling   boccia

Paralympic Games

Paralympic Competitors

Paralympic competitors are athletes with disabilities. Much like Olympians, Paralympians compete for gold, silver, and bronze medals against the best
5 athletes with disabilities in the world.

Since the Seoul Games (1988), the Paralympics have taken place in the same country and year as the Olympic Games (every four years), shortly after them, using the same venues
10 and facilities. In 1976, the Winter Paralympic Games were created and until 1992 they were celebrated every four years in the same year as their summer counterpart, just as the Olympics were. However, since 1994, both the Winter
15 Paralympics and the Winter Olympics have been held once every four years, alternating with the Summer Games.

The Games have emphasized the importance of physical activity for people with disabilities and have
20 promoted equality, inclusion, and accessibility.

A neurosurgeon organized the 1948 International Wheelchair Games to coincide with the 1948 London Olympics. The competitors were British World War II veterans with spinal cord injuries.
25 Throughout the years, more and more competitors from other countries joined the Games, which only became official in 1960.

In 1960, in Rome, 400 athletes from 23 countries competed in 8 different sports. In London, in 2012,
30 there were 4,237 athletes from 164 countries competing in 20 different sports. By 2020, more than 40,000 competitors will have participated in both the Summer and Winter Paralympic Games. These athletes will have shown the world the
35 power of their determination.

Paralympic Vision

According to the International Paralympic Committee, the objective of the Paralympic Games is "to enable Paralympic athletes to achieve sporting excellence
40 and inspire and excite the world".

Paralympic Sports

Paralympic summer sports include archery, athletics, wheelchair basketball, boccia, road and track cycling, equestrian events, judo, sailing,
45 shooting, sitting volleyball, and swimming, among others. Paralympic winter sports are alpine skiing, biathlon, cross-country skiing, ice sledge hockey, snowboard, and wheelchair curling.

Based on <www.paralympic.org/paralympic-games>; <www.paralympic.org/the-ipc/history-of-the-movement>; <www.paralympic.org/sites/default/files/document/120203111830492_sec_i_chapter_1.1_paralympic_vision_and_mission_0.pdf>.
Accessed on December 1, 2015.

Vocabulary

counterpart: correspondente, semelhante	**hold:** realizar, promover	**spinal cord:** medula espinhal
gold: ouro	**silver:** prata	**throughout:** ao longo de, no decorrer de

After Reading

1 Check the correct alternative to complete the sentences according to the text.

1 The Paralympic Games now take place _____ the Olympic Games.

   a ☐ shortly after   b ☐ shortly before   c ☐ at the same time as

2 The Paralympics and the Olympics use _____ facilities.

   a ☐ different   b ☐ the same   c ☐ distant

3 The Winter and the Summer Paralympic Games began to take place in different years in _____.

   a ☐ 1976   b ☐ 1992   c ☐ 1994

> **Observar a coesão por meio de referentes**
>
> Os referentes textuais – pronomes pessoais/possessivos/demonstrativos/relativos etc. – são elementos linguísticos que estabelecem a retomada de ideias, dando coesão ao texto. Identificar a que esses termos se referem é fundamental para compreender como as ideias do texto estão articuladas.

2 What do the words in bold refer to?

1 *"Since the Seoul Games (1988), the Paralympics have taken place in the same country and year as the Olympic Games (every four years), shortly after **them** [...]"* (lines 6-9).

   a ☐ the Olympic Games   b ☐ the Paralympic Games   c ☐ the Seoul Games

2 *"Throughout the years, more and more competitors from other countries joined the Games, **which** only became official in 1960"* (lines 25-27).

   a ☐ 1960   b ☐ competitors   c ☐ the Games

3 *"These athletes will have shown the world the power of **their** determination"* (lines 34-35).

   a ☐ determination   b ☐ the world   c ☐ these athletes

3 Answer the questions.

1 What are the origins of the Paralympic Games?

   _____

2 Which values have the Paralympics promoted throughout the years?

   _____

3 What is the goal of the Paralympic Games?

   _____

Vocabulary Expansion

1 **Read the information in the box. Then write new words based on the ones in parentheses to complete the sentences.**

1 Leona looked at the stranger with _____ (trust) and fear.

2 Grandpa's speech was full of words that have fallen into _____ (use).

3 I _____ (like) meat, but unfortunately it is all we have to eat.

4 Things _____ (appear) from my desk easily!

5 You must not _____ (obey) your parents.

> **Prefix *dis-***
>
> O prefixo *dis-* descreve um processo, uma qualidade ou um estado negativo.
> ability– **dis**ability
> connect – **dis**connect
> honest – **dis**honest

2 **Check the correct meaning of the words in bold.**

1 An **official** will come and explain the rules to us.

   a ☐ oficial   b ☐ funcionário(a) público(a)

2 Members of the Parliament are on an **official** visit to India.

   a ☐ oficial   b ☐ funcionário(a) público(a)

3 Math is her favorite school **subject**.

   a ☐ assunto   b ☐ disciplina escolar

4 What is the **subject** of our meeting today?

   a ☐ assunto   b ☐ disciplina escolar

> **Words with Two Meanings**
>
> **official:** oficial; funcionário(a) público(a)
> **subject:** assunto; disciplina escolar

3 **Read the explanation and complete the sentences with the words from the box.**

| therefore | because | additionally | however |

1 The singer was expected to be here. _____, he hasn't shown up.

2 He trained hard for several years, _____ he got the gold medal in the competition.

3 I did what I could for them _____ they are very good friends of mine.

4 Many facilities are not equipped for people with disabilities. _____, these people face a lot of prejudice.

> **Connectives**
>
> Os conectivos são palavras usadas para ligar as ideias expressas em duas orações.
> I am very tired, **but** I have to finish this task.

Extra Practice 9

1 **Underline the correct options. In some cases more than one answer is correct.**

1 David fixed the table **who** / **that** was broken.

2 The horses **which** / **who** / **that** / **X** were in the stable belonged to the farmer.

3 She bought a violin **whom** / **X** / **which** / **who** cost U$1,500.

4 That's the lady to **whom** / **which** / **that** / **who** / **X** we gave the keys.

5 Children **that** / **who** / **X** / **whom** don't brush their teeth may have many cavities.

6 The book **that** / **X** / **who** / **which** / **whom** he's reading belongs to me.

2 **Check the correct alternative.**

1 He has a house _____ was built in 1940.

a ☐ that   c ☐ who

b ☐ whose   d ☐ whom

2 Dr. Braun, _____ works in the laboratory, has received a Nobel Prize.

a ☐ whose   c ☐ whom

b ☐ X   d ☐ who

3 Technology, _____ provides us comfort, is the result of scientific investigation.

a ☐ that   c ☐ which

b ☐ who   d ☐ X

4 The man _____ baby is sleeping is an excellent father.

a ☐ that   c ☐ who

b ☐ whose   d ☐ whom

5 The salesperson _____ showed us the products is sick.

a ☐ whose   c ☐ who

b ☐ X   d ☐ which

6 Helen, _____ husband is in England, is taking an English course now.

a ☐ who   c ☐ that

b ☐ which   d ☐ whose

3 Complete the sentences with the correct relative pronoun.

1 The Theory of Relativity, _____ changed the course of modern science, was developed by Albert Einstein.

2 Julia, about _____ we were talking during the conference, has written two books on the impacts of global warming.

3 My father, _____ was born in Spain, doesn't speak a word of Spanish, since he came to Brazil when he was still very young.

4 We often visit our uncle in Dublin, _____ is in Ireland.

5 Jeff is studying a gas _____ damages the ozone layer.

6 The singer _____ we listened to is Australian.

4 Choose the alternative with all the possibilities that complete each sentence.

1 It's a poem _____ was written by a famous Portuguese writer.

a ☐ who/whom/that/X   c ☐ which/that   e ☐ whom

b ☐ who/that   d ☐ which/that/X

2 The girl _____ we know will help us.

a ☐ who/whom/that/X   c ☐ which/that   e ☐ whom

b ☐ who/that   d ☐ which/that/X

3 These are the tests _____ her doctor needed.

a ☐ who/whom/that/X   c ☐ which/that   e ☐ whom

b ☐ who/that   d ☐ which/that/X

4 The boy to _____ we are writing lives in Germany.

a ☐ who/whom/that/X   c ☐ which/that   e ☐ whom

b ☐ who/that   d ☐ which/that/X

5 The motorcycle _____ Joan bought was made in Japan.

a ☐ who/whom/that/X   c ☐ which/that   e ☐ whom

b ☐ who/that   d ☐ which/that/X

6 I called the director _____ also wrote the movie we saw last week.

a ☐ who/whom/that/X   c ☐ which/that   e ☐ whom

b ☐ who/that   d ☐ which/that/X

5 Connect the sentences using *which*.

1 The dentist bought that white chair in the waiting room. It is very expensive.
That white chair in the waiting room, which the dentist bought, is very expensive.

2 He gave me those red roses in the white vase. They are beautiful.

_____

3 That red car with a sticker on it is in front of the house. It is mine.

_____

4 Venice is considered a very romantic city. It is located in Italy.

_____

5 My sister's room is full of posters. It is near the kitchen.

_____

6 Rewrite the sentences according to the instructions in parentheses.

1 I will have finished the test by 4 o'clock. (negative)
I will not/won't have finished the test by 4 o'clock.

2 They will have gone to Miami by March. (interrogative)

_____

3 She will have finished dinner by the time you arrive. (negative)

_____

4 It will have stopped snowing by April. (interrogative)

_____

5 My father will have made lunch by 1 o'clock. (negative)

_____

7 Complete the sentences using the verbs in parentheses in the Future Perfect.

1 We _____ (meet) the new teacher by the end of this week.

2 By 2 o'clock tomorrow, she _____ (read) my letter.

3 By the time he comes back, I _____ (finish) my homework.

4 I _____ (have) lunch by the time he arrives.

5 They _____ (talk) by the time I get there.

6 We _____ (buy) a new house by the end of the year.

8 **There are mistakes in some of the sentences below. Circle these mistakes and rewrite the sentences correcting them.**

1   Will you have finished everything by the time I come back from school?

_____

2   By this time next year, I have graduated.

_____

3   By the time I am 30, I'll have visited most countries in South America.

_____

4   We are late. By the time we get to the party, everyone will leave.

_____

5   By the time we return to Brazil, Sally will have have her baby.

_____

9 **Complete the sentences using the words/expressions from the box.**

| will go   don't like   rains   waiting   has just left   were studying   is taking   am writing |

1   Tomorrow after work I _____ to the beach.

2   While you _____ at home, your friends were in class.

3   I _____ a book about my adventures in Africa.

4   I _____ to live in London because it _____ a lot here.

5   **A:** Are you _____ for Mr. Britt?

     B: Yes, I am.

     A: Sorry to tell you, but he _____.

6   Look, that man _____ your magazine away!

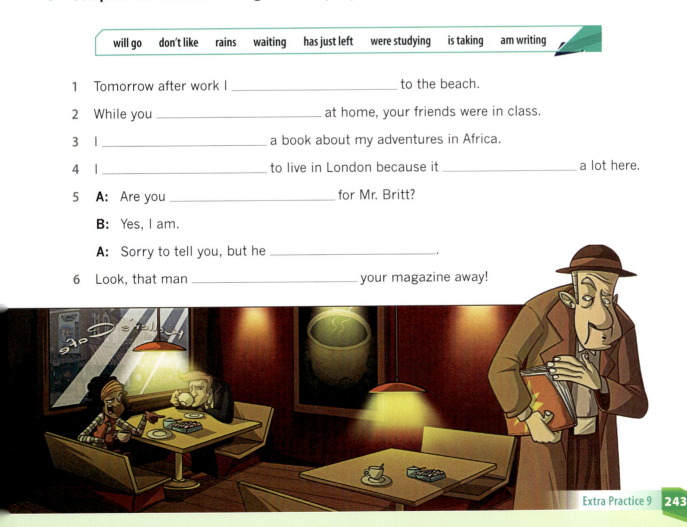

10 Check the corresponding question for each of the answers below.

1 I was sleeping.

    a ☐ What were you doing when the accident happened?

    b ☐ What do you usually do at 10 p.m.?

2 When you called yesterday, I was watching my favorite TV show.

    a ☐ What were you doing when I called yesterday?

    b ☐ Who did you call yesterday when I was watching TV?

3 When I arrive in São Paulo next week, I will stay in a hotel.

    a ☐ Where did you stay in São Paulo?

    b ☐ Where will you stay in São Paulo?

11 Choose the best alternative to complete the sentences.

1 It _____ heavily yesterday. We can _____ skiing tomorrow.

    a ☐ snowed – to go   c ☐ snowed – go

    b ☐ snows – goes   d ☐ was snowing – went

2 My brother _____ in India for more than a year.

    a ☐ has been living   c ☐ had living

    b ☐ was lived   d ☐ can to live

3 Silence, please! Mom _____.

    a ☐ had slept   c ☐ sleeps

    b ☐ is sleeping   d ☐ will slept

4 I have _____ to the Modern Art Museum many times.

    a ☐ be   c ☐ was

    b ☐ went   d ☐ been

5 I had _____ pictures of the Iguaçu Falls before I went to Foz do Iguaçu, but the place is much more beautiful than in the pictures.

    a ☐ seen   c ☐ sawed

    b ☐ saw   d ☐ seeing

Job Corner 9

Physical Education

Students that majored in Physical Education in the past had little choice; most of them ended up working as Physical Education teachers – and very few found opportunities in sports clubs.

However, things are quite different today. Physical Education is recognized as an ally of healthcare and esthetics, thus the area of physical fitness offers employment positions for many professionals. Most of the opportunities are in fitness centers and spas, but the physical educator can also work independently as a personal trainer.

Another area with plenty of jobs is that of groups with special needs. Employers in this area are entities and NGOs that care for children with special needs and take care of the elderly. In Brazil, São Paulo and Rio de Janeiro are the best markets for these specializations.

In southern and northeastern Brazil, tourism promotes the specialization in recreation and leisure activities. Professionals that also have knowledge and experience in hiking, horseback riding, canoeing, and other sports can find excellent jobs.

Based on <http://vestibular.brasilescola.uol.com.br/guia-de-profissoes/educacao-fisica.htm>;
<http://guiadoestudante.abril.com.br/profissoes/saude/educacao-fisica-684908.shtml>.
Accessed on March 14, 2016.

Vocabulary

ally: aliado(a)
care for: cuidar de
elderly: idosos(as)
employment: emprego

fitness center: academia de ginástica
healthcare: cuidados com a saúde
hiking: caminhada
leisure: lazer

major: formar-se (em curso universitário)
NGO: organização não governamental (ONG)
plenty of: muitos(as)
take care of: tomar conta de

19 Beauty Standards

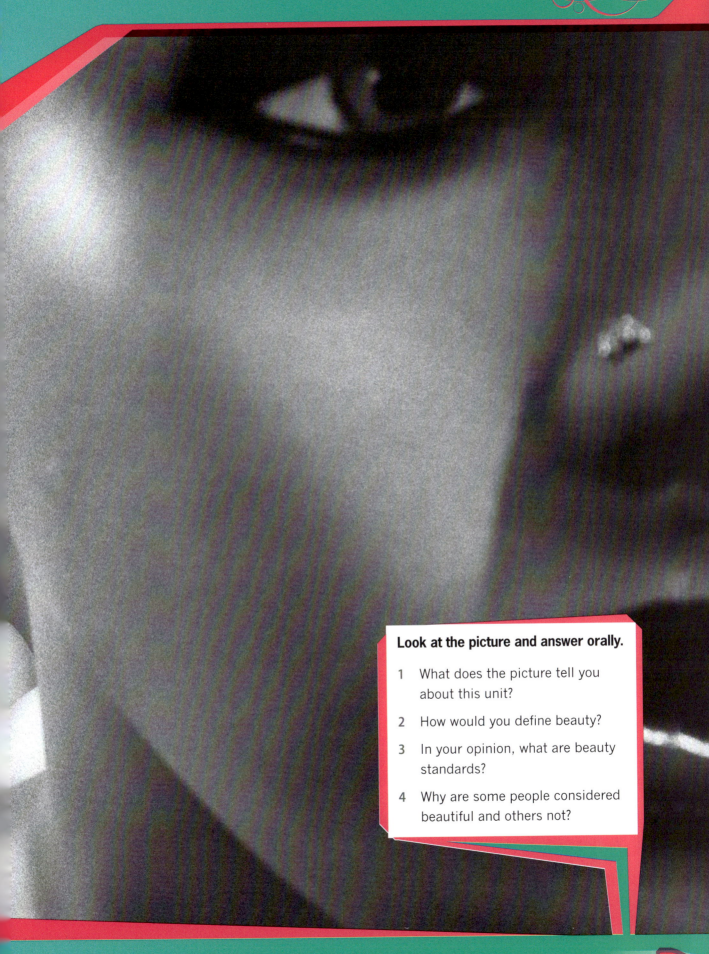

Look at the picture and answer orally.

1 What does the picture tell you about this unit?

2 How would you define beauty?

3 In your opinion, what are beauty standards?

4 Why are some people considered beautiful and others not?

Language in Context

1 **Take a look at the text.**

www.sheknows.com

How the Media Affects Girls' Body Image

Body images and beauty standards presented by the media affect both adults and teenagers, also having a strong effect even on very young children. Hatch program, an initiative of SheKnows media, asked some girls to produce a video in which they discuss the topic. "In the media you see all these images of the ideal body type and how you should be really skinny and look a certain way and be a certain weight," says one of the girls. They comment on how things they did when they were younger were scary consequences of these unrealistic beauty standards, such as weighing themselves at birthday parties and competing on who lost more weight at camp. The video states that if these standards continue to be promoted, even more girls and women will be affected by issues such as eating disorders and high suicide rates. At the end, the girls drew self-portraits of themselves, emphasizing what they wouldn't change about their bodies.

Based on <www.sheknows.com/parenting/articles/1078249/media-affects-girls-body-image>. Accessed on March 18, 2016.

2 **Give your opinion about the text.**

1 How do the girls feel about the beauty standards they see in the media?

2 Do you think only girls are affected by these beauty standards?

3 **Read, think, and answer orally.**

1 If these standards continue to be promoted, even more girls and women will be affected.

2 If these standards continued to be promoted, even more girls and women would be affected.

a Which will most probably happen: the action in sentence 1 or the one in sentence 2?

b What verb tenses were used in sentence 1?

c What verb tenses were used in sentence 2?

Vocabulary

eating disorder: distúrbio alimentar
scary: assustador(a)
self-portrait: autorretrato
skinny: muito magro(a)
standard: padrão

Language Practice

Sentences with *Would*

Would é um verbo modal e, sozinho, não tem tradução. Assim como os outros verbos modais, ele aparece sempre ligado a outro verbo.

Would + verbo / **Would have** + verbo no **Past Participle**

Afirmativa: I **would go** to the party. (Eu iria à festa.)

I **would have gone** to the party. (Eu teria ido à festa.)

Interrogativa: **Would** you **go** to the party?

Would you **have gone** to the party?

Negativa: I **would not go** to the party.

I **would not have gone** to the party.

Forma abreviada: wouldn't (would not)

---

1 **Rewrite the sentences using *would* + verb and *would have* + Past Participle.**

1 I will visit her.

I would visit her.

I would have visited her.

2 They will not sell the house.

_____

_____

3 Will she run to the park?

_____

_____

4 He will not meet us.

_____

_____

5 Will they invite us?

_____

_____

Language Practice

Conditional Sentences (I)

A oração condicional (*if clause*) expressa uma condição e vem sempre ligada a uma oração principal (*main clause*).

If she comes, I will talk to her.   I will talk to her **if she comes.**

    [*if clause*]   [main clause]   [main clause]   [*if clause*]

As estruturas condicionais podem expressar:

Condição provável (*first conditional*): If he has the money, he will buy a car.
Condição improvável (*second conditional*): If he had the money, he would buy a car.
Condição impossível (*third conditional*): If he had had the money, he would have bought a car.

---

2 **Complete the sentences using the verbs in parentheses in the correct form to indicate a probable condition.**

1   If we protest, they _____ (cut down – neg.) the trees.

2   If you pay attention, you _____ (learn) how to do it.

3   If she has the money, she _____ (go) to the movies.

4   We _____ (save) time if we take the subway.

5   He _____ (find) his book if he looks for it in his bedroom.

3 **Complete the sentences using the verbs in parentheses in the correct form to indicate an improbable condition.**

1   If you asked her, she _____ (tell) you the whole story.

2   I _____ (teach) you if I had time.

3   They _____ (play) in the park if it wasn't raining.

4   We _____ (help) her if she asked us.

4 **Complete the sentences using the verbs in parentheses in the correct form to indicate an impossible condition.**

1   If he had accepted the idea, they _____ (approve) the project.

2   I _____ (go) to the supermarket if it hadn't rained.

3   She _____ (come) to the party if you had invited her.

4   If I had known about your birthday, I _____ (buy) you a present.

5   If you had arrived earlier, you _____ (get) a good seat.

5 **Check the correct verb form to complete the sentences.**

1 I _____ the house if you bought some paint.

   a ☐ would have painted

   b ☐ would paint

2 If they had asked, I _____ their refrigerator.

   a ☐ will fix

   b ☐ would have fixed

3 If we _____ late, she will look after the children.

   a ☐ arrive

   b ☐ arrived

4 I would make a chocolate cake if I _____ the recipe.

   a ☐ have

   b ☐ had

5 She would have been tired if she _____ hard.

   a ☐ had worked

   b ☐ worked

6 The gate _____ if you press the button.

   a ☐ would unlock

   b ☐ will unlock

6 **Do the sentences in the previous activity present a probable condition, an improbable condition, or an impossible condition?**

1 _____

2 _____

3 _____

4 _____

5 _____

6 _____

Go to page 266 for Extra Practice.

Reading

Before Reading

1 **Discuss the questions below in Portuguese.**

    1   Do you think the concept of beauty varies from place to place?

    2   In your opinion, is beauty important? Why?

    3   What can works of art teach us about the concept of beauty?

    4   Should works of art only represent beautiful people and things? Why?

2 **Look at the pictures and the text on page 253. What are they about? Check the correct alternative.**

    a ☐ The current pressures of the media on people (especially women) about their looks.

    b ☐ The work of an artist that comments on the idea of beauty standards.

    c ☐ How the Photoshop culture forces people to look perfect under any circumstances.

    d ☐ The notion of beauty according to personal taste and cultural settings.

3 **How does the writer begin and finish the text?**

    a ☐ With doubts he/she has on the topic.

    b ☐ With quotations from famous researchers.

    c ☐ With questions for the reader.

4 **Why does he/she do that?**

    a ☐ In order to involve the reader in the discussion of the topic.

    b ☐ In order to justify the ideas presented in the text.

    c ☐ In order to give credibility to his/her text.

5 **Match the words from the text to their correspondent in Portuguese.**

1	makeover	a	☐	transformação estética
2	slim-waisted	b	☐	muito magro(a)
3	plump	c	☐	que tem cintura fina
4	waif-thin	d	☐	curvilíneo(a)
5	voluptuous	e	☐	rechonchudo(a)

Classic Beauties Get a Shocking Photoshop Treatment

"What would have happened if the aesthetic standard of our society had belonged to the collective unconscious of the great artists of the past?" So asks Italian artist Anna Giordano
5   in her Venus project, which reimagines classic artistic representations of Venus with a modern and extreme Photoshop makeover. The original Rubenesque beauties are transformed into busty, slim-waisted figures more closely matching the
10 ideals we are bombarded with today.

Giordano's reworking of the classics raises numerous questions about the aesthetic standards of our current society and its obsession with almost impossible figures. Is our current ideal healthy or
15 even possible for most men and women? Is today's preference even as attractive as the more "natural" figures in the original versions of these paintings? As the standards of beauty have evolved through history,

we have seen vast changes in ideals. From the
20 plump beauty standards of China's Tang Dynasty to the waif-thin ideals of the 1920s and the voluptuous 1950s, we've seen standards change for a long, long time. When does a certain body type stop being considered beautiful?

25 In our current era, we are marketed standards of beauty like never before. Advertisements showing that ideal are on every corner of the street and internet, subtly effecting our perceptions of what looks beautiful and determining standards that put
30 pressure on men and women alike. How do the beautiful women in these classic paintings hold up to a modern treatment? While some may appear to have found some healthy improvement with their digital nip and tuck, others turn out looking disturbingly thin.
35 Which do you find more attractive?

Adapted from <www.visualnews.com/2012/02/08/classic-beauties-get-a-shocking-photoshop-treatment>. Accessed on November 13, 2015.

Vocabulary

belong: pertencer
disturbingly: perturbadoramente

effect: afetar, impactar
hold up to: sair-se, desempenhar

nip and tuck: cirurgia plástica
Rubenesque beauty: beleza curvilínea

After Reading

1 Find information in the text to support the following statements.

1 *"As the standards of beauty have evolved through history, we have seen vast changes in ideals"* (lines 17-19).

_____

_____

2 *"In our current era, we are marketed standards of beauty like never before"* (lines 25-26).

_____

_____

2 Check the alternative that could best substitute the sentences below.

1 *"What would have happened if the aesthetic standard of our society had belonged to the collective unconscious of the great artists of the past?"* (lines 1-4).

a ☐ What would happen if the current beauty standards were determined by the collective unconscious of great artists?

b ☐ What would great artists have done if they had known how much society's aesthetic standards have changed?

c ☐ What would have been the consequences if the great artists of the past had had in mind our current beauty standards?

2 *"In our current era, we are marketed standards of beauty like never before"* (lines 25-26).

a ☐ Marketing standards show us that being thin has been considered beautiful throughout history.

b ☐ People have never before been so influenced to believe that certain beauty standards should be pursued.

c ☐ The beauty standards currently marketed are similar to the ones marketed before.

3 Discuss the following questions with your classmates.

1 Is our current ideal of beauty healthy or even possible for most people?

2 Which figure do you find more attractive: the original or the digitally modified one?

3 Do the same beauty standards apply to men and women? Why?

Vocabulary Expansion

1 **Read the information in the box. Then underline the correct option in each sentence.**

> ### To stop
> Quando seguido de outro verbo, o verbo **to stop** assume um significado diferente dependendo da forma do termo que o sucede.
> Sandra **stopped drinking** coffee. (Sandra parou de tomar café.)
> Sandra **stopped to drink** coffee. (Sandra parou para tomar café.)

1 Kids, stop **to talk** / **talking** and do your homework!

2 Johnny was thirsty, so he stopped **drinking** / **to drink** some water.

3 Fiona stopped **to read** / **reading** when her mother entered the room.

4 Kirk fell from that tree and I stopped **to help** / **helping** him.

5 It was cold and he stopped **making** / **to make** some hot tea.

6 Many people are now trying to stop **smoking** / **to smoke**.

2 **Complete the sentences with the correct form of the verbs in parentheses.**

1 Those employees stop _____ (work) at 5:30 p.m.

2 She stopped everything she was doing _____ (buy) him a present.

3 I stopped _____ (believe) her the third time I found out she was lying.

4 My cousin usually stops _____ (have) lunch around 1 p.m.

5 We need to stop _____ (try) to impress our classmates.

3 **Read the information in the box. Then write new words based on the ones in parentheses to complete the sentences.**

> ### Suffix -y
> O sufixo **-y** pode ser acrescentado a substantivos para formar adjetivos.
> health – health**y**   sun – sun**ny**

1 The weather was a bit _____ (cloud), so we decided not to go to the beach that morning.

2 I was still feeling a bit _____ (sleep) when I heard the doorbell.

3 The morning was too _____ (fog), so the airport was closed for some hours.

4 My sister is too _____ (mess)! She can't find anything she needs.

5 They were very _____ (thirst), so they decided to buy some water.

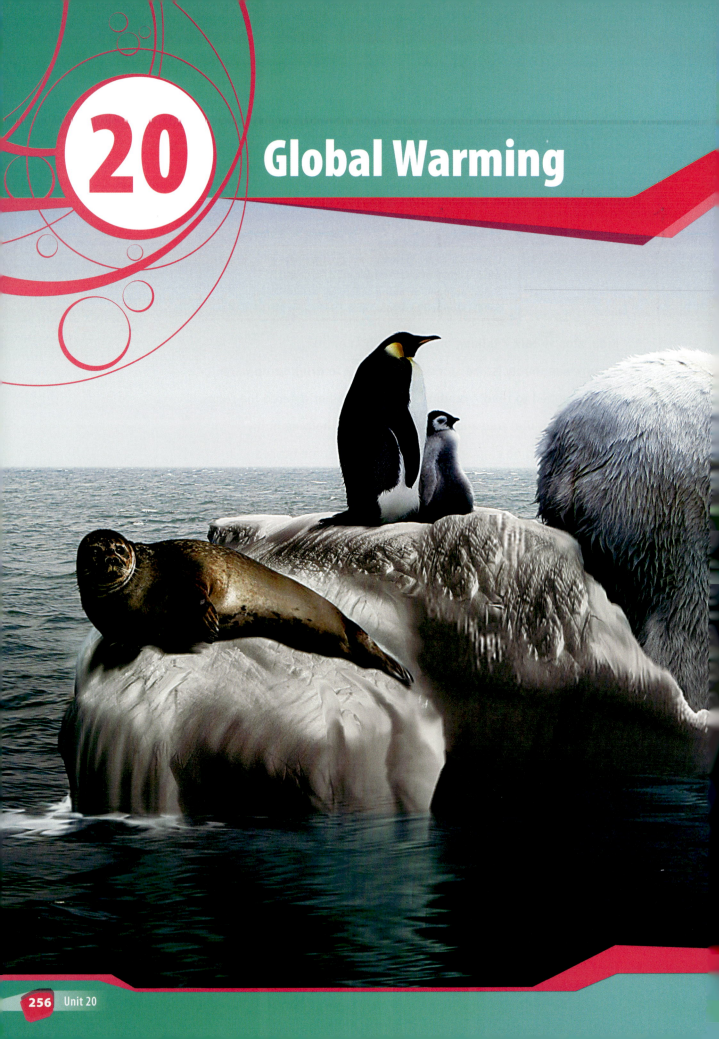

20 Global Warming

Look at the picture and answer orally.

1 What does the picture tell you about this unit?

2 How would you define global warming?

3 What can cause it?

4 What are its impacts on our lives (climate, rainfall, health, etc.)?

Language in Context

1 **Take a look at the text.**

> Dear Phil,
>
> In response to your letter of last May 16, I would not plant rice if I were you. Rice will not grow well unless there is abundant rainfall. Rice growers lose money when there is little water. Weather specialists forecast a very dry year next year, so choose something that doesn't need much water. Alternatively, you can plant rice provided that you irrigate your land.
>
> > Yours cordially,
>
> > > Jeff Owens
> > > Agriculture Consultant

2 **Give your opinion about the text.**

1 What's Phil's profession?

2 Does Phil plant rice now?

3 What did Phil ask Jeff Owens?

Vocabulary

forecast: prever
provided that: desde que
unless: a menos que

3 **Read, think, and answer orally.**

1 I would not plant rice if I were you.

2 Rice will not grow well unless there is abundant rainfall.

3 You can plant rice provided that you irrigate your land.

a Underline the conditional clauses.

b *If* is not used in sentences 2 and 3. What words/expressions introduce the conditional clauses?

Language Practice

Conditional Sentences (II)

Uso

Podemos verificar várias ocorrências nas orações principais usadas com as estruturas condicionais.

Modals – Verbos modais como *may*, *might*, *can* e *could* podem ser usados.

> If you go out in the rain, you **may** catch a cold.

> If we had asked her, she **could** have come.

Imperative – Usado para dar uma ordem ou instrução.

> If you have any problems, **call** me.

Simple Present – Usado para expressar leis naturais e verdades universais (*zero conditional*).

> If you heat iron, it **melts**.

Were – Geralmente é usado em vez de *was* em orações condicionais (*second conditional*), independentemente do sujeito.

> If I **were** your mother, I would punish you.

Já nas orações subordinadas, ***unless*** (se não, a menos que) e ***provided that*** (desde que) podem ser usados em vez de *if... not* e *if*, respectivamente.

> **Unless** we study, we won't pass the exam. (= If we don't study, we won't pass the exam.)

> **Provided that** we study, we will pass the exam. (= If we study, we will pass the exam.)

If – Em condições impossíveis (*third conditional*), *if* pode ser omitido invertendo-se o sujeito e o verbo auxiliar. Essa construção é formal e mais comum em textos escritos.

> **If** we had preserved the environment, we could have avoided global warming.

> **Had we** preserved the environment, we could have avoided global warming.

---

1 **Rewrite the following sentence using the information in parentheses. Make the necessary changes.**

If you make an effort, you will win the game.

1   (made) If you made an effort, you would win the game.

2   (had made) _____

3   (had you) _____

4   (may) _____

5   (provided that) _____

6   (won't win) _____

2 Check the best alternative.

1 _____ me if you need any help.

  a ☐ Will call   c ☐ Would call

  b ☐ Call   d ☐ Called

2 If you heat ice, it _____ .

  a ☐ would melt   c ☐ would have melted

  b ☐ melted   d ☐ melts

3 I _____ if I were 18.

  a ☐ would drive   c ☐ drove

  b ☐ will drive   d ☐ drive

4 If she knew about your past, she _____ very proud.

  a ☐ would be   c ☐ was

  b ☐ would have been   d ☐ will be

5 _____ you help me, I won't be able to finish all these tasks on time.

  a ☐ If   c ☐ Unless

  b ☐ Provided that   d ☐ Only if

6 If we leave now, we _____ get there on time.

  a ☐ had   c ☐ would

  b ☐ might   d ☐ could have

3 Complete the sentences using the phrases from the box.

> ask for another one   it boils   unless you pay them   if he had been kind to me
> if I were you   had we known about the engagement

1 I would have helped him _____.

2 If you heat water to 100° C, _____.

3 If your hamburger doesn't taste good, _____.

4 I would sell this car _____.

5 They won't work on Sunday _____.

6 _____, we would have called her.

4 Underline the correct option.

1 I won't buy a new house unless I **save** / **saved** enough money.

2 Rice growers **may lose** / **would lose** money if there is little rain.

3 Had he known the truth, he **would have told** / **will tell** us.

4 If I **had been** / **were** you, I wouldn't talk to Dad now.

5 **Raise** / **Will raise** your hands if you have a question.

6 They **won't go** / **will go** to the movies unless they help me first.

5 Complete the sentences using the correct form of the verbs in parentheses.

1 If the kids disturb you, _____ (call) me.

2 If they had arrived earlier, they _____ (see) the entire show.

3 Plants _____ (grow – neg.) if you leave them in the dark.

4 She _____ (come – neg.) unless we invite her.

5 I would not travel in this weather if I _____ (be) you.

6 If I _____ (have) enough money, I might go to Europe.

Go to page 266 for Extra Practice.

The man said the flowers would grow if they got enough water.

Reading

Before Reading

1 **Discuss the questions below in Portuguese.**

1 Have you noticed any climate changes in the last few years? If so, which ones?

2 In your opinion, what practices in your community contribute to global warming?

3 How is your community directly affected by global warming?

4 Do you do anything to fight global warming? If so, what?

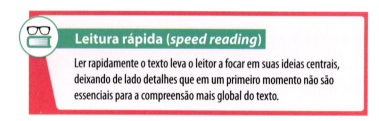

Leitura rápida (*speed reading*)

Ler rapidamente o texto leva o leitor a focar em suas ideias centrais, deixando de lado detalhes que em um primeiro momento não são essenciais para a compreensão mais global do texto.

2 **Read the text on page 263 as fast as you can in order to understand its main ideas. Complete the task in up to 4 minutes.**

3 **Read the text again. This time you must take less than 3.5 minutes. Then write one sentence saying what the text is about.**

_____

_____

4 **Match the words from the box to the corresponding definition.**

| downpour   flooding   fossil fuel   wildfire   coal   deforestation |

1 a large fire that spreads quickly _____

2 heavy rainfall _____

3 the clearing of a large area of trees _____

4 fuel formed from the remains of living organisms _____

5 inundation _____

6 a combustible black material used as fuel _____

Confronting the Realities of Climate Change:

The Consequences of Global Warming Are Already Here

Global warming is happening now. The planet's temperature is rising in a clear and unmistakable trend. Every one of the past 38 years has been warmer than the 20th century average. The 12 warmest years on record have all occurred since 1998. The hottest year ever recorded for the United States occurred in 2012. We are the cause. We are overloading our atmosphere with carbon dioxide, which traps heat and steadily drives up the planet's temperature. All this carbon comes from the fossil fuels we burn for energy – coal, natural gas, and oil – plus the loss of forests due to deforestation, especially in the tropics.

Impacts

Global warming is already having significant and costly effects that will only intensify as the planet's temperature continues to rise.

- **Accelerating Sea Level Rise**
  Global warming is dramatically increasing coastal flooding risks.

- **Longer and More Damaging Wildfire Seasons**
  Wildfires are increasing as temperatures rise.

- **More Frequent and Intense Heat Waves**
  Dangerously hot weather is already occurring more frequently than it did 60 years ago.

- **Heavier Precipitation and Flooding**
  As temperatures increase, more rain falls during the heaviest downpours, increasing the risk of flooding.

Solutions

- _____
  As individuals, we can help by taking action to reduce our personal carbon emissions. But we can't address the threat of global warming unless we demand action from our elected leaders, in an attempt to avoid malpractice and negligence.

- _____
  Tropical deforestation accounts for about 10 percent of the world's heat-trapping emissions. If we reduce tropical deforestation, we can significantly lower global warming emissions.

- _____
  Media experts and special interest groups raise doubts about the truth of global warming. Coming across such misinformation confuses the public – and makes it more difficult to implement effective solutions.

- _____
  Certain consequences of global warming are now inevitable, including sea level rise, more frequent and severe heat waves, and growing wildfire risks. Even as we work to reduce global warming emissions, we must also prepare to face this dangerous new reality without giving up.

Adapted from <www.ucsusa.org/global_warming#.VkOIVberTIV>. Accessed on November 11, 2015.

Vocabulary

heat-trapping: que retém o calor
heat wave: onda de calor
misinformation: informação incorreta
overload: sobrecarregar
precipitation: precipitação atmosférica, chuva
unmistakable: inconfundível, evidente

After Reading

1 **Which fact cannot be linked to the global warming trend?**

a ☐ The year 2012 was extremely hot in the United States.

b ☐ The emission of too much carbon dioxide traps heat in the atmosphere.

c ☐ It is impossible not to notice the temperature rising trend.

d ☐ The burning of fossil fuels causes deforestation in the tropics.

e ☐ The past three decades were warmer than the 20th century average temperature.

2 **Decide if the following statements regarding the impacts of global warming are true (T) or false (F).**

1 ☐ Fossil fuels burn carbon dioxide in order to produce energy.

2 ☐ Forest fires are more devastating today than they were before.

3 ☐ Coastline flooding is a direct consequence of sea level rise.

4 ☐ Temperatures increase as a consequence of heavier rainfalls and flooding.

5 ☐ About one tenth of the heat-trapping emissions in the atmosphere is a result of tropical deforestation.

6 ☐ Experts should still raise doubts about the truth of global warming.

3 **Write the subtitles below in the correct place in the text.**

> Fight Misinformation   Stop Deforestation   Reduce Emissions   Prepare for Impacts

4 **Answer the questions based on the text.**

1 What will happen if people reduce tropical deforestation?

_____

2 Which consequences of global warming can't be reversed?

_____

3 Besides working to reduce global warming, what must we do?

_____

5 **Why do you think it is so difficult to reduce carbon dioxide emissions at global levels? Make a list of factors and discuss in Portuguese.**

Vocabulary Expansion

1 Read the information in the box. Then write new words based on the ones in parentheses to complete the sentences.

> **Prefix *mal-***
>
> O prefixo **mal-** indica coisas desagradáveis, ruins ou imperfeitas e ações malsucedidas.
> adjusted – **mal**adjusted   practice – **mal**practice

1 About ten percent of the world population suffers from _____ (nutrition).

2 The animals at the zoo died because of _____ (treatment).

3 Who is responsible for the _____ (nourishment) of these children?

4 Last month he accused the committee of _____ (administration).

5 The doctor told the mother her son had a small _____ (formation) on his lips.

6 The police investigated the mayor after he was accused of _____ (practice).

2 Match the columns according to the meaning of the words in bold.

1	He went on **stage** and started to sing.	a ☐	enfrentar
2	They are not accepting any job applications at this **stage**.	b ☐	fase
3	I am too tired to **face** another problem like this.	c ☐	palco
4	She had a beautiful and delicate **face**.	d ☐	remédio
5	He wasn't sure if he wanted a career in **medicine**.	e ☐	medicina
6	The young child died because there was no **medicine**.	f ☐	rosto

3 Complete the sentences using the phrasal verbs from the box. Make any necessary changes.

> **Phrasal Verbs**
>
> | | | | |
> |---|---|---|---|
> | **come:** vir | **come out:** ser publicado(a) | **give:** dar | **give out:** distribuir |
> | **come across:** encontrar por acaso | **come up:** surgir | **give in:** ceder | **give up:** desistir |

1 The executive _____ to the pressure and quit.

2 Because of the accident, they had to _____ their dreams.

3 I _____ your brother at the party last weekend.

4 Ann is going to _____ lots of candy on Halloween.

5 Kirk's new book will _____ next year.

6 That subject has _____ at a meeting in the office.

Extra Practice 10

1 **Complete the chart about conditional sentences.**

Condition	If Clause	Main Clause
	Simple Present	*will* + verb in the base form
improbable		
	Past Perfect	+ verb in the Past Participle

2 **Classify the condition expressed in each sentence as probable (A), improbable (B), or impossible (C).**

1 ☐ If I knew her address, I would send her a postcard.

2 ☐ If you had locked the car, nobody would have stolen it.

3 ☐ I will drive you home if I find my driver's license.

4 ☐ If he doesn't get here soon, we will start the meeting without him.

5 ☐ She would go with us on the boat if she knew how to swim.

6 ☐ We wouldn't have gone out if it had snowed heavily.

3 **Rewrite the sentences according to the information in parentheses.**

1 If he had found the money, he would have given it to me. (improbable condition)
If he found the money, he would give it to me.

2 They will win the game if they play well. (impossible condition)
_____

3 If it had rained, we wouldn't have gone to the beach. (probable condition)
_____

4 You will arrive earlier if you take a taxi. (impossible condition)
_____

5 If you teach me, I will learn how to drive. (improbable condition)
_____

6 I would eat the cake if you made it. (probable condition)
_____

4 **Choose the best alternative to complete each sentence.**

1 We _____ in the afternoon if I have time.

   a ☐ will talk   c ☐ would have talked

   b ☐ would talk   d ☐ talk

2 They _____ the room if she had come back.

   a ☐ will leave   c ☐ left

   b ☐ would leave   d ☐ would have left

3 I would visit my friends if I _____ their address.

   a ☐ have   c ☐ had had

   b ☐ had   d ☐ would have

4 He would answer your question if he _____ the answer.

   a ☐ knows   c ☐ had known

   b ☐ knew   d ☐ will know

5 They _____ you the whole story if you had had time to listen to them.

   a ☐ will tell   c ☐ would have told

   b ☐ would tell   d ☐ told

6 She will hurt herself if she _____ over the gate.

   a ☐ jumps   c ☐ had jumped

   b ☐ jumped   d ☐ would jump

5 **There are mistakes in some of the sentences below. Circle these mistakes and rewrite the sentences correcting them.**

1 You would have missed the flight if you won't arrive earlier.

_____

2 She may get sick if she isn't vaccinated.

_____

3 We will go to the beach if the weather is nice.

_____

4 They came up with a new plan if you gave them some ideas.

_____

6 **Complete the sentences using the verbs in parentheses in the correct form.**

1 I _____ (trust) you if you didn't tell so many lies.

2 You _____ (get) lost if you don't pay attention to the map.

3 If he hadn't read so many books, he wouldn't _____ (be) a good writer.

4 If I had gone to the bank, I _____ (talk) to the manager.

5 You would like this book if you _____ (read) it.

7 **Rewrite the sentences using *unless*.**

1 You won't be a healthy person if you don't eat vegetables.
   You won't be a healthy person unless you eat vegetables.

2 Don't write to Mark if you don't like him.
   _____

3 He wouldn't be rich if he didn't work hard.
   _____

4 The kids won't come back for lunch if you don't call them.
   _____

5 She will get a cold if she doesn't stay home in this weather.
   _____

6 I wouldn't be happy if I didn't talk to them.
   _____

8 **Check the alternative that presents the correct conditional sentence with an inversion.**

1 If I had been tired, I would have taken a nap.

   a ☐ Had I been tired, I would have taken a nap.

   b ☐ Would I have taken a nap if I had been tired.

2 If he had studied, he would have passed the final exams.

   a ☐ Had he studied, he would have passed the final exams.

   b ☐ Were he studied, he would have passed the final exams.

3 The cats would have escaped if you had opened the door.

   a ☐ Had the cats escaped, you would have opened the door.

   b ☐ Had you opened the door, the cats would have escaped.

9 **Match the columns to form sentences.**

1 If you are late,

2 Rice grows

3 Wood floats if

4 Please wait for him

5 If you want to have dinner,

6 Don't call them if

a ☐ if the weather is not dry.

b ☐ wash your hands.

c ☐ take a taxi.

d ☐ if he is late.

e ☐ you put it in water.

f ☐ it's too early.

10 **Check the word that corresponds to the following definitions.**

1 A mixture of gases surrounding the Earth.

   a ☐ century

   b ☐ atmosphere

2 To make something hotter.

   a ☐ to warm

   b ☐ to precipitate

3 An idea or thing used as a measure or model.

   a ☐ skinny

   b ☐ standard

4 A condition caused by lack of food.

   a ☐ evaporation

   b ☐ malnutrition

11 Check the correct alternative.

1 You won't enjoy yourself unless you _____ during spring.

   a ☐ will travel   c ☐ travel

   b ☐ had traveled   d ☐ would travel

2 If you like skiing, you _____ to Colorado.

   a ☐ had gone   c ☐ would go

   b ☐ can go   d ☐ would have gone

3 If it rains, he _____ fishing.

   a ☐ had gone   c ☐ would go

   b ☐ would have gone   d ☐ won't go

4 If it rains, he _____ fishing.

   a ☐ can't go   c ☐ go

   b ☐ couldn't   d ☐ didn't

5 _____ known, she would have stayed for the film.

   a ☐ If she   c ☐ Had she

   b ☐ May she   d ☐ If she was

6 I'll visit London _____ I can buy the tickets.

   a ☐ unless   c ☐ provided that

   b ☐ if not   d ☐ could

Tourism ✈

As is the case in many areas, you can take a two-year or a four-year course in Tourism. There are many courses for tourism careers both in Brazil and abroad. It all depends on what you want to do.

Tourism graduates can work in travel agencies. They organize tours with detailed information on means of transportation, lodging options, places to visit, and local attractions. Some agents offer specialized packages, such as educational tourism or ecotourism.

Professionals in this area may also work with the marketing side of tourism. They can make market analyses in order to meet the needs of their clients, creating projects to advertise a city, a state, or a region. They may also announce a product to attract visitors and investments.

On the planning side, specialists identify the tourism possibilities of a place (which they call a destination). They are responsible for analyzing the environmental and cultural impacts of tourism activities there.

Tourism professionals also organize events, such as fairs, exhibits, seminars, and conferences. This is known as business tourism.

01A

BOARDING PASS

Based on <http://vestibular.brasilescola.uol.com.br/guia-de-profissoes/turismo.htm>; <http://guiadoestudante.abril.com.br/profissoes/administracao-negocios/turismo-gestao-turismo-682697.shtml>. Accessed on March 18, 2016.

Vocabulary

abroad: no exterior
advertise: anunciar, fazer propaganda
both… and…: tanto… quanto…

conference: conferência, congresso
exhibit: exposição
lodging: acomodação, hospedagem

meet the needs: atender as necessidades
package: pacote
side: lado, aspecto

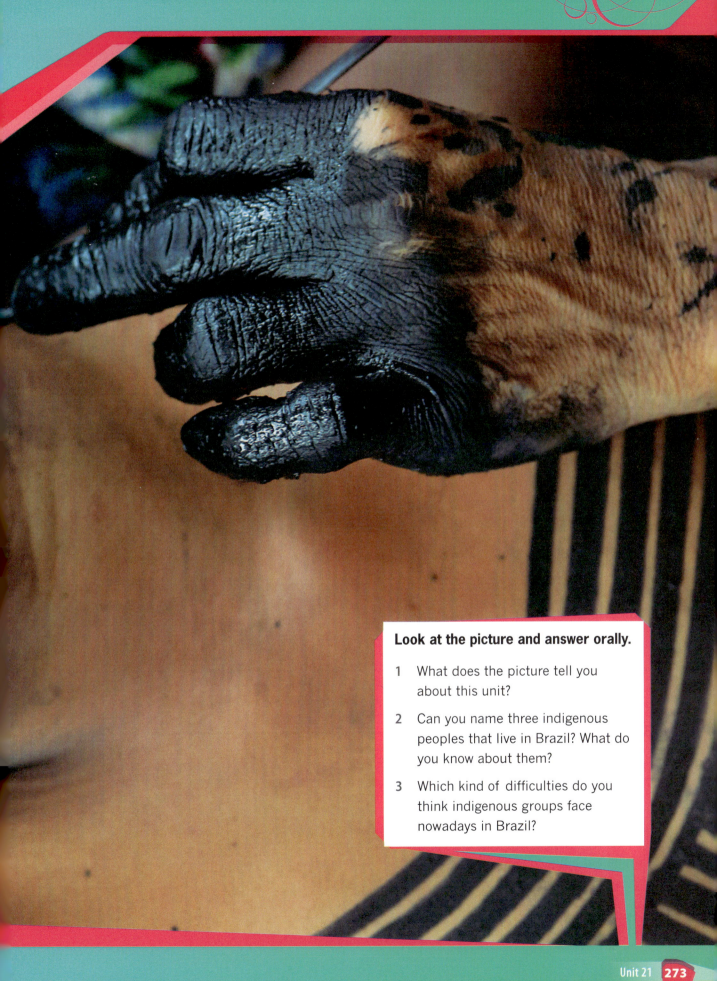

Look at the picture and answer orally.

1 What does the picture tell you about this unit?

2 Can you name three indigenous peoples that live in Brazil? What do you know about them?

3 Which kind of difficulties do you think indigenous groups face nowadays in Brazil?

Language in Context

1 Take a look at the text.

Sacrificing the Amazon and Its Peoples for Dirty Energy

The Brazilian government is building one of the world's largest hydroelectric dams on the Xingu River (an Amazon tributary), the Belo Monte complex. The whole Xingu basin is in theory protected due to its indigenous reserves and conservation units. However, the area is severely impacted by cattle ranching and soy monocultures. This dam is the first in a series of projects that will cause considerable devastation to a region that already faces environmental problems.

As a result of it, more than 1,500 km² of Brazilian rainforest will be devastated and, besides the environmental impacts, it is estimated that about 40,000 people will be displaced.

The Belo Monte complex has a huge impact on the land and livelihoods of thousands of families and communities, also affecting indigenous peoples from a number of neighboring areas.

Based on <http://amazonwatch.org/work/belo-monte-dam>. Accessed on April 1, 2016.

2 Give your opinion about the text.

1 Which environmental impacts can the Belo Monte complex bring to the Xingu basin?

2 What could the indigenous peoples living in the region do to avoid the impacts of the project?

Vocabulary

basin: bacia
cattle: gado
soy: soja
tributary: afluente

3 Read, think, and answer orally.

A (Active Voice)	B (Passive Voice)
The government is building a dam.	A dam is being built.
The dam will affect the population.	The population will be affected.
Initiatives protect the basin.	The basin is protected.

1 Observe the sentences in column A. Then underline the subjects and circle the objects.

2 Observe the sentences in column B and underline the subjects.

3 What happened to the verbs and objects when changing the sentences from the active to the passive voice?

Language Practice

Passive Voice (I)

> **To be** (no mesmo tempo do verbo principal da voz ativa) **+ Past Participle**
>
> John **broke** the vase. ⟶ The vase **was broken**.
>   ↓   ↓   ↓
> Simple Past   Simple Past Past Participle

Uso

A voz de um verbo mostra se o sujeito faz ou recebe a ação.

Voz ativa – o sujeito executa ou realiza a ação: He **wrote** a message in French.

Voz passiva – o sujeito recebe a ação: A message **was written** in French.

A voz passiva é usada quando o agente/autor da ação é desconhecido, não é importante ou quando não se deseja mencioná-lo ou enfatizá-lo.

1 Based on the information above, complete the following chart.

Verb Tense	Active Voice	Passive Voice
Simple Present	write / writes	is written / are
Present Continuous	am/is/are writing	is/are being
Simple Past	wrote	was written /
Past Continuous	was/were writing	
Present Perfect	have/has written	have/has been
Past Perfect	had written	
Simple Future	will write	
Modal	can write	can be

2 Complete the sentences in the active voice.

1 The lecture on Brazilian History was given yesterday.

The professor _____.

2 My mother's vase has been broken.

My brother _____.

3 A cake will be made to celebrate his 30th birthday.

His sister _____.

3 Rewrite the sentences in the passive voice.

1   The students were writing a beautiful song.
    <u>A beautiful song was being written.</u>

2   A tornado has destroyed several houses in southern Oklahoma.
    _____

3   The Geography teacher taught the main topics in the unit.
    _____

4   Don't worry. Someone will open the door.
    _____

5   They grow coffee in Kenya.
    _____

6   People are destroying the forests in Indonesia.
    _____

Language Practice

Passive Voice (II)

Observações

Quando uma frase passa da voz ativa para a voz passiva:

- o objeto da voz ativa passa a ser sujeito na voz passiva.

    Someone stole **my bag**. ⟶ **My bag** was stolen.

    sujeito objeto   sujeito

- pode-se mencionar quem realizou a ação usando-se a preposição **by**.
    My bag was stolen <u>by</u> **someone**.

    Iracema was written <u>by</u> **José de Alencar**.

    The village was built <u>by</u> **some of its members**.

- se houver dois objetos (direto e indireto), qualquer um deles pode ser o sujeito da passiva.
    John told **me a story**.

    I was told a story (by John).

    A story was told to me (by John).

4 **Rewrite the sentences using the passive voice without *by*.**

1 They sent the letters yesterday.

_____

2 Someone has established the agenda for the next meeting.

_____

3 The monkey is eating the bananas.

_____

4 They make good shoes in Franca, São Paulo.

_____

5 The committee has approved the new medical program.

_____

6 He is selling that big house on the corner.

_____

5 **Rewrite each sentence twice using the passive voice.**

1 She sent us a letter.
We were sent a letter.
A letter was sent to us.

2 Grandma told me a secret.

_____

_____

3 They will give the kids new shoes.

_____

_____

4 I have asked John a question.

_____

_____

5 The salesperson showed me an expensive book.

_____

_____

Go to page 292 for Extra Practice.

Reading

Before Reading

1 **Discuss the questions below in Portuguese.**

1 What do you know about the living conditions of the Guarani?

2 Which factors might threaten the culture of indigenous peoples in Brazil?

3 How do these peoples fight for their rights and for preserving their culture?

2 **Refer to the text on page 279 and find these expressions in bold. Then match the sentences halves to define them.**

1 If you **forge ahead with** something,

2 If you **deprive** someone **of** something,

3 If someone is **poised to** do something,

4 If you **prevent** someone **from** doing something,

5 If there is a **lack of** something,

6 If you **run** something,

a ☐ you manage, are the chief, or are the owner of it.

b ☐ you impede that person from acting.

c ☐ the person is ready to take action because he/she has prepared for it.

d ☐ there is not enough of it.

e ☐ you take something away from him/her.

f ☐ you make strong and steady progress in it.

3 **Scan the text and find the following information.**

1 Current Brazilian plans for the Amazon.

_____

2 Results of building hydroelectric dam complexes.

_____

3 An example of a project by indigenous groups to defend their rights.

_____

www.survivalinternational.org

home   news   about us   🔍

Threats and Challenges Today

Since Europeans arrived in Brazil over 500 years ago, native peoples have experienced genocide on a huge scale and the loss of most of their land.

Today, as Brazil forges ahead with aggressive plans to develop and industrialize the Amazon, even the remotest territories are now under threat. Several hydroelectric dam complexes are being built near uncontacted indigenous groups; they will also deprive thousands of other indigenous people of land, water, and livelihood. The dam complexes will provide cheap energy to mining companies, which are poised to carry out large-scale mining on indigenous lands if Congress passes a draft bill that is being pushed hard by mining lobbyists.

In the south, many tribes, such as the Guarani, live in appalling conditions under tarpaulin shacks along the roadside. Their leaders are being systematically targeted and killed by private militias of gunmen hired by the ranchers to prevent them from occupying their ancestral land. Many Guarani have committed suicide in despair at the lack of any meaningful future.

"In the old days, we were free. Now we are no longer. So our young people think there is nothing left. They sit down and think, they lose themselves, and then commit suicide."
Rosalino Ortiz, Guarani

Indigenous Resistance and Organizations

Today, there are over 200 indigenous organizations, which are at the forefront of the battle to defend their hard-won rights. They have protested against the government's plans to weaken their rights. Many run their own projects, health clinics, and bilingual schools. The Tikuna established a museum to showcase their technologies, art, culture, and language to white people.

Despite these achievements, there is still endemic racism towards indigenous peoples in Brazil. Their most important goal is to gain control over their own lands – Brazil is one of only two South American countries that do not recognize tribal land ownership.

"We do exist. I want to say to the world that we are alive and we want to be respected as a people."
Marta, Guarani

Adapted from <www.survivalinternational.org/tribes/brazilian>. Accessed on November 13, 2015.

Vocabulary

appalling: espantoso(a), terrível	**despite:** apesar de	**gunman:** pistoleiro	**shack:** cabana
dam: represa, barragem	**draft bill:** projeto de lei	**livelihood:** meio de vida	**showcase:** exibir
despair: desespero	**forefront:** frente, vanguarda	**ownership:** propriedade	**tarpaulin:** tipo de lona

After Reading

1 **What is the main topic of the text? Answer in Portuguese.**

_____

_____

> **Identificar o tom do texto**
>
> "Tom" é a atitude do autor em relação ao tópico abordado no texto e pode ser notado por suas escolhas lexicais e semânticas.

2 **Identify in the text words and expressions that convey the author's attitude about the topic.**

_____

_____

_____

3 **Based on your understanding, check what the text's tone is.**

a ☐ condescending   b ☐ critical   c ☐ sarcastic

4 **Decide if the following statements are true (T) or false (F), according to the text.**

1 ☐ Native populations in the industrialized areas of the Amazon are pushing indigenous peoples to the remotest territories.

2 ☐ Dams may be built in the Amazon to meet the energy needs of mining companies.

3 ☐ The Guarani have engaged in wars against gunmen to win back their ancestral lands.

4 ☐ Suicide is an extreme measure many Guarani have resorted to because they no longer feel free and hopeful.

5 **Based on the last paragraph of the text, it is possible to state that...**

a ☐ racism and lack of land ownership are still big issues for indigenous peoples in Brazil, in spite of the victories they have achieved.

b ☐ more than 200 Tikuna organizations have managed to win battles against racism and homelessness.

c ☐ even as the government tries to pass laws in favor of indigenous peoples, they still believe they need to fight for widespread land ownership.

d ☐ the Tikuna have established museums and health clinics to fight for their rights, the most important of which is tribal land ownership.

Vocabulary Expansion

1 **Read the information in the box and change the words in parentheses into adjectives.**

> **Adjectives ending in -ed and -ing**
>
> Alguns adjetivos podem terminar em **-ed** ou **-ing**, mudando ligeiramente de significado.
>
> **bored:** entediado(a) **challenged:** desafiado(a) **excited:** empolgado(a) **interested:** interessado(a)
>
> **boring:** entediante **challenging:** desafiador(a) **exciting:** empolgante **interesting:** interessante
>
> The kids were **excited** about the trip to the beach.
> Our trip to the beach was **exciting**.

1 **A:** Do you want to know more about Australia?

   B: Sure, my friends and I are very _____ (interest) in it.

2 **A:** I don't want to talk about this movie. It's so _____ (bore).

   B: I don't agree with you. In my opinion, it is very _____ (interest).

3 **A:** The more difficult the task, the better.

   B: You're right. I like _____ (challenge) tasks too.

4 **A:** The children look _____ (bore) today. What happened?

   B: They have nothing _____ (excite) to do.

2 **Check the correct meaning of the words in bold.**

1 When you live abroad, you **miss** your family and friends.

   a ☐ Senhorita

   b ☐ sente falta

2 Could you please come here, **Miss** Brown? I need to ask you a question.

   a ☐ Senhorita

   b ☐ sente falta

3 If you run that way, your shoes won't **last** very long.

   a ☐ durar

   b ☐ últimos(as)

4 They were the **last** passengers to leave the plane.

   a ☐ durar

   b ☐ últimos(as)

5 They tried **hard** to make the relationship work, but ended up getting a divorce.

   a ☐ intensamente

   b ☐ duros(as)

6 Those nuts are as **hard** as a rock. I can't crack them.

   a ☐ intensamente

   b ☐ duros(as)

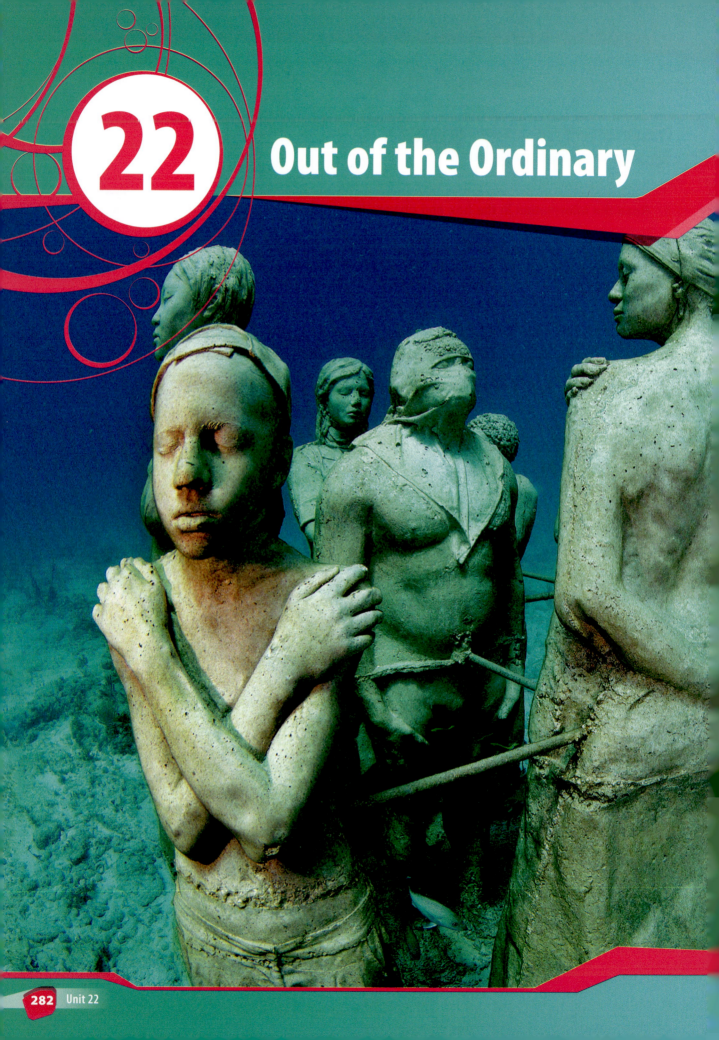

22 Out of the Ordinary

Look at the picture and answer orally.

1   What does the picture tell you about this unit?

2   What do you expect to find in a museum?

3   Should only works of art be exposed in museums? What else can be found in them?

Language in Context

1 Take a look at the text.

Chat

ramona_on_the_web	Hey, I'm Ramona. What's your name?
simon_online	Simon.
ramona_on_the_web	Hi, Simon. Ask me a question.
simon_online	Do you have a family?
ramona_on_the_web	Of course I do.
simon_online	What is your favorite thing, Ramona?
ramona_on_the_web	I like chatting with people online.
simon_online	What was your biggest disappointment?
ramona_on_the_web	I do not know what a biggest disappointment is.
simon_online	I want to ask you another question.
ramona_on_the_web	Ask me another question.
simon_online	Do you have problems with words, Ramona?
ramona_on_the_web	I don't think I have problems with words, Simon.
simon_online	Are you real?
ramona_on_the_web	What do you think?
simon_online	Well, my friends say that you're virtual.
ramona_on_the_web	Maybe they are right.
simon_online	What do you mean?
ramona_on_the_web	I mean I am a real virtual person. What about you, Simon? Are you human?

ramona_on_the_web

simon_online

2 Give your opinion about the text.

1 How did you identify the real person?

2 Have you ever chatted with a virtual person?

Vocabulary

chat: conversar
disappointment: decepção
mean: querer dizer

3 Read, think, and answer orally.

A	B
She said, "I like chatting with people online."	She said (that) she liked chatting with people online.
He said, "I want to ask you another question."	He said (that) he wanted to ask her another question.

1 Circle the verbs in the sentences above.

2 Observe the verbs in the sentences in column B. What changed in comparison with the sentences in column A?

3 Now observe the pronouns in column B. What changed in comparison with the ones in column A?

Language Practice

Direct and Indirect Speech (I)

Há duas formas de relatar o que alguém disse:

- usando o **discurso direto** (*direct speech*) – Quando relatamos o que foi dito usando as mesmas palavras da pessoa, entre aspas: She said, "I love you."
- usando o **discurso indireto** (*indirect speech*) – Quando contamos com nossas próprias palavras o que foi dito: She said (that) she loved me. (*That* pode ou não ser usado.)

Quando usamos o discurso indireto, geralmente modificamos o tempo verbal, alguns pronomes e advérbios. Observe:

Direct Speech	Indirect Speech
She said, "I **am** happy today."	She said (that) she **was** happy that day.
She said, "I **worked** yesterday."	She said (that) she **had worked** the day before.
She said, "I'**ll study** tomorrow."	She said (that) she **would study** the next day.
They said, "We **are leaving** now."	They said (that) they **were leaving** then.
He said, "I **was reading** an hour ago."	He said (that) he **had been reading** an hour before.
I said, "I **have lived** here."	I said (that) I **had lived** there.
He said, "I **can go** with you."	He said (that) he **could go** with me.
He said, "I **must buy** these books."	He said (that) he **had to buy** those books.

A mudança no tempo verbal não é obrigatória quando:

- a situação relatada ainda existe no presente;
- o verbo usado para relatar (por exemplo, *say*) estiver no *Simple Present*, no *Present Perfect* ou no *Simple Future*.

    He says, "I **come** from Brazil."

    He says (that) he **comes** from Brazil.

1 Rewrite the sentences using direct speech.

1   Vivian said that she had studied the day before.

    _____

2   Tony said that he would study that day.

    _____

3   Virginia said that it was going to rain.

    _____

2 Complete the chart with information on verb tense changes.

Direct Speech	Indirect Speech
Simple Present	Simple Past
Present Continuous	
Simple Past	
Past Continuous	Past Perfect Continuous
Present Perfect	
will	
can	
must	*have to*

3 Fill in the blanks according to the changes observed on page 285.

1 today _____

2 now _____

3 here _____

4 these _____

5 yesterday _____

6 ago _____

7 tomorrow _____

4 Report what people have said using indirect speech.

1 Carla said, "I am studying French now."

_____

2 She said, "I watch TV every day."

_____

3 He said, "I've worked here for a long time."

_____

4 I said, "I am going to leave early today."

_____

5 Natalie said, "You can trust me."

_____

5 **Fill in the blanks with the missing verb(s).**

1   She said, "I want to go out today."

   She said that she _____ to go out that day.

2   He said, "The boys are sleeping in their room."

   He said that the boys _____ in their room.

3   She said, "I will visit my friends next week."

   She said she _____ her friends the following week.

4   They said, "We've lived here for a long time."

   They said they _____ there for a long time.

5   She said, "I was waiting for you."

   She said she _____ for me.

6   He said, "I can come tonight."

   He said he _____ that night.

6 **Check the correct alternative.**

1   Mary said, "I want to bring my books today."

   a   ☐ Mary said she wants to bring her books that day.

   b   ☐ Mary said that she wanted to bring her books that day.

2   The girl said, "I am studying a lot at the moment."

   a   ☐ The girl said that she had been studying a lot at that moment.

   b   ☐ The girl said that she was studying a lot at that moment.

3   She said, "The test was very difficult."

   a   ☐ She said that the test had been very difficult.

   b   ☐ She said that the test was being very difficult.

4   They said, "We will help you."

   a   ☐ They said they would help me.

   b   ☐ They said they were helping me.

5   Mary said, "I made this cake for your birthday."

   a   ☐ Mary said she made that cake for her birthday.

   b   ☐ Mary said that she had made that cake for my birthday.

Go to page 292 for Extra Practice.

Reading

Before Reading

1 **Discuss the questions below in Portuguese.**

   1 What are the main characteristics of a museum?

   2 Why do people visit museums?

   3 Do you and your family visit museums? If so, how often?

2 **Take a quick look at the texts on page 289. What do the museums mentioned in them have in common? Answer in Portuguese.**

_____

_____

3 **Choose the best synonym for the words in bold.**

1 *"Museum of Bad Art: A Home for **Forlorn** Paintings"* (text A).

   a ☐ happy

   b ☐ hopeless

   c ☐ rich

2 *"There has to be something about it that makes you [...] **wonder** why the artist continued [...]"* (text A, lines 11-14).

   a ☐ believe

   b ☐ ignore

   c ☐ think

3 *"[...] when her brother [...] hung up a painting that an antiques **dealer** was about to throw away"* (text A, lines 18-21).

   a ☐ artist

   b ☐ customer

   c ☐ merchant

4 *"[...] the language is presented as a dynamic cultural **heritage** [...]"* (text B, lines 7-9).

   a ☐ attempt

   b ☐ merchandise

   c ☐ tradition

4 **Find in the text words that correspond to the following definitions.**

   1 The structure surrounding a picture or photograph. _____

   2 An educational talk or speech on a given subject. _____

   3 A definite expression of someone's opinions or ideas. _____

Text A

MUSEUM OF BAD ART: A HOME FOR FORLORN PAINTINGS

What makes a work of art bad? According to Michael Frank, head of the Museum of Bad Art (located in Boston, U.S.),
5 he knows it when he sees it.

"We look for pieces of work that are produced in an attempt to make some sort of artistic statement – but clearly
10 something has gone wrong," he says. "There has to be something about it that makes you stop, and very often wonder why the artist continued down the path
15 to produce what he or she did."

Louise Reilly Sacco, one of the museum's cofounders, said the idea began in 1994, when her brother, Jerry Reilly, hung up a
20 painting that an antiques dealer was about to throw away. The dealer had only wanted the frame, not the dubious picture it contained.

Visitors can now expect to find
25 works like *Dog*. When asked to describe the piece, Sacco hesitated. "Uh… It's a puppy who's staring straight ahead with bright yellow eyes," she says, "but then at the top, it seems to turn
30 into a mountain covered in snow that melds into the puppy's head."

Text B

MUSEUM OF THE PORTUGUESE LANGUAGE

Designing exhibits for a museum whose purpose is to celebrate a language is a challenge. At the Museum of the
5 Portuguese Language, the world's first museum of its kind, the language is presented as a dynamic cultural heritage, using technology
10 to emphasize its permanent state of transformation.

The goal was to create a "democratic" space that would go far beyond the notion of
15 right and wrong ways to speak. Visitors take part in a journey

through language using audiovisuals, lectures, virtual experiences, and
20 interactive opportunities.

The Language Plaza mixes texts from Brazil's most important literary figures with lyrics of
25 popular songs, which are projected onto the ceiling and read by popular singers and writers.

A 120-meter projection screen shows the Portuguese language
30 in daily life and there are eight totems representing the influences of languages that contributed

to the formation of Brazilian Portuguese. Furthermore,
35 the Etymology Table is an interactive game that allows visitors to play with the creation of words and learn about the origins of words they use.

Adapted from <https://segd.org/content/museum-portuguese-language>. Accessed on December 3, 2015.

Vocabulary

antique: antiguidade	**cofounder:** cofundador(a)	**furthermore:** ademais, além disso	**meld:** fundir, misturar
attempt: tentativa	**dubious:** duvidoso(a), questionável	**head:** chefe, dirigente	**path:** caminho, trilha
ceiling: teto	**exhibit:** exposição	**lyrics:** letra de música	**screen:** tela

After Reading

1 **It is possible to affirm that the Museum of Bad Art…**

a ☐ exhibits the works of artists that intentionally produce art to confront the establishment and shock people.

b ☐ exhibits the works of artists that were condemned by merchants and critics but have great artistic value.

c ☐ showcases works of art that originally intended to make an artistic statement but didn't exactly reach their objectives.

d ☐ understands that it is impossible to know when a work of art is good or bad if the artist is unknown.

Scan this QR code to see a few works by contemporary artists and a discussion on what can be considered art.

2 **Which of the following statements is related to the origins of the Museum of Bad Art?**

a ☐ Michael Frank was looking for works of art in which something has clearly gone wrong.

b ☐ Jerry Reilly kept a picture that was almost thrown away by a dealer who was only interested in its frame.

c ☐ Ms. Sacco's antiques dealer bought a discarded painting and her brother decided to hang it up.

d ☐ Jerry Reilly, an antiques dealer, was about to throw away a valuable work of art he wasn't fond of.

> ### Observar listagens
> Em textos descritivos, observar elementos ou características de determinado elemento que foram listados pelo autor auxilia o leitor a ter uma imagem mais clara dos objetos ou itens descritos.

3 Text B mentions a series of elements through which visitors can learn about the Portuguese language. List them below.

_____

4 **According to text B, the Museum of the Portuguese Language…**

a ☐ is one of several museums whose purpose is to celebrate a challenging language.

b ☐ aims at helping preserve the cultural heritage of the correct way to speak Portuguese.

c ☐ assumes that Portuguese is an international language that influences many others.

d ☐ uses interactive materials to celebrate the language's permanent state of transformation.

e ☐ presents a clear view about the way Portuguese should be spoken to preserve its traditions.

Vocabulary Expansion

1 **Read the information in the box and match the sentence halves.**

Phrasal Verbs

turn: girar; virar(-se)
turn against: voltar-se contra
turn around: virar-se
turn away: expulsar, afastar
turn back: voltar

turn down: recusar
turn into: transformar-se em
turn off: desligar
turn on: ligar
turn out: resultar; acontecer

1 It was a good offer, but unfortunately

2 Can you turn around and

3 The snow forced them

4 He's managed

5 The machine will

a ☐ to turn his wife against you.

b ☐ to turn back and return home.

c ☐ I had to turn it down.

d ☐ turn this wheel.

e ☐ look at me, please?

2 **Complete the sentences using the phrasal verbs from the box in the correct form.**

| turn off | turn away | turn into | turn out | turn on |

1 The house is too quiet today. _____ the TV, please.

2 She is disappointed because things didn't _____ the way she had expected.

3 I have to study. Would you mind _____ the radio, please?

4 Fans who tried to photograph the pop star were _____ by his bodyguards.

5 Last week I read a book in which the main character had the power to _____ all kinds of mystic creatures.

3 **Read the information in the box and complete the sentences.**

1 She was born a few days _____ Christmas.

2 What you have done is _____ my comprehension.

3 We lived in Rome _____ moving to Milan.

4 Go along this street and turn right one block _____ the park.

5 He could see _____ the mountains and the sea.

6 My grandpa kept working _____ the age of 60. He liked his job.

before: antes
beyond: além; do outro lado

Extra Practice 11

1 Read the text and circle all the verbs that are in the passive voice.

The American bison, which is also known as buffalo, used to dominate the North American territory in the past. It is estimated that between 20 and 30 million of them lived in the area when European settlers arrived. However, by the end of the 19th century they were almost extinct. They were killed mainly by Native Americans, farmers, a severe drought, and the construction of railroads that went through their territory. There are currently about 500,000 buffaloes living in North America, but most of these animals have been crossbred with cattle and are semidomesticated.

Based on <www.defenders.org/bison/basic-facts>; <www.pbs.org/wnet/need-to-know/five-things/the-great-american-bison/8950>. Accessed on April 2, 2016.

2 Complete the sentences in the passive voice without using *by*.

1 They teach Medieval History at the local university.

Medieval History _____ at the local university.

2 Scientists researched this subject two years ago.

This subject _____ two years ago.

3 The surgeon is operating on my friend.

My friend _____ on.

4 We will have decided everything by tomorrow.

Everything _____ by tomorrow.

5 They have rented their house for two years.

Their house _____ for two years.

6 I sold my car for $20,000.

My car _____ for $20,000.

3 **Rewrite the sentences in the passive voice using *by*.**

1 This movie fascinates me.
   I am fascinated by this movie.

2 The show surprised them.

3 They were cleaning the house when I arrived.

4 This company has produced new car models in the past years.

5 I will paint the door tomorrow.

6 The storm damaged the house.

4 **There is a mistake in each sentence in the passive voice. Circle these mistakes and rewrite the sentences correcting them.**

1 Many people are talking about globalization in the meetings.

   Globalization is talking about in the meetings.

   Globalization is being talked about in the meetings.

2 Fire may destroy forests.

   Forests may destroyed by fire.

3 That enormous dog licked the baby.

   The baby were licked by that enormous dog.

4 The judge must punish the criminal.

   The criminal must be punish by the judge.

5 The movie bored Jack.

   Jack has been bored by the movie.

5 Check the correct alternative.

1 I am going to prepare some sandwiches.

Some sandwiches _____ prepared.

a ☐ will be to   b ☐ are going to be   c ☐ will

2 They will speak Chinese at the meeting.

Chinese _____ at the meeting.

a ☐ will be spoken   b ☐ would speak   c ☐ is going to speak

3 They make this product in Japan.

This product _____ in Japan.

a ☐ is making   b ☐ is make   c ☐ is made

4 She had completed her task when I arrived.

Her task _____ when I arrived.

a ☐ was completed   b ☐ had been completed   c ☐ has been completed

5 Someone was blocking the street this morning.

The street _____ this morning.

a ☐ was being blocked   b ☐ did block   c ☐ had blocking

6 Choose the correct passive voice version of the sentences.

1 Susan will write her paper in July.

a ☐ Her paper will be written in July.

b ☐ Her paper would written in July.

2 They built this bridge in 1890.

a ☐ They were built in 1890.

b ☐ This bridge was built in 1890.

3 Jorge Amado wrote *Capitães da areia*.

a ☐ *Capitães da areia* was written by Jorge Amado.

b ☐ Jorge Amado was written by *Capitães da areia*.

4 They were painting the room when I left.

a ☐ The room has being painted when I left.

b ☐ The room was being painted when I left.

7 **Check two passive voice possibilities for each of the sentences below.**

1 I'll give my mother a new pair of shoes for her birthday.

   a ☐ My mother will be given a new pair of shoes.

   b ☐ My mother will give me a new pair of shoes.

   c ☐ A new pair of shoes will be given to my mother.

   d ☐ I will be given a new pair of shoes by my mother.

2 She is going to tell me a secret.

   a ☐ A secret is going to be told to her.

   b ☐ A secret is going to be told to me.

   c ☐ I am going to be told a secret.

   d ☐ She is going to be told a secret.

3 They sang a song for the baby.

   a ☐ The baby was sung a song.

   b ☐ A song was sung for the baby.

   c ☐ We sang them a song.

   d ☐ They had sung a song.

4 We sent flowers to Jessica.

   a ☐ Flowers were sent to us.

   b ☐ Jessica has sent us flowers.

   c ☐ Jessica was sent flowers.

   d ☐ Flowers were sent to Jessica.

5 He gave Paul tickets to the game.

   a ☐ Tickets to the game were given by Paul.

   b ☐ Tickets to the game were given to Paul.

   c ☐ He has given tickets to the game to Paul.

   d ☐ Paul was given tickets to the game.

8 **Complete the sentences using reported speech.**

1 My friend said, "I will receive a postcard from my boyfriend."

My friend said that she _____.

2 Mom said, "I can't do that."

Mom said that she _____.

3 Ted said, "I have studied here for two years."

Ted said that he _____.

4 I said, "I am going to arrive late."

I said that I _____.

5 Tim said, "I didn't work yesterday."

Tim said that he _____.

6 Paul said, "Sally doesn't like vegetables."

Paul said that Sally _____.

9 **Check the alternative with the correct use of indirect speech.**

1 He said, "I may bring someone with me to the party."

a ☐ He said that he might bring someone with him to the party.

b ☐ He said that I may bring someone with me to the party.

2 She said, "I bought these shoes in a garage sale."

a ☐ She said that she had bought those shoes in a garage sale.

b ☐ She said that I have bought those shoes in a garage sale.

3 I said, "These flowers are for him."

a ☐ He said that these flowers were for you.

b ☐ I said that those flowers were for him.

4 I said, "I will think about it."

a ☐ I said I will have thought about it.

b ☐ I said that I would think about it.

5 He said, "I have been cleaning these windows for two hours."

a ☐ He said that he had been cleaning those windows for two hours.

b ☐ He said I have been cleaning these windows for two hours.

BIOTECHNOLOGY

Biotechnology is a course that started being offered fairly recently by universities. It uses knowledge of Chemistry, Biology, and new technologies in the healthcare, food, chemical, and environmental industries. Biotechnology graduates are multidisciplinary professionals, since they study Biology, Chemistry, Physics, Statistics, and Information Technology.

In the area of microbiology, these professionals study fungi, bacteria, viruses, and protozoa and the diseases that they cause in plants, animals, and human beings. They also research how such microorganisms can be used in the production of foods and beverages – such as dairy products, beer, and wine.

Biotechnologists specializing in immunology use microorganisms in the production of vaccines and kits for diagnosis. In the food and pharmaceutical industries, they improve safety and hygiene at the workplace by controlling microbial growth. They also research the development of new pharmaceutical drugs.

These professionals may also work in the environmental area, to evaluate and prevent water and soil contamination.

Based on <http://vestibular.brasilescola.uol.com.br/guia-de-profissoes/biotecnologia.htm>; <http://guiadoestudante.abril.com.br/profissoes/meio-ambiente-ciencias-agrarias/bioquimica-741140.shtml>. Accessed on April 2, 2016.

Vocabulary

diagnosis: diagnóstico
fairly: razoavelmente
graduate: graduado(a), formado(a)
healthcare: cuidados com a saúde
improve: aumentar, melhorar
prevent: prevenir, evitar
safety: segurança
since: visto que, uma vez que

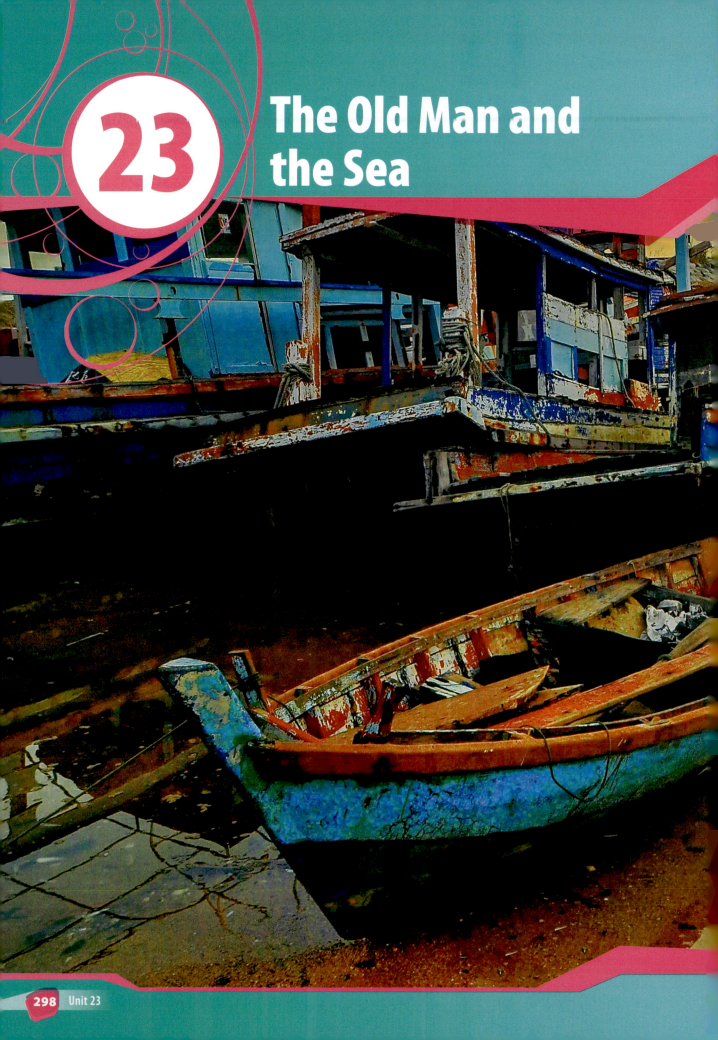

23

The Old Man and the Sea

Look at the picture and answer orally.

1   What does the picture tell you about this unit?

2   In your opinion, what is a fisher's routine like?

3   What are some of the challenges fishers face when they go out to sea?

Language in Context

1 Take a look at the dialogue.

Father:	Mom called from London last night.
Daughter:	Is she enjoying her trip?
Father:	I guess so…
Daughter:	You guess so? Didn't she say if she's having a good time?
Father:	No, she didn't.
Daughter:	What did she say, then?
Father:	She told me not to forget to lock the doors at night. And she told you to visit Grandma every other day.
Daughter:	Was that all?
Father:	No, she asked if you were studying. She asked if your brother had gone to his piano lesson. She also asked me if I had taken the dog for a walk, if I had phoned the dentist, and if you had talked to Aunt Julia.
Daughter:	That's Mom!

2 Give your opinion about the dialogue.

1 Has the mother been away for a long time? Why do you think so?

2 Why does the daughter say "That's Mom!"?

> **Vocabulary**
>
> **every other day:** dia sim, dia não
> **guess:** achar; supor

3 Read, think, and answer orally.

A (Direct Speech)	B (Indirect Speech)
Ela disse: "Você levou o cão para passear?"	Ela perguntou se eu tinha levado o cão para passear.
She said, "Did you walk the dog?"	She asked if I had walked the dog.

1 What changes do you notice in the first line of the chart?

2 Do the same changes occur in the second line?

Language Practice

Direct and Indirect Speech (II)

Uso

Para relatar uma pergunta, colocamos a frase na forma afirmativa.

He said, "Does she study?"	**He asked if she studied.**
He said, "Where does she live?"	**He asked where she lived.**

Para relatar ordens e pedidos, geralmente usamos **tell**, **ask** ou **order**.

He said, "Open the door."	He **told** me to open the door.
He said, "Don't go."	He **asked** me not to go.
He said, "Don't call me later!"	He **ordered** me not to call him later.

Say/**Tell** – Explicitar o objeto indireto é obrigatório quando usamos *tell*.

He **told** <u>me</u> that he was sick.

He **said** that he was sick.

Os modais **would**, **could**, **should**, **might** e **ought to** não mudam de forma.

He said, "I **could** help you."   He said that he **could** help me.

---

1 **Rewrite the sentences using direct speech.**

1   She asked me if I was reading the book.

   She said, _____

2   He told me not to smoke.

   He said, _____

3   She asked me when I would leave.

   She said, _____

4   He told me to go home.

   He said, _____

5   She asked me where I studied.

   She said, _____

6   He asked me what they were saying.

   He said, _____

2 Rewrite the sentences using indirect speech.

1 Mary said to me, "Don't speak to me."

Mary asked me _____.

2 Mom said to me, "Turn on the TV."

Mom told me _____.

3 She said to Jane, "What time is it?"

She asked Jane _____.

4 The woman said, "Are you a student?"

The woman asked _____.

5 She said, "Did you make the cake?"

She asked _____.

3 Check the correct alternative to complete the sentences.

1 He told us _____ up.

a ☐ to stand

b ☐ stand

c ☐ standing

2 They asked me when I _____ to leave.

a ☐ will want

b ☐ wanted

c ☐ to want

3 She asked if we _____ that film the day before.

a ☐ saw

b ☐ see

c ☐ had seen

4 He told me _____ the dog.

a ☐ don't touch

b ☐ not to touch

c ☐ didn't touch

4 Circle the appropriate form of the verbs in the sentences in indirect speech.

1 "Do you know the answer?"

He asked me if I **knew** / **to know** the answer.

2 "Will you help me?"

He asked me if I **will to** / **would** help him.

3 "Could you give her the money?"

He asked if I **could** / **had** give her the money.

4 "Where did you meet her?"

He asked me where I **had met** / **met** her.

Language Practice

Would Rather, Had Better, It Takes

Would rather (*'d rather*) – Expressa preferência.
> I **would rather** walk to school. (Prefiro andar até a escola.)

Had better (*'d better*) – Expressa conselho ou recomendação.
> You **had better** go home. (É melhor você ir para casa.)

It takes… – Expressa o tempo que alguém leva para praticar uma ação ou que algum evento leva para ocorrer.
> **It takes** me <u>10 minutes</u> to get ready. (Levo 10 minutos para ficar pronto.)

> **It took** us <u>one day</u> to get there. (Levamos um dia para chegar lá.)

> **It will take** him <u>one hour</u> to have lunch. (Ele levará uma hora para almoçar.)

O pronome pessoal objeto pode ser eliminado se não for essencial para a compreensão da frase.
> **It took** 45 minutes to bake the cake. (O bolo levou 45 minutos para assar.)

5 **Complete the sentences using *would rather* or *had better*.**

1 I love blue, so I _____ wear the blue dress.

2 It is raining. You _____ take an umbrella.

3 It's a beautiful day. I _____ walk home.

4 I have a headache. I _____ take an aspirin.

6 **Answer the questions using the information in parentheses.**

1 How long did it take you to go home yesterday?

(30 minutes) <u>It took (me) 30 minutes.</u>

2 How long will it take us to get there by train?

(one day) _____

3 How long does it take Jane to wash the dog?

(one hour) _____

4 How long did it take Hemingway to win the Nobel Prize in Literature?

(55 years) _____

5 How long did it take to cook the meat?

(2 hours) _____

Go to page 318 for
Extra Practice.

Reading

Before Reading

1 **Discuss the questions below in Portuguese.**

1 Have you ever been fishing in the open sea? If so, how was it? If not, would you like to?

2 How is professional fishing different from fishing for pleasure?

3 What would you do if you caught a huge fish and were alone on the boat? How would you take the fish to shore?

2 **Scan the text and check the best alternative.**

1 The story takes place...

a ☐ in the city of Santiago, Chile.   b ☐ in the sea near Havana, Cuba.

2 The old man...

a ☐ always went fishing alone.   b ☐ went fishing alone that time.

3 The fisherman struggled with the fish for...

a ☐ two days and two nights.   b ☐ one day and one night.

3 **Write the meaning of the words below. Use the glossary.**

1 fisherman _____   3 hook _____

2 sail _____   4 aloud _____

4 **Read the box to learn about the author.**

Ernest Hemingway

Ernest Miller Hemingway (1899-1961) was an American author and journalist. Having participated in World War I as an ambulance driver and in World War II as a war correspondent, he is remembered both for his economical style and for his personal adventures. Some of his most famous works include *A Farewell to Arms* (1929) and *The Old Man and the Sea* (1952), which took him less than a year to write. He received the Nobel Prize in Literature in 1954.

Based on <www.goodreads.com/author/show/1455.Ernest_Hemingway>. Accessed on December 10, 2015.

The Old Man and the Sea

SUMMARY

This is the story of Santiago, an aging fisherman. One day, after 84 days of bad luck, Santiago decides to sail far out to sea in search of a big fish. This time, he goes alone. The boy who is his best friend can't go away with him. Later that day, his luck turns and he hooks a giant marlin. For two days and two nights, 5 the fish pulls the old man further out to sea.

The fish never changed his course all that day. Santiago looked behind him and saw that no land was visible. I have no cramps and I feel strong, he thought. I wish I could see him once to know what I have against me.

It was cold after the sun went down. He could feel the strength of the fish
10 through the line he held across his shoulders. They were moving more slowly now, and the glow of Havana was not so strong. We must be going to the eastward, he thought.

Then, he said aloud, "I wish I had the boy here. To help me and to see this." Then he began to think about the great fish that he had hooked. "He is
15 wonderful and strange, and who knows how old he is," he told himself. "But he cannot know that it is only one man against him, nor that it is an old man. Oh, I had better remember to eat the tuna in order to keep strong. I must remember," he said to himself. No one should be alone in their old age, he thought. But it is unavoidable.

20 It was very cold now in the time before daylight and the old man pushed against the wood to be warm. "Fish," he said softly, aloud, "I'll stay with you until I am dead." He'll stay with me too, I suppose, the old man thought, and he waited for it to be light.

51

Adapted from HEMINGWAY, E. *The Old Man and the Sea*. New York: Charles Scribner's Sons, 1952.

► Vocabulary

cramp: cãibra	**further:** mais longe	**strength:** força	**tuna:** atum
eastward: na direção leste	**glow:** brilho	**suppose:** supor	**unavoidable:** inevitável

After Reading

Reconhecer as vozes do texto

Em textos literários, é comum haver uma sobreposição de vozes na narrativa, dependendo do estilo do autor. Destacar as diferentes vozes é uma importante estratégia na interlocução com o texto.

1 Check the voices that you notice in the text.

a ☐ Santiago's voice.

b ☐ Santiago's thoughts.

c ☐ The boy's voice.

d ☐ The fish's thoughts.

e ☐ The narrator's voice.

2 Answer the questions.

1 Does the author separate Santiago's thoughts from the other sentences of the text? If so, how?

_____

2 What about what Santiago says aloud, is it separated from the text? If so, how?

_____

3 Complete the statements based on the text.

1 Santiago, the fisherman...

a ☐ controlled the fish with the strength of his arms.

b ☐ was pulled away from the land by the fish.

2 In the sentence "*I wish I could see him once to know what I have against me*" (line 8), we can infer that Santiago...

a ☐ had already seen the fish.

b ☐ had not seen the fish yet.

Scan this QR code to watch a video about the challenges and expectations of getting older.

4 Decide if the following statements are true (T) or false (F).

1 ☐ Santiago was sure about his location.

2 ☐ Santiago's wish was to have the boy there with him.

3 ☐ Santiago admired and respected the fish.

4 ☐ Santiago knew how old the fish was.

Vocabulary Expansion

1 **Write the meaning of the phrasal verbs in bold. Use the words from the box.**

| approach | leave | proceed | pass | examine |

1 "Time **goes by** so slowly," says a famous song. _____

2 I'll **go over** the books to determine our real situation. _____

3 I don't know how to **go about** this problem. _____

4 They have decided to **go ahead** with the plan. _____

5 Can we **go away** to the beach next weekend? _____

2 **Complete the sentences using the words/phrases from the box.**

| getting sick | unhappy | isn't working | to a lower level |

1 If you are **feeling down**, you are _____.

2 If the computer **is down**, it _____.

3 If you **are coming down with** the flu, you are _____.

4 If you are **going down** a hill, you are going _____.

3 **Read the box and complete the chart.**

Suffix **-able**

Acrescentado a verbos, o sufixo **-able** significa "capaz de" e forma adjetivos.
avoid – avoid**able**   believe – belie**vable**

	Verb	Adjective	Translation
1	to admire	admirable	admirável
2	to accept	_____	_____
3	to suit	_____	_____

4 **Now fill in the blanks with the words from the previous activity.**

1 We tried to find a solution that was _____ to everyone.

2 They demonstrated an _____ courage when dealing with the problem.

3 I'm not sure if this movie is _____ for such a young child.

24

Teenagers Changing the World

Look at the picture and answer orally.

1   What does the picture tell you about this unit?

2   What makes some people want to change the world?

3   Do you know anyone who has made a difference and improved the lives of others?

Language in Context

1 Take a look at the dialogue.

🎧 48

Official:	Mr. Rodrigues, why are you coming to this country?
Luis Rodrigues:	I want to study here.
Official:	Do you intend to work too?
Luis Rodrigues:	No. I want to study and surf.
Official:	Where are you going to stay?
Luis Rodrigues:	At the university dormitory.
Official:	How long do you want to stay?
Luis Rodrigues:	Four years.
Official:	Did you bring enough money?
Luis Rodrigues:	Yes, I did.
Official:	Did you leave your luggage unattended after landing?
Luis Rodrigues:	No, sir. I've kept my luggage near me all the time.
Official:	Did anybody give you anything to carry after landing?
Luis Rodrigues:	No, sir.
Official:	Welcome, Mr. Rodrigues. Here is your passport. Enjoy your stay.

2 Give your opinion about the dialogue.

1 Did Luis enter the country?

2 Why did the official ask if Luis had left his luggage unattended?

> **Vocabulary**
>
> **landing:** aterrissagem
> **luggage:** bagagem
> **unattended:** desacompanhado(a)

3 Read, think, and answer orally.

1 I want to study here.

2 Do you intend to work too?

3 Did you leave your luggage unattended after landing?

a Find in the sentences examples of infinitive with *to*, infinitive without *to*, and gerund.

b Underline the words that might have required these structures to be used.

Language Practice

Infinitive: (*to*) + verb

O infinitivo é uma forma do verbo e pode conter ou não a partícula *to*.

Uso

Usa-se o infinitivo com *to* na maioria dos casos.

She wants **to leave**.

We decided not **to go**.

He was the first **to arrive**.

You are too young **to drive**.

What a nice thing **to say**!

It's time **to leave**.

I am pleased **to meet** you.

It took us one hour **to get** there.

Usa-se o infinitivo sem *to*:

- após os verbos modais (*can*, *may*, etc.), os verbos auxiliares (*do* e *will*) e os verbos *make* e *let*

She <u>can</u> **dance**.

He <u>made</u> me **cry**.

<u>Do</u> you **like** tea?

<u>Let</u> me **go**.

> **Nota**
> **To help** pode ser seguido de infinitivo com ou sem *to*:
> Help me **(to) push** the car.

- após *but* e *except*

We did nothing <u>but</u> **cry**.

You should do nothing <u>except</u> **wait**.

---

1 **Match the sentence halves.**

1 There's nothing they can

2 What time do you

3 We must

4 It's very difficult

a ☐ leave for school?

b ☐ do except hope for the best.

c ☐ to answer this question.

d ☐ finish our homework before dinner.

2 **Answer the questions using *not* and the expressions in parentheses.**

1 What did he decide?

(go to the beach) He decided not to go to the beach.

2 What did she promise?

(arrive late) _____

3 What do they expect?

(fail the examination) _____

4 Why did they hurry?

(miss the train) _____

3 Circle the correct infinitive form to complete the sentences.

1 Can I **offer** / **to offer** you something to drink?

2 He made me **to laugh** / **laugh** at the party.

3 Grandma was the first woman **to drive** / **drive** a bus in her town.

4 Let's **to talk** / **talk** to Mr. Johnson.

5 Last Sunday we did nothing but **work** / **to work**.

6 She's too young **to drive** / **drive**.

Language Practice

Gerund: verb + -ing

O gerúndio é uma forma verbal caracterizada pela terminação -ing e que pode funcionar como substantivo.

Uso

Pode ser usado:
- como sujeito – **Painting** is a good hobby.
- como objeto – I love **dancing**.
- após preposição – He is tired <u>of</u> **working**.
- após os verbos *come* e *go* (indicando atividade física) – I <u>went</u> **skiing**.
- após expressões como *can't help* (não conseguir evitar) e *it's no use* (não adianta) – I <u>can't help</u> **being** upset. <u>It's no use</u> **talking** to him when he's angry.
- após verbos como *appreciate, avoid, consider, enjoy, finish, mind* etc. – I <u>avoid</u> **sleeping** late because I <u>enjoy</u> **working out** early in the morning.

4 Check the correct alternative.

1 I don't mind _____ a little longer.

   a ☐ waiting

   b ☐ to wait

2 She dedicates her time to _____.

   a ☐ paint

   b ☐ painting

3 Go home and _____ writing the letter.

   a ☐ finish

   b ☐ finishing

4 They decided not _____ early.

   a ☐ to arrive

   b ☐ arriving

Language Practice

Infinitive and Gerund

Alguns verbos podem ser seguidos por gerúndio ou infinitivo sem *to*, como *feel, hear, notice, see, observe* e *watch*.

> I <u>heard</u> him **crying/cry**.

> I <u>saw</u> it **falling/fall**.

Outros verbos podem ser seguidos por gerúndio ou infinitivo com *to*, como *advise, allow, attempt, begin, continue, dislike, forget, hate, intend, like, love, permit, prefer, remember, start, stop* e *try*.

> He <u>likes</u> **studying/to study**.

> He <u>started</u> **eating/to eat**.

> **Nota**
>
> Alguns verbos, como *forget, remember* e *stop*, mudam de significado dependendo da forma verbal que os sucede.
> He <u>stopped</u> **talking**. (Ele parou de falar.)
> He <u>stopped</u> **to talk**. (Ele parou para conversar.)

5 **Circle the correct option to complete the sentences.**

1   We intend **to go** / **go** out after dinner.

2   I asked the boys to stop **talk** / **talking**.

3   I can't imagine Grandpa **to go** / **going** to work by bike.

4   He saw the little girl **crossing** / **to cross** the street.

5   The man asked me how **get** / **to get** to the airport.

6   Carol loves **working** / **work** in Hawaii.

6 **Fill in the blanks with the verbs in parentheses in the correct form.**

1   I like _____ (swim) in the lake.

2   _____ (read) is her favorite pastime.

3   Are you thinking of _____ (go) out now?

4   I hate _____ (take) this medicine.

5   We went _____ (fish) last vacation.

6   In the end we decided _____ (stay).

Go to page 318 for Extra Practice.

Reading

Before Reading

1 **Discuss the questions below in Portuguese.**

    1 Is it possible for ordinary people to change their communities? How?

    2 What would you like to change in your community? What could you do to help?

2 **Which words from the texts correspond to the following definitions?**

Text A

    1 A stock of a resource that is necessary or desired. _____

    2 Somebody/Something that calls attention. _____

    3 Careful study or investigation of a given subject, field, or problem. _____

Text B

    4 A common but oversimplified conception, opinion, or image. _____

    5 Representing the prevalent ideas and practices of a society. _____

    6 Financial support for a project, event, or organization. _____

3 **Refer to the texts and match the sentence halves.**

    1 When a person **takes part in** something,

    2 If someone **comes up with** something,

    3 If someone **sets** something **up**,

    a ☐ he/she makes it ready to work.

    b ☐ he/she participates in it.

    c ☐ he/she creates or develops it.

4 **Find in text B an English correspondent to the word *favela*.**

    a ☐ shortcoming

    b ☐ crossfire

    c ☐ shantytown

Beyond Malala:
Teenagers Changing the World

Text A

Kelvin Doe was born during the civil war in Sierra Leone. Now in his early twenties, he personifies how the country is trying to rebuild and look forward. A short film about him has more than 5 million views on YouTube.

Doe is a self-taught engineer who began early in life. Frustrated with the unreliable electricity supply in his neighborhood, he built a generator using parts that were homemade or rescued from the trash. It also powered a community radio station that he built from recycled materials. He acts as a DJ and employs his friends as journalists and station managers.

In 2012, he was picked for a trip to America, where he presented his inventions, took part in research, and lectured to Engineering students.

His mentor, David Sengeh, said, "The inspirational effects of the original YouTube video have been remarkable. In Sierra Leone, other young people suddenly feel they can be like Kelvin."

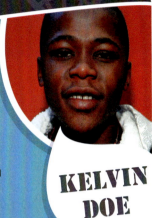

KELVIN DOE

Text B

RENE SILVA

While most Brazilian teenagers are interested in computer games, homework, football, or *baile funk*, Rene Silva has dedicated himself to fighting negative stereotypes about his *favela* community.

Conscious of the shortcomings of the mainstream media, one of his teachers asked him to set up a community newspaper in 2005, so he came up with *Voz das Comunidades*. Five years later, he live-tweeted a huge military and police operation to "pacify" the Alemão *favela*, where he lived. Silva corrected mistakes made by TV reporters and raised warnings about a young boy who was caught in the crossfire between the police and gangsters. This initiative secured sponsorship for his newspaper – now largely online.

Silva has published a book, *A voz do Alemão*, about the residents of his *favela*, which he hopes will further change perceptions of Rio's shantytowns and expose the problems they continue to face after pacification. "The important thing about being young and doing what I do in the *favelas* is to create new points of reference," he said. "In the past, it was drug trafficking. Today, there is more recognition of the people who are trying to do good and change the reality of the place where they live."

Adapted from <www.theguardian.com/world/2013/oct/18/teenagers-changing-world-malala-yousafzai>. Accessed on December 10, 2015.

Vocabulary

crossfire: fogo cruzado
homemade: caseiro(a)
pick: escolher
raise: criar, despertar
secure: garantir
self-taught: autodidata
shortcoming: defeito, deficiência
unreliable: não confiável

After Reading

1 Check the <u>wrong</u> statement about Kelvin Doe.

a ☐ He built a power supply for his neighborhood using old parts.

b ☐ He hasn't attended formal Engineering school in his home country.

c ☐ He directed a film about his work which has more than 5 million views.

d ☐ He built a radio station that provides job opportunities for his friends.

e ☐ He is a positive example to other young people in Sierra Leone.

2 One of Rene Silva's objectives in his activities is to…

a ☐ inform about potential sponsors interested in funding communication initiatives in the *favelas*.

b ☐ show that shantytowns are also inhabited by people who want to do good and improve society.

c ☐ reveal that pacification put an end to the problems in underprivileged communities.

d ☐ raise funds to publish the book *A voz do Alemão*, in which he depicts life in the *favelas*.

e ☐ establish the *Voz das Comunidades* newspaper to discuss conflicts with gangsters.

3 What similarities are there between Kelvin and Rene? Answer in Portuguese.

_____

_____

> **Ler criticamente**
>
> É importante que o leitor não aceite toda e qualquer afirmação apresentada por um texto como uma verdade absoluta. Ele deve procurar verificar essas informações e buscar no texto fatos que deem suporte às opiniões emitidas.

4 Think about these propositions and discuss in Portuguese.

1 Text B mentions "*negative stereotypes about his* favela *community*". Can stereotypes be positive? If so, give some examples.

2 Find a statement in this text that can be considered a stereotype.

3 Do you think the author was conscious that he/she was conveying a stereotype? Why?

4 What do you think about this stereotype? Do you agree with it? Do you think it represents you and the Brazilian teenagers you know?

Vocabulary Expansion

1 Read the information in the box and match the expressions to their meaning.

> **To make**
> É geralmente usado no sentido de "criar", "construir", "produzir" ou em determinadas expressões.
> Mom is **making** dinner early today.

1	make the bed	a		cometer um erro/engano
2	make a decision	b		fazer chá/café/almoço
3	make fun of	c		arrumar a cama
4	make a mess	d		tomar uma decisão
5	make a mistake	e		caçoar de
6	make tea/coffee/lunch	f		fazer bagunça

2 Read the information in the box and match the expressions to the corresponding meaning.

> **To do**
> É geralmente usado em ações mais abstratas, com o sentido de "realizar", ou em determinadas expressões.
> I **did** everything I could to help her.

1	do my best	a		fazer as tarefas domésticas
2	do the housework	b		ir bem na escola
3	do well at school	c		fazer o meu melhor
4	do the shopping	d		fazer um bom trabalho
5	do an exercise	e		fazer as compras
6	do a good job	f		fazer um exercício

3 Complete the sentences using *do* or *make* in the correct form/tense.

1 I always _____ my best to organize everything here.

2 Julie, don't leave without _____ your bed, OK?

3 Don't worry, from now on I will _____ all my duties.

4 Last weekend he _____ lunch and I _____ the dishes.

5 The teacher told us not to _____ the experiment at home.

6 I don't know why they keep _____ fun of the others.

Extra Practice 12

1 Choose the best alternative to complete each sentence.

1 She said to me, "You should sign this letter."

She told me that I _____ sign that letter.

a ☐ should   b ☐ can't   c ☐ would

2 He said, "I'm working now."

He said that he was working _____.

a ☐ now   b ☐ then   c ☐ there

3 Linda said, "Bob was ill."

Linda said that Bob _____ ill.

a ☐ were   b ☐ was being   c ☐ had been

4 We said to Karen, "We have cleaned your room."

We told Karen that we had cleaned _____ room.

a ☐ your   b ☐ my   c ☐ her

2 Rewrite the sentences using reported speech.

1 Tess said, "My teacher will go to China tomorrow."

Tess said that _____.

2 I said to the officer, "I was reading a book in my room yesterday."

I told the officer that _____.

3 She said, "My friend flew to Paris last night."

She said that _____.

4 He said to me, "We didn't see you at school two days ago."

He told me that _____.

5 Leo said, "She has already been there."

Leo said that _____.

6 I said to them, "I often read this book."

I told them that _____.

3 Check the correct alternative.

1 He asked _____.

   a ☐ where is the bus stop

   b ☐ where the bus stop was

   c ☐ where stops the bus

2 He asked _____.

   a ☐ that we liked the movie

   b ☐ that we to like the movie

   c ☐ if we had liked the movie

3 He said _____.

   a ☐ the plane will been on time

   b ☐ the plane to be on time

   c ☐ the plane would be on time

4 He said _____.

   a ☐ he had gone downtown the day before

   b ☐ he is going downtown yesterday

   c ☐ he goes downtown the day before

5 Mom told me _____.

   a ☐ clean the kitchen

   b ☐ not clean the kitchen

   c ☐ to clean the kitchen

6 She asked me _____.

   a ☐ to do my homework

   b ☐ did my homework

   c ☐ had done my homework

7 She said _____.

   a ☐ she visited her relatives next afternoon

   b ☐ she had visited her relatives two days before

   c ☐ she visits her relatives one hour before

4 **What piece of advice would you give to someone who…**

1   feels sick? (see a doctor)

You'd better see a doctor. _____

2   feels stressed? (go for a walk)

_____

3   is hungry? (eat something)

_____

4   feels sad? (talk to a friend)

_____

5   is late? (hurry)

_____

5 **Write sentences using *would rather* or *had better*, according to the information in parentheses.**

1   I / go by plane (preference)

I'd rather go by plane. _____

2   She / arrive early (advice)

_____

3   You / work tomorrow morning (advice)

_____

4   He / wake up early (preference)

_____

5   We / walk in the park (preference)

_____

6 **Answer the questions.**

1   How long does it take you to go from home to school?

_____

2   How long did it take you to shower yesterday?

_____

3   How long will it take you to finish high school?

_____

7 Rewrite the sentences according to the information in parentheses.

1 It took me an hour to do my homework.

(present) _____

2 It will take them 2 years to build a new house.

(past) _____

3 It took us three years to write a book.

(future) _____

4 It will take her 20 minutes to make a cake.

(present) _____

8 Answer the questions using the words in parentheses and one of the forms in the example.

1 Why does she want the money? (buy a car)

She wants the money to buy a car. / She wants the money in order to buy a car.

2 Why is he working hard? (get a promotion)

_____

3 Why are you saving money? (buy a new house)

_____

4 Why does she study in the evening? (work in the afternoon)

_____

9 Combine the sentences using *and*.

1 He decided to rest. He decided to watch some TV.

He decided to rest and to watch some TV.

2 She could come. She could see her new room.

_____

3 I stopped talking. I stopped laughing.

_____

4 We like to run. We like to swim.

_____

5 My cousin is good at playing soccer. My cousin is good at solving puzzles.

_____

10 **Complete the sentences using the infinitive of the verbs in parentheses with or without to.**

1 It's difficult _____ (learn) Greek.

2 Jennifer may _____ (visit) us next month.

3 He'll do anything except _____ (wash) the dog.

4 Can you _____ (teach) me how _____ (play) baseball?

5 I was the last one _____ (arrive) yesterday.

6 He will _____ (tell) us where _____ (go) after the show.

11 **Fill in the blanks using the verbs in parentheses in the infinitive (with or without to) or in the gerund.**

1 My brother's passion is _____ (swim).

2 I want _____ (talk) to you before the end of the week.

3 She couldn't stand _____ (look) at those bright lights.

4 They helped me _____ (do) my homework.

5 I really enjoy _____ (meet) new people.

6 There is nothing you can _____ (do) but _____ (hope) for the best.

12 **Check the correct alternative to complete each sentence.**

1 He was the first _____ the question.

   a ☐ to answer   b ☐ answer   c ☐ answering

2 _____ hard is something we all have to do.

   a ☐ To working   b ☐ Work   c ☐ Working

3 You should _____ to the dentist before lunch.

   a ☐ to go   b ☐ go   c ☐ going

4 They hope _____ to a restaurant for dinner.

   a ☐ to go   b ☐ go   c ☐ going

5 My father is interested in _____ another language.

   a ☐ to learn   b ☐ learn   c ☐ learning

6 We both stopped _____ about 5 years ago.

   a ☐ to smoke   b ☐ smoke   c ☐ smoking

Job Corner 12

Professions in the Media

If you decide to work in the media industry, you can choose among a variety of areas: social communications, news coverage, investigative journalism, news editing, cinema and video, photography, multimedia, editorial production, radio and TV, public relations, and many others.

You can also work as a spokesperson, making the link between a company and the media. This is the area that offers the most job opportunities, since companies are always looking for more visibility for their brands and products. A spokesperson can also be responsible for communication aimed at employees, customers, and suppliers.

If you work as an editor, you can define the focus, the approach, and the length of pieces of news, and you can write or approve the final text. In the printed media and on the internet, you are responsible for choosing the photos and illustrations that will accompany a text. On the radio and on TV, you are the one who selects soundtracks and images that will be presented in news shows.

As a reporter, you can collect information and write texts to be presented on the radio, on television, and online – or to be published in newspapers and magazines.

Based on <http://vestibular.brasilescola.uol.com.br/guia-de-profissoes/ciencias-sociais-aplicadas.htm>;
<http://guiadoestudante.abril.com.br/profissoes/comunicacao-informacao/estudos-midia-686062.shtml>. Accessed on April 4, 2016.

Vocabulary

aimed at: voltado(a) para
approach: abordagem
brand: marca
coverage: cobertura
customer: cliente
focus: foco, enfoque
length: comprimento, duração
news show: noticiário
printed: impresso(a)
soundtrack: trilha sonora
spokesperson: porta-voz
supplier: fornecedor(a)

GREGG SEGAL 📷

7 Days of Garbage

[...]

In January, I set out to create pictures that make the trash problem impossible to ignore. I asked family, friends, neighbors and other acquaintances to save their trash and recyclables for a week and then to lie down and be photographed in it. [...] I asked people to include their recyclables for several reasons: much of what is designated recyclable is not recycled, recycling plastic has environmental costs, and packaging is excessive. [...]

By asking us to look at ourselves, I've found that some are considering the issue more deeply. Many have said the process of saving their garbage and then laying in it reconciled them to a need for change. Others have commented how powerless they feel. [...]

Still, some of us are making small steps to mitigate the crisis. Reflecting on the pictures I've made so far, I see 7 Days of Garbage as instant archeology, a record not only of our waste but of our values – values that may be evolving a little.

Disponível em <www.greggsegal.com>. Acesso em 16 de fevereiro de 2016.

Habilidades

H5: Associar vocábulos e expressões de um texto em LEM ao seu tema.

H6: Utilizar os conhecimentos da LEM e de seus mecanismos como meio de ampliar as possibilidades de acesso a informações, tecnologias e culturas.

H8: Reconhecer a importância da produção cultural em LEM como representação da diversidade cultural e linguística.

Gregg Segal é um fotógrafo norte-americano preocupado com o acúmulo de lixo produzido pelo nosso modo de vida. É possível dizer que seu projeto 7 Days of Garbage (2014)...

a ☐ estimula nas pessoas um sentimento de reconciliação com o lixo produzido.

b ☐ detalha os padrões de consumo de produtos não recicláveis dos norte-americanos.

c ☐ revela o lixo que alguns de seus vizinhos e amigos produzem em uma semana.

d ☐ demonstra como algumas pessoas estão aos poucos mudando seus hábitos.

e ☐ registra como os valores da nossa sociedade são impactados pelo consumo.

VOLUNTARY GLOBAL TARGETS

 A **25%** relative reduction in risk of premature mortality from cardiovascular diseases, cancer, diabetes, or chronic respiratory diseases.

 At least **10%** relative reduction in the harmful use of alcohol, as appropriate, within the national context.

 A **10%** relative reduction in prevalence of insufficient physical activity.

 A **30%** relative reduction in mean population intake of salt/sodium.

A **30%** relative reduction in prevalence of current tobacco use in persons aged 15+ years.

 A **25%** relative reduction in the prevalence of raised blood pressure or contain the prevalence of raised blood pressure, according to national circumstances.

 Halt the rise in diabetes and obesity.

 At least **50%** of eligible people receive drug therapy and counselling (including glycaemic control) to prevent heart attacks and strokes.

 An **80%** availability of the affordable basic technologies and essential medicines, including generics, required to treat major noncommunicable diseases in both public and private facilities.

Disponível em <http://apps.who.int/iris/bitstream/10665/94384/1/9789241506236_eng.pdf?ua=1>. Acesso em 20 de abril de 2016.

Habilidades

H5: Associar vocábulos e expressões de um texto em LEM ao seu tema.

H6: Utilizar os conhecimentos da LEM e de seus mecanismos como meio de ampliar as possibilidades de acesso a informações, tecnologias e culturas.

O quadro acima foi publicado no *Global Action Plan for the Prevention and Control of Noncommunicable Diseases 2013-2020*, da Organização Mundial da Saúde. Dentre os objetivos dessa ação estão...

a ☐ a redução relativa de 25% no consumo de bebidas alcoólicas e a diminuição dos casos de diabetes e obesidade causados pelo consumo de álcool.

b ☐ a disponibilização de remédios básicos na maioria das instituições de saúde e a redução da incidência de prática insuficiente de atividades físicas.

c ☐ a redução do número de mortes prematuras por todas as causas e a diminuição da ingestão de sódio e bebidas alcoólicas em 30%.

d ☐ o fornecimento de medicamentos para metade dos pacientes com doenças cardíacas e a diminuição de 30% no uso de tabaco por menores de 15 anos.

e ☐ o aumento relativo de 10% na prática de atividades físicas e a diminuição de 25% dos números absolutos de casos de pressão alta.

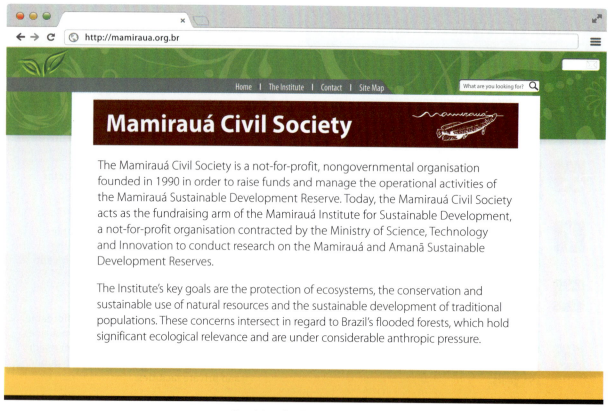

← → C   🌐 http://mamiraua.org.br   ≡

Home | The Institute | Contact | Site Map

What are you looking for? 🔍

Mamirauá Civil Society

The Mamirauá Civil Society is a not-for-profit, nongovernmental organisation founded in 1990 in order to raise funds and manage the operational activities of the Mamirauá Sustainable Development Reserve. Today, the Mamirauá Civil Society acts as the fundraising arm of the Mamirauá Institute for Sustainable Development, a not-for-profit organisation contracted by the Ministry of Science, Technology and Innovation to conduct research on the Mamirauá and Amanã Sustainable Development Reserves.

The Institute's key goals are the protection of ecosystems, the conservation and sustainable use of natural resources and the sustainable development of traditional populations. These concerns intersect in regard to Brazil's flooded forests, which hold significant ecological relevance and are under considerable anthropic pressure.

Disponível em <http://mamiraua.org.br/en-us/institution/mamiraua-civil-society>. Acesso em 3 de agosto de 2015.

Habilidades

H5: Associar vocábulos e expressões de um texto em LEM ao seu tema.

H6: Utilizar os conhecimentos da LEM e de seus mecanismos como meio de ampliar as possibilidades de acesso a informações, tecnologias e culturas.

Várias organizações não governamentais mantêm páginas na internet para informar o público sobre suas atividades. Que informação é possível depreender a partir do texto acima?

a ☐ A Sociedade Civil Mamirauá abriga o Instituto de Desenvolvimento Sustentável Mamirauá e foi contratada pelo Ministério da Ciência, Tecnologia e Inovação.

b ☐ Conservar recursos naturais e promover a sustentabilidade entre populações nativas são os únicos objetivos da Sociedade Civil Mamirauá.

c ☐ O Instituto de Desenvolvimento Sustentável Mamirauá foi contratado pelo Ministério da Ciência, Tecnologia e Inovação para criar a reserva Mamirauá.

d ☐ A Sociedade Civil Mamirauá se dedica prioritariamente à captação de recursos para pesquisas feitas pelo Instituto de Desenvolvimento Sustentável Mamirauá.

e ☐ Sociedade Civil Mamirauá e Instituto de Desenvolvimento Sustentável Mamirauá são dois nomes diferentes de uma mesma instituição.

"The legal system can force open doors and sometimes even knock down walls. But it cannot build bridges. That job belongs to you and me."

Justice Thurgood Marshall

Disponível em <www.upenn.edu/pennpress/book/toc/13833.html>. Acesso em 2 de março de 2016.

Habilidades

H5: Associar vocábulos e expressões de um texto em LEM ao seu tema.

H6: Utilizar os conhecimentos da LEM e de seus mecanismos como meio de ampliar as possibilidades de acesso a informações, tecnologias e culturas.

H7: Relacionar, em um texto em LEM, as estruturas linguísticas, sua função e seu uso social.

H8: Reconhecer a importância da produção cultural em LEM como representação da diversidade cultural e linguística.

Thurgood Marshall foi o primeiro negro a ser juiz da Suprema Corte norte-americana, em 1967. Defensor do movimento dos direitos civis, disse, ao receber a Medalha da Liberdade em 1992, as palavras imortalizadas no Virginia Civil Rights Memorial. Qual ideia abaixo mais se alinha à sua fala?

a ☐ O sistema judiciário é capaz de ajudar as pessoas a se unir por um objetivo comum, mesmo contra a vontade de alguns.

b ☐ Apenas as atitudes das pessoas podem abrir portas e derrubar barreiras. O sistema judiciário não é capaz de fazer isso.

c ☐ O sistema judiciário não pode forçar as pessoas a se unir contra a segregação ou o preconceito.

d ☐ O sistema judiciário pode garantir a aplicação da lei, mas cabe às pessoas colocar em prática a dessegregação.

e ☐ Abrir portas, derrubar paredes e construir pontes são atribuições fundamentais do sistema judiciário.

BIOGRAPHY

João Carlos
Martins
Pianist, Conductor

Born: June 25, 1940, São Paulo, Brazil

[...]

Between 1979 and 1998, João Carlos Martins devoted himself to recording J. S. Bach's complete works for keyboard [...]. Following a recording session in Sofia in 1995, he was beaten senseless by two Bulgarian thugs. He received injuries to his skull and brain, causing the loss of use of his right arm. Therapy and biofeedback in the next few years brought back much movement. In 1996 he returned to the concert stage with an appearance at New York's Carnegie Hall. But an operation in early 2000 rendered his hand essentially useless. Instead of retiring completely from the piano, Martins turned to recording the complete repertoire for the left hand. The series began with a disc of Ravel's concerto, Camille Saint-Saëns' Etudes, and Johannes Brahms' transcription of the J. S. Bach Chaconne in June 2001.

Disponível em <www.bach-cantatas.com/Bio/Martins-Joao-Carlos.htm>. Acesso em 20 de abril de 2016.

Habilidades

H5: Associar vocábulos e expressões de um texto em LEM ao seu tema.

H6: Utilizar os conhecimentos da LEM e de seus mecanismos como meio de ampliar as possibilidades de acesso a informações, tecnologias e culturas.

Biografias geralmente destacam os momentos mais importantes da vida de personalidades notáveis. No caso de João Carlos Martins, esses momentos são marcados...

a ☐ pelo constante embate entre a vida e a morte e pela maneira como isso é representado em sua arte.

b ☐ pela violência urbana com a qual pessoas que seguem a carreira artística muitas vezes sofrem.

c ☐ pelo uso da música como meio de buscar soluções para os problemas físicos enfrentados por ele.

d ☐ pela influência e colaboração de artistas búlgaros em projetos relacionados à música de Bach.

e ☐ por uma autodeterminação irrefreável que o motiva a superar os mais diversos obstáculos.

A SOCIAL NEUROSCIENCE PERSPECTIVE ON
ADOLESCENT
RISK-TAKING

The teen years are a time of intense brain changes. Interestingly, two of the primary brain functions develop at different rates. Recent brain research indicates that the part of the brain that perceives rewards from risk, the limbic system, kicks into high gear in early adolescence. The part of the brain that controls impulses and engages in longer-term perspective, the frontal lobes, matures later. This may explain why teens in mid-adolescence take more risks than older teens. As the frontal lobes become more developed, two things happen. First, self-control develops as teens are better able to assess cause and effect. Second, more areas of the brain become involved in processing emotions, and teens become better at accurately interpreting others' emotions.

Disponível em <www.jhsph.edu/research/centers-and-institutes/center-for-adolescent-health/_includes/Interactive%20Guide.pdf>.
Acesso em 21 de abril de 2016.

Habilidades

H5: Associar vocábulos e expressões de um texto em LEM ao seu tema.

H6: Utilizar os conhecimentos da LEM e de seus mecanismos como meio de ampliar as possibilidades de acesso a informações, tecnologias e culturas.

O comportamento de adolescentes é tema de diversos estudos científicos. Baseando-se nos dados apresentados pelo texto, é correto afirmar que...

a ☐ o sistema límbico se desenvolve antes dos lóbulos frontais, o que leva adolescentes mais jovens a se arriscar mais.

b ☐ adolescentes mais novos se arriscam menos devido ao controle dos impulsos exercido pelo sistema límbico.

c ☐ a capacidade de compreender relações de causa e efeito aumenta quando o sistema límbico para de crescer.

d ☐ o desenvolvimento dos lóbulos frontais causa nos adolescentes dificuldades em lidar com suas emoções.

e ☐ o autocontrole e a percepção dos sentimentos alheios não caracterizam o comportamento adolescente de forma geral.

THE STEM CELL DEBATE: IS IT OVER?

Stem cell therapies are not new. Doctors have been performing bone marrow stem cell transplants for decades. But when scientists learned how to remove stem cells from human embryos in 1998, both excitement and controversy ensued.

The excitement was due to the huge potential these cells have for curing human disease. The controversy centered on the moral implications of destroying human embryos. Political leaders began to debate over how to regulate and fund research involving human embryonic stem (hES) cells.

Newer breakthroughs may bring this debate to an end. In 2006 scientists learned how to stimulate a patient's own cells to behave like embryonic stem cells. These cells are reducing the need for human embryos in research and opening up exciting new possibilities for stem cell therapies.

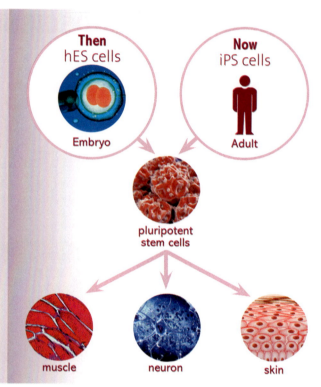

Disponível em <http://learn.genetics.utah.edu/content/stemcells/scissues>. Acesso em 5 de julho de 2015.

Habilidades

H5: Associar vocábulos e expressões de um texto em LEM ao seu tema.

H6: Utilizar os conhecimentos da LEM e de seus mecanismos como meio de ampliar as possibilidades de acesso a informações, tecnologias e culturas.

Até recentemente, os cientistas conseguiam usar células-tronco pluripotentes apenas se as extraíssem de um embrião, suscitando debates morais, religiosos e ideológicos. Que desenvolvimento pode pôr fim a esses debates?

a ☐ Os cientistas finalmente conseguiram usar células-tronco de embriões para a realização de transplantes de medula.

b ☐ As células-tronco passaram a ser utilizadas para curar doenças, o que minimiza as chances de destruição de embriões.

c ☐ Os cientistas passaram a retirar células-tronco de embriões sem precisar destruí-los.

d ☐ As células de um paciente podem agora ser estimuladas a se comportar como células-tronco embrionárias.

e ☐ O uso de embriões não é mais necessário, pois os cientistas passaram a transplantar células-tronco de medulas ósseas.

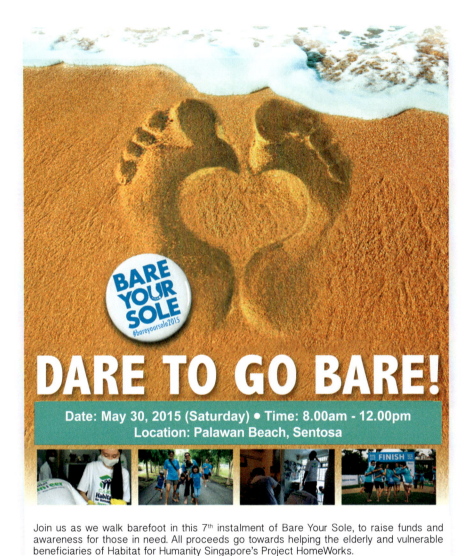

Join us as we walk barefoot in this 7th instalment of Bare Your Sole, to raise funds and awareness for those in need. All proceeds go towards helping the elderly and vulnerable beneficiaries of Habitat for Humanity Singapore's Project HomeWorks.

Find out more and register at www.bareyoursole.org.sg today! Food, music, games and entertainment will be available from 8am.

Disponível em <www.give2habitat.org/singapore/bys2015>. Acesso em 6 de julho de 2015.

Habilidades

H5: Associar vocábulos e expressões de um texto em LEM ao seu tema.

H6: Utilizar os conhecimentos da LEM e de seus mecanismos como meio de ampliar as possibilidades de acesso a informações, tecnologias e culturas.

H7: Relacionar, em um texto em LEM, as estruturas linguísticas, sua função e seu uso social.

H8: Reconhecer a importância da produção cultural em LEM como representação da diversidade cultural e linguística.

A iniciativa Bare Your Sole, organizada pela Habitat for Humanity Singapore, destina-se a...

a ☐ convidar as pessoas a andar descalças e observar como esse hábito pode afetar sua saúde.

b ☐ angariar recursos para pessoas idosas e em situação de vulnerabilidade em Cingapura.

c ☐ organizar eventos nas praias de Cingapura com comida, música, jogos e entretenimento.

d ☐ promover pela primeira vez uma caminhada em que os participantes devem andar descalços.

e ☐ solicitar a doação de sapatos para pessoas desassistidas por programas governamentais.

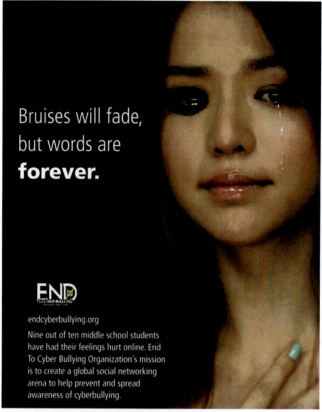

Bruises will fade,
but words are
forever.

END
TO CYBER BULLYING
ORGANIZATION

endcyberbullying.org
Nine out of ten middle school students
have had their feelings hurt online. End
To Cyber Bullying Organization's mission
is to create a global social networking
arena to help prevent and spread
awareness of cyberbullying.

Disponível em <http://cargocollective.com/jindesign/End-to-Cyberbullying-Ad-Campaign>.
Acesso em 21 de abril de 2016.

Habilidades

H5: Associar vocábulos e expressões de um texto em LEM ao seu tema.

H6: Utilizar os conhecimentos da LEM e de seus mecanismos como meio de ampliar as possibilidades de acesso a informações, tecnologias e culturas.

Cyberbullying **é a ação de intimidar ou humilhar alguém persistentemente por mensagens de texto, pela internet ou por outro meio de comunicação eletrônico. Em vista disso, a organização End To Cyber Bullying objetiva...**

a ☐ mostrar que nove entre dez jovens foram agredidos fisicamente por pessoas que conheceram *online*.

b ☐ identificar nove entre dez jovens que praticam *cyberbullying* contra alunos da Educação Básica.

c ☐ eliminar completamente a prática de *cyberbullying* nas redes sociais por meio de ações educativas.

d ☐ criar uma comunidade mundial para ajudar na conscientização sobre o *cyberbullying* e em sua prevenção.

e ☐ expor pessoas que tenham ajudado a disseminar o *cyberbullying* contra alunos da Educação Básica.

On Marriage

Khalil Gibran

Love one another, but make not a bond of love:
Let it rather be a moving sea between the shores of your souls.
Fill each other's cup but drink not from one cup.
Give one another of your bread but eat not from the same loaf.
Sing and dance together and be joyous, but let each one of you be alone,
Even as the strings of a lute are alone though they quiver with the same music.

Give your hearts, but not into each other's keeping.
For only the hand of Life can contain your hearts.
And stand together yet not too near together:
For the pillars of the temple stand apart,
And the oak tree and the cypress grow not in each other's shadow.

GIBRAN, K. On Marriage. *The Prophet*. New York: Alfred A. Knopf, Inc., 2001, p. 15-16.

Habilidades

H5: Associar vocábulos e expressões de um texto em LEM ao seu tema.
H7: Relacionar, em um texto em LEM, as estruturas linguísticas, sua função e seu uso social.
H8: Reconhecer a importância da produção cultural em LEM como representação da diversidade cultural e linguística.

Em seu livro *O profeta*, Khalil Gibran discorre sobre vários aspectos da vida, inclusive os relacionamentos afetivos. A esse respeito, o texto acima, repleto de metáforas, leva o leitor a considerar que...

a ☐ duas pessoas em um relacionamento amoroso devem compartilhar tudo o que têm e manter-se o mais próximas possível.

b ☐ não se deve abrir o coração para outra pessoa nem ficar muito preso a ela, pois isso pode gerar muito sofrimento.

c ☐ uma pessoa precisa manter sua individualidade mesmo quando está envolvida em um relacionamento amoroso.

d ☐ duas pessoas apaixonadas devem sempre estar juntas, divertir-se e dançar, aproveitando os bons momentos da vida.

e ☐ relacionamentos amorosos são semelhantes aos pilares de um templo e às árvores que crescem na natureza.

Benjamin felt a nose nuzzling at his shoulder. He looked round. It was Clover. Her old eyes looked dimmer than ever. Without saying anything, she tugged gently at his mane and led him round to the end of the big barn, where the Seven Commandments were written. For a minute or two they stood gazing at the tatted wall with its white lettering.

"My sight is failing," she said finally. "Even when I was young I could not have read what was written there. But it appears to me that that wall looks different. Are the Seven Commandments the same as they used to be, Benjamin?"

For once Benjamin consented to break his rule, and he read out to her what was written on the wall. There was nothing there now except a single Commandment. It ran:

ALL ANIMALS ARE EQUAL

BUT SOME ANIMALS ARE MORE EQUAL

THAN OTHERS

Chapter X

ORWELL, G. *Animal Farm.* New York: Signet Classics, 2012, p. 108-109.

Habilidades

H5: Associar vocábulos e expressões de um texto em LEM ao seu tema.

H7: Relacionar, em um texto em LEM, as estruturas linguísticas, sua função e seu uso social.

George Orwell usou alegorias em seu livro *A revolução dos bichos* para denunciar governos autoritários. Qual das alternativas melhor descreve o trecho acima?

a ☐ Sete mandamentos foram resumidos em apenas um, que defende a igualdade incondicional de todos os animais.

b ☐ Sete mandamentos foram reduzidos a somente um, e este garante, por meio de um jogo de palavras, o poder para apenas alguns animais.

c ☐ A idade e a visão embaçada impedem que Benjamin tenha certeza de que as regras mudaram sem que ele soubesse.

d ☐ Benjamin e Clover são velhos amigos que discordam sobre as alterações que precisam ser feitas aos sete mandamentos.

e ☐ Benjamin procura Clover para que ela o ajude a desvendar quem foi responsável pela alteração dos sete mandamentos.

WATER CONSERVATION
as a Way of Life

Also as a reminder, the state has mandated that we all comply with the following four prohibited activities:

1. Outdoor irrigation that causes run-off such that water flows onto adjacent property, non-irrigated areas, private and public walkways, roadways, parking lots or structures.

2. Using a hose to wash an automobile unless the hose has an automatic shut off nozzle.

3. Application of water to any hard surface including but not limited to driveways, sidewalks and asphalt.

4. Using potable water in a fountain or decorative water feature unless the feature has a recirculating system.

As California continues to face extreme drought conditions, it is important we do our part to conserve water.

Here are several tips on saving water and decreasing your water bill:

Find leaks and fix them. Check your water meter and examine faucet gaskets and pipe fittings.

Keep a container of drinking water in the refrigerator instead of running the tap.

Wash only full loads in both dishwasher and washing machines.

Wash fruits and vegetables in a basin instead of running water from the tap.

Turn the water off when brushing teeth or shaving.

Collect the water you use from washing fruits and vegetables and use it for your plants.

Avoid water run-off at any time.

UPPER SAN GABRIEL VALLEY
MUNICIPAL WATER DISTRICT

Disponível em <www.ci.el-monte.ca.us/LinkClick.aspx?fileticket=SI4KLf5Kmss%3d&tabid=718>. Acesso em 22 de abril de 2016.

Habilidades

H5: Associar vocábulos e expressões de um texto em LEM ao seu tema.

H6: Utilizar os conhecimentos da LEM e de seus mecanismos como meio de ampliar as possibilidades de acesso a informações, tecnologias e culturas.

H7: Relacionar, em um texto em LEM, as estruturas linguísticas, sua função e seu uso social.

A água é um recurso finito, o que nos obriga a consumi-la de forma consciente. Qual das alternativas abaixo corresponde ao que é expresso na campanha californiana para economizar água?

a ☐ Utilize a água da lavagem de frutas e vegetais para lavar a louça.

b ☐ Sempre tome água em copos, e não diretamente da torneira.

c ☐ Nunca use a mangueira para lavar seu automóvel.

d ☐ É proibido ter fontes decorativas e lavar calçadas.

e ☐ Use máquinas de lavar roupa e louça em sua capacidade total.

4 • The Power of Myth

[...]

MOYERS: I came to understand from reading your books – *The Masks of God* or *The Hero with a Thousand Faces*, for example – that what human beings have in common is revealed in myths. Myths are stories of our search through the ages for truth, for meaning, for significance. We all need to tell our story and to understand our story. We all need to understand death and to cope with death, and we all need help in our passages from birth to life and then to death. We need for life to signify, to touch the eternal, to understand the mysterious, to find out who we are.

CAMPBELL: People say that what we're all seeking is a meaning for life. I don't think that's what we're really seeking. I think that what we're seeking is an experience of being alive, so that our life experiences on the purely physical plane will have resonances within our own innermost being and reality, so that we actually feel the rapture of being alive. That's what it's all finally about, and that's what these clues help us to find within ourselves.

[...]

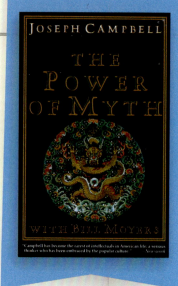

CAMPBELL, J.; MOYERS, B. *The Power of Myth*. New York: Anchor Books, 1991, p. 4-5.

Habilidades

H5: Associar vocábulos e expressões de um texto em LEM ao seu tema.

H6: Utilizar os conhecimentos da LEM e de seus mecanismos como meio de ampliar as possibilidades de acesso a informações, tecnologias e culturas.

H7: Relacionar, em um texto em LEM, as estruturas linguísticas, sua função e seu uso social.

***O poder do mito* é um livro editado a partir de uma entrevista do jornalista Bill Moyers com o escritor e palestrante Joseph Campbell. Tendo como base o trecho acima, é possível afirmar que...**

a ☐ Moyers e Campbell concordam que o ser humano busca um sentido para a vida e que esse sentido está revelado nos mitos.

b ☐ Moyers e Campbell discordam sobre aspectos fundamentais dos mitos, como sua importância para eventos como o nascimento e a morte.

c ☐ Moyers pensa que todos precisamos de ajuda para aceitar a existência de mitos sobre o nascimento e a morte.

d ☐ para Campbell, a plenitude da vida é uma experiência exclusivamente física, centrada no aspecto material da existência.

e ☐ na opinião de Campbell, os mitos nos ajudam a conciliar nossa existência material com nosso mundo interior.

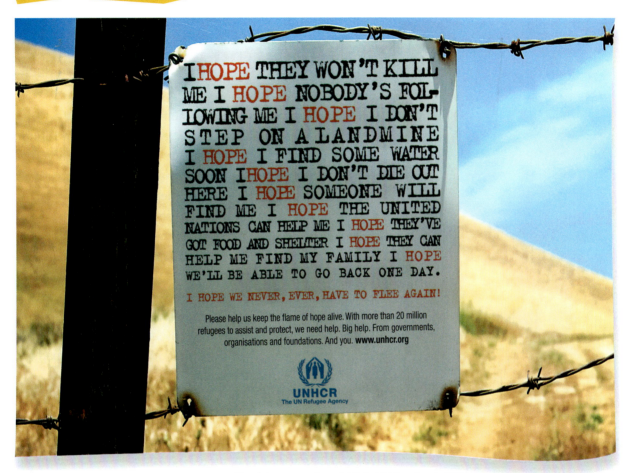

Disponível em <www.unhcr.org/cgi-bin/texis/vtx/home/opendocPDFViewer.html?docid=462dcfa22&query=posters>.
Acesso em 22 de abril de 2016.

Habilidades

H5: Associar vocábulos e expressões de um texto em LEM ao seu tema.

H6: Utilizar os conhecimentos da LEM e de seus mecanismos como meio de ampliar as possibilidades de acesso a informações, tecnologias e culturas.

H7: Relacionar, em um texto em LEM, as estruturas linguísticas, sua função e seu uso social.

H8: Reconhecer a importância da produção cultural em LEM como representação da diversidade cultural e linguística.

Cartazes devem ser chamativos e ter uma linguagem direta. Com esse objetivo, o cartaz da Agência da ONU para Refugiados (Acnur) reproduz enfaticamente o pensamento de uma pessoa. Esse indivíduo...

a ☐ é um refugiado que está escapando de uma região de conflito e sente medo.

b ☐ é um soldado que está indo para uma região de conflito ajudar refugiados.

c ☐ é alguém que está feliz em migrar para outro país por um futuro melhor.

d ☐ está sob ameaça de morte e nunca mais verá sua terra natal e sua família.

e ☐ perdeu as esperanças de ser ajudado e não vê mais meios de sobreviver.

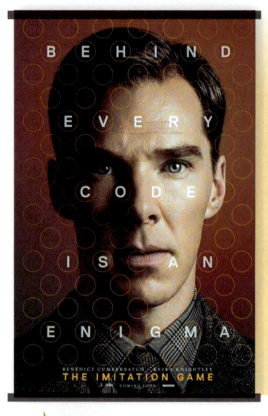

The Imitation Game
📽 2014

During the winter of 1952, British authorities entered the home of mathematician, cryptanalyst and war hero Alan Turing (Benedict Cumberbatch) to investigate a reported burglary. They instead ended up arresting Turing himself on charges of "gross indecency", an accusation that would lead to his devastating conviction for the criminal offense of homosexuality – little did officials know, they were actually incriminating the pioneer of modern-day computing. Famously leading a motley group of scholars, linguists, chess champions and intelligence officers, he was credited with cracking the so-called unbreakable codes of Germany's World War II Enigma machine. An intense and haunting portrayal of a brilliant, complicated man, *The Imitation Game* follows a genius who under nail-biting pressure helped to shorten the war and, in turn, save thousands of lives.

Disponível em <www.rottentomatoes.com/m/the_imitation_game>. Acesso em 22 de abril de 2016.

Habilidades

H5: Associar vocábulos e expressões de um texto em LEM ao seu tema.

H6: Utilizar os conhecimentos da LEM e de seus mecanismos como meio de ampliar as possibilidades de acesso a informações, tecnologias e culturas.

Resenhas de filme procuram informar o leitor a respeito das histórias contadas por essas obras. O filme *O jogo da imitação* se baseia na biografia de Alan Turing, controverso matemático inglês, e inclui aspectos como...

a ☐ sua contribuição para desvendar códigos alemães durante a Segunda Guerra Mundial, salvando milhares de vidas.

b ☐ sua tendência a cometer pequenos roubos, o que lhe causou problemas legais junto à polícia inglesa.

c ☐ sua investigação e prisão devido às ofensas e atitudes indecentes que cometeu contra homossexuais.

d ☐ a forma como motivou intelectuais, linguistas e campeões de xadrez a criar a máquina chamada Enigma.

e ☐ a pressão sofrida por policiais ingleses por prenderem, após inúmeras tentativas, o criador dos computadores atuais.

• INDUSTRY •

How Can We End Child Labor in the Fields? Pay Farmers Better

A few weeks ago a request for internal documents from the chocolate giant Hershey's Co moved forward, with a judge ruling that the company will have to share confidential information with its shareholders. The Louisiana Municipal Police Employees' Retirement System brought legal action against the company in 2012, asserting that the company knowingly bought cocoa from areas plagued with child labor issues.

Even though Hershey's is the company targeted in the lawsuit, human rights abuses like child labor are still rampant throughout the food supply chain. Although companies like Mars or Nestlé now publicly discuss child labor in their supply chains, these issues are unlikely to go away when these same companies rely upon cheap land and labor to operate. […]

Disponível em <www.forbes.com/sites/bethhoffman/2014/04/08/how-can-we-end-child-labor-in-the-fields-pay-farmers-better>.
Acesso em 22 de abril de 2016.

Habilidades

H5: Associar vocábulos e expressões de um texto em LEM ao seu tema.
H6: Utilizar os conhecimentos da LEM e de seus mecanismos como meio de ampliar as possibilidades de acesso a informações, tecnologias e culturas.

Revistas impressas ou *online* procuram relatar e analisar fatos correntes. No texto acima, publicado pela revista *Forbes*, comenta-se que...

a ☐ empresas alimentícias continuarão se confrontando com o trabalho infantil se mantiverem a utilização de mão de obra barata.

b ☐ há provas de que a Hershey's sabia do emprego de mão de obra infantil em sua linha de produção na Louisiana.

c ☐ a Hershey's precisou recorrer a documentos confidenciais para provar sua inocência em uma ação pública.

d ☐ comprar cacau de fazendas que empregam mão de obra infantil é prática corriqueira de empresas como Hershey's, Mars e Nestlé.

e ☐ um juiz recentemente sentenciou a Hershey's a compartilhar documentos confidenciais de 2012 com seus consumidores.

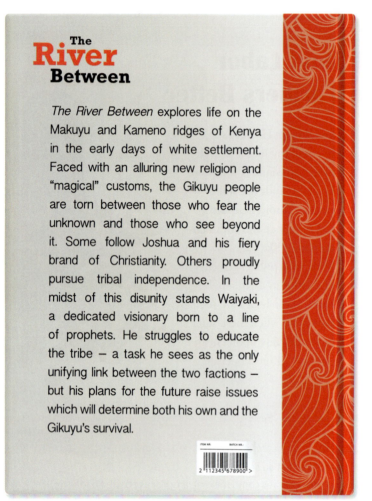

The River Between

The River Between explores life on the Makuyu and Kameno ridges of Kenya in the early days of white settlement. Faced with an alluring new religion and "magical" customs, the Gikuyu people are torn between those who fear the unknown and those who see beyond it. Some follow Joshua and his fiery brand of Christianity. Others proudly pursue tribal independence. In the midst of this disunity stands Waiyaki, a dedicated visionary born to a line of prophets. He struggles to educate the tribe — a task he sees as the only unifying link between the two factions — but his plans for the future raise issues which will determine both his own and the Gikuyu's survival.

THIONG'O, N. *The River Between*. Portsmouth: Heinemann, 1989.

Habilidades

H5: Associar vocábulos e expressões de um texto em LEM ao seu tema.

H6: Utilizar os conhecimentos da LEM e de seus mecanismos como meio de ampliar as possibilidades de acesso a informações, tecnologias e culturas.

H8: Reconhecer a importância da produção cultural em LEM como representação da diversidade cultural e linguística.

A quarta capa de um livro geralmente traz um panorama da obra, que visa atrair um possível leitor. Qual informação é possível obter a partir da leitura da quarta capa acima?

a ☐ O livro explora a vida e a cultura dos negros no Quênia antes da chegada dos colonizadores brancos.

b ☐ Waiyaki defende a educação como instrumento de união em meio a um embate entre o cristianismo e a independência tribal.

c ☐ O foco da obra é mostrar os fatos históricos que marcaram a imposição do cristianismo no Quênia.

d ☐ O livro é uma biografia de Waiyaki, filho de profetas que lutou contra a influência do cristianismo.

e ☐ A luta pela educação de um povo muitas vezes levanta questões intrinsicamente atreladas a crenças religiosas.

Online growth in 2014

During 2014, the whole Paralympic Movement enjoyed phenomenal online growth, here are a few facts for you to digest.

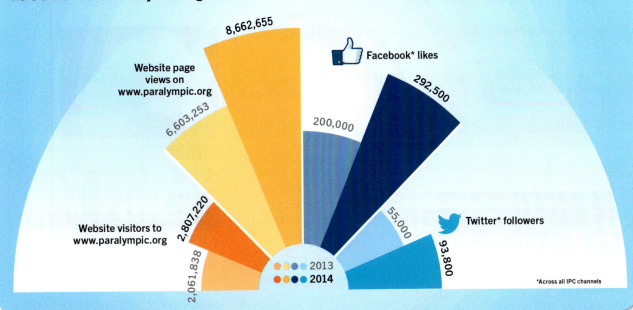

Disponível em <http://paralympics.uberflip.com/i/493093-the-paralympian-issue-no-1-2015>.
Acesso em 23 de abril de 2016.

Habilidades

H5: Associar vocábulos e expressões de um texto em LEM ao seu tema.
H6: Utilizar os conhecimentos da LEM e de seus mecanismos como meio de ampliar as possibilidades de acesso a informações, tecnologias e culturas.

Gráficos geralmente são usados para apresentar informações de forma clara e objetiva. Com base no gráfico sobre o crescimento *online* do Movimento Paralímpico em 2014, é possível inferir que...

a ☐ o número de curtidas na página do movimento no Facebook praticamente dobrou em relação a 2013.

b ☐ o aumento dos visitantes ao *site* www.paralympic.org foi maior que o do número de visitas em termos absolutos.

c ☐ em 2014 o Facebook foi o meio eletrônico mais utilizado para divulgar o Movimento Paralímpico.

d ☐ o gráfico compara visitas ao *site* do movimento com visitas às suas páginas no Facebook e no Twitter.

e ☐ vários internautas visitam mais de uma página dentro do *site* do Movimento Paralímpico.

New Documentary Puts Beauty in Spotlight

Emmy-nominated director Joanna Rudnick has a new documentary that aims to challenge society's notions of beauty and inclusiveness.

The film, *On Beauty*, follows photographer Rick Guidotti as he seeks to redefine beauty through a series of photos portraying people with genetic, physical and behavioral conditions that many would think excludes them from the world of modeling and fashion. [...]

Guidotti had previously been a fashion photographer [...]. He explains that he became jaded with the lack of inclusiveness and narrow perceptions of the fashion industry. "As an artist, I don't just see beauty on the covers of magazines," says Guidotti. "I see beauty everywhere."

[...]

Upon researching albinism and other genetic conditions, Guidotti was able to find only "images of sadness." The photographer says the pictures he found were dehumanizing and often exploitative: "I couldn't find one positive image of a person with albinism."

When used in the right way, Guidotti believes, photography can be empowering and a tool for social progress.

[...]

Guidotti wants the film to be an agent for social change, encouraging discourse on society's perceptions of beauty and normality. "It's going to go to every classroom nationwide, and it's going to introduce this notion of diversity," he says. [...]

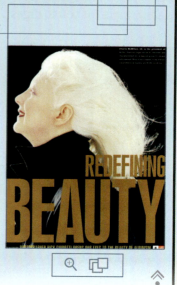

Disponível em <www.newsweek.com/new-documentary-puts-beauty-spotlight-356720>. Acesso em 23 de abril de 2016.

Habilidades

H5: Associar vocábulos e expressões de um texto em LEM ao seu tema.

H6: Utilizar os conhecimentos da LEM e de seus mecanismos como meio de ampliar as possibilidades de acesso a informações, tecnologias e culturas.

H8: Reconhecer a importância da produção cultural em LEM como representação da diversidade cultural e linguística.

Rick Guidotti é um fotógrafo cujo trabalho é documentado no filme *On Beauty*, dirigido por Joanna Rudnick. Um dos objetivos desse documentário é...

a ☐ defender a publicação de novas imagens de pessoas albinas em livros didáticos, retratando a beleza no diferente.

b ☐ empoderar instituições para que divulguem uma imagem positiva de pessoas com disfunções genéticas.

c ☐ problematizar os padrões de beleza de nossa sociedade para promover as noções de inclusão e diversidade.

d ☐ contestar os atuais padrões de magreza instituídos e promovidos pela indústria da moda no cinema.

e ☐ difundir diferentes percepções de beleza nas escolas para que crianças acima do peso não sofram preconceito.

Q: How much will the Earth warm if emissions of greenhouse gases continue to rise?

A: If humans continue to emit greenhouse gases at or above the current pace, we will probably see an average global temperature increase of 3 to 7° F by 2100, and greater warming after that. Temperatures in some parts of the globe (e.g., over land and in the polar regions) are expected to rise even more.

Even if we were to drastically reduce greenhouse gas emissions, returning them to year 2000 levels and holding them constant, the Earth would still warm about 1° F over the next 100 years. This is due to the long lifetime of many greenhouse gases and the slow cycling of heat from the ocean to the atmosphere.

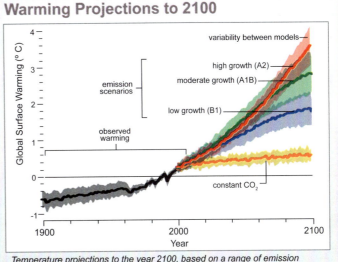

Warming Projections to 2100

Temperature projections to the year 2100, based on a range of emission scenarios and global climate models. Scenarios that assume the highest growth in greenhouse gas emissions provide the estimates in the top end of the temperature range. The orange line ("constant CO_2") projects global temperatures with greenhouse gas concentrations stabilized at year 2000 levels. Source: NASA (adapted from IPCC, 2007)

Disponível em <www.epa.gov/climatechange/Downloads/wycd/Climate_Basics.pdf>. Acesso em 23 de abril de 2016.

Habilidades

H5: Associar vocábulos e expressões de um texto em LEM ao seu tema.

H6: Utilizar os conhecimentos da LEM e de seus mecanismos como meio de ampliar as possibilidades de acesso a informações, tecnologias e culturas.

H7: Relacionar, em um texto em LEM, as estruturas linguísticas, sua função e seu uso social.

A EPA é um órgão governamental norte-americano responsável pela proteção ao meio ambiente. Que informação é possível depreender do trecho acima, retirado de sua cartilha "Frequently Asked Questions about Global Warming and Climate Change: Back to Basics"?

a ☐ Mesmo que as emissões de CO_2 fossem reduzidas aos níveis do ano 2000, continuaríamos testemunhando um aumento na temperatura média do planeta.

b ☐ Em um cenário de baixa elevação na emissão de CO_2, pode-se estimar um aumento na temperatura global de mais de 2 °C até o ano de 2100.

c ☐ Caso a emissão de poluentes continue aumentando no ritmo que se observa hoje, pode--se prever um aumento na temperatura global de até 7 °C até 2100.

d ☐ Se a emissão de poluentes se mantiver no ritmo atual, as temperaturas globais aumentarão de 3 a 7 °F até 2100, quando finalmente irão se estabilizar.

e ☐ Devido ao lento ciclo de resfriamento dos oceanos, qualquer cenário futuro aponta para um aumento da temperatura global de pelo menos 4 °C até 2100.

The Ainu: Reviving the Indigenous Spirit of Japan

[...]

The Ainu people are historically residents of parts of Hokkaido (the northern island of Japan), the Kuril Islands, and Sakhalin. According to the government, there are currently 25,000 Ainu living in Japan, but other sources claim there are up to 200,000. The origin of the Ainu people and language is, for the most part, unknown. [...]

During the Tokugawa Period (1600–1868) the Ainu [...] were able to maintain their culture and way of life to a certain extent, although there is some evidence that the Ainu became slaves.

However, the Meiji restoration brought great change upon the Ainu people in 1899. As Japan began reforming to Western standards, the government decided to unify Japan, [...] creating a law that restricted the Ainu from participating in their own cultural activities. [...] It wasn't until 1997 that this law was lifted and the Ainu people were allowed to practice their own customs again [...].

It seems that while there is still some discrimination of the Ainu people, those who rejected their heritage before are beginning to admit it openly or even embrace their identity with pride. [...]

These days, young Ainu [...] are doing their best to create a new identity for their people and a Japan more open to minorities. [...]

Disponível em <www.tofugu.com/japan/ainu-japan>. Acesso em 23 de abril de 2016.

Habilidades

H5: Associar vocábulos e expressões de um texto em LEM ao seu tema.

H6: Utilizar os conhecimentos da LEM e de seus mecanismos como meio de ampliar as possibilidades de acesso a informações, tecnologias e culturas.

Os ainus são um grupo indígena japonês que se distingue do restante da população do país por suas características culturais e até físicas. De acordo com o texto acima, pode-se afirmar que esse povo...

a ☐ sempre pôde manter sua cultura e seu estilo de vida, mesmo quando algumas etnias foram escravizadas.

b ☐ manteve vivas suas tradições até 1997, quando seus membros foram proibidos de realizar determinados rituais.

c ☐ não busca se expressar culturalmente devido à discriminação que sofre dos japoneses de outras etnias.

d ☐ foi proibido de participar de algumas de suas manifestações culturais quando o governo decidiu unificar o Japão.

e ☐ tem recriado sua própria identidade, mesclando elementos da cultura japonesa a outros da cultura ocidental.

The Museum of the Person

by Karen Worcman

Director and cofounder of the Museum of the Person, São Paulo, Brazil

[...]
The Museum of the Person was founded in São Paulo, Brazil, in 1991. Its aim is to record, preserve and transform into information life stories of any and every person in society, thus bringing about social change through valorising individuals and communities. Today, it has 4,000 texts and over 10,000 photographs in digital format from personal collections – collected during projects, events, open sessions to record statements, as well as stories received through the Internet.

From its inception, the Museum of the Person aimed to establish a virtual network of life stories. The idea of building a museum of life stories led us to reconsider the notion of "space", since people are innumerable and stories intangible. At first, we thought we would establish a multimedia databank and disseminate information on CD-ROM. As the Internet became increasingly popular, our project expanded. Besides guaranteeing access to the collection, the Internet is now the tool that allows people to be not only receivers of information, but also to become agents of their own history. Through the Internet, individuals and groups become part of a larger community. Their histories are no longer solely theirs and become part of collective memory. A memory pervaded by multiple voices, including histories of people from all sectors of society.
[...]

Disponível em <http://icom.museum/fileadmin/user_upload/pdf/ICOM_News/2004-3/ENG/p4b_2004-3.pdf>. Acesso em 23 de abril de 2016.

Habilidades

H5: Associar vocábulos e expressões de um texto em LEM ao seu tema.

H6: Utilizar os conhecimentos da LEM e de seus mecanismos como meio de ampliar as possibilidades de acesso a informações, tecnologias e culturas.

Com base nas palavras de Karen Worcman, diretora do Museu da Pessoa, é possível afirmar que...

a embora tivesse o intuito de ser um museu virtual, o Museu da Pessoa nunca conseguiu cumprir esse objetivo, pois surgiu antes do advento da internet.

b o objetivo do Museu da Pessoa atualmente é construir uma sede física para abrigar seu acervo de 4.000 textos e mais de 10.000 fotografias.

c o Museu da Pessoa foi criado inicialmente para registrar histórias de vida, mas posteriormente passou a visar à criação de uma rede virtual para unir pessoas.

d tendo em vista sua proposta de registrar as intangíveis histórias de vida de inúmeras pessoas, o museu precisou repensar a noção de espaço.

e os objetivos iniciais do Museu da Pessoa de catalogar e divulgar histórias pessoais em CD-ROM foram prejudicados com o advento da internet.

ENEM Practice 23

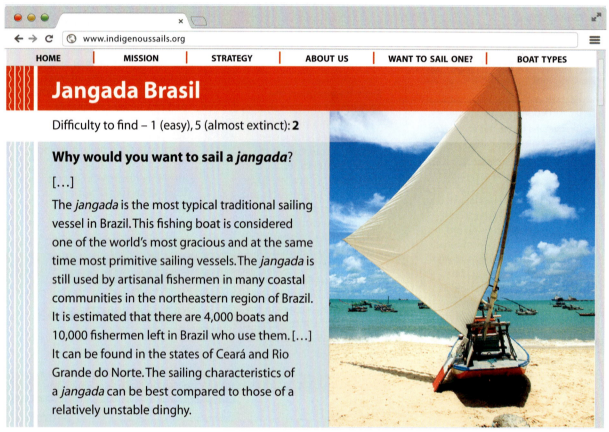

← → C 🌐 www.indigenoussails.org   ☰

| HOME | MISSION | STRATEGY | ABOUT US | WANT TO SAIL ONE? | BOAT TYPES |

Jangada Brasil

Difficulty to find – 1 (easy), 5 (almost extinct): **2**

Why would you want to sail a *jangada*?

[…]

The *jangada* is the most typical traditional sailing vessel in Brazil. This fishing boat is considered one of the world's most gracious and at the same time most primitive sailing vessels. The *jangada* is still used by artisanal fishermen in many coastal communities in the northeastern region of Brazil. It is estimated that there are 4,000 boats and 10,000 fishermen left in Brazil who use them. […] It can be found in the states of Ceará and Rio Grande do Norte. The sailing characteristics of a *jangada* can be best compared to those of a relatively unstable dinghy.

Disponível em <www.indigenoussails.org/boat-types/jangada-brasil>. Acesso em 23 de abril de 2016.

Habilidades

H5: Associar vocábulos e expressões de um texto em LEM ao seu tema.

H6: Utilizar os conhecimentos da LEM e de seus mecanismos como meio de ampliar as possibilidades de acesso a informações, tecnologias e culturas.

Com base nas informações apresentadas no *site* acima, pode-se afirmar que as jangadas...

a ☐ são raramente empregadas por pescadores hoje em dia, por serem embarcações mais tradicionais.

b ☐ são utilizadas atualmente por 4.000 pescadores nos estados do Ceará e do Rio Grande do Norte.

c ☐ são usadas por cerca de 10.000 pescadores no Brasil, sobretudo no litoral da região nordeste.

d ☐ são consideradas as embarcações mais belas dentre as embarcações primitivas para pesca.

e ☐ são mais instáveis que botes em termos de navegabilidade, porém são melhores para a pesca.

South Bay Community College Students Create a Device to Help Boy Bend His Arms

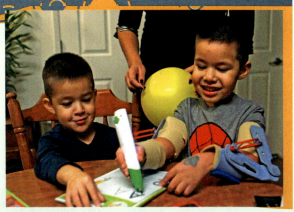

SAN JOSE – Kevin Godines never pictured himself as the kind of guy who could give superhero powers to a little boy – until he met Noel Gaeta.

The 22-year-old Foothill College student and the 4-year-old San Jose boy made an unlikely and life-changing connection through a new community college program that teaches students how to design biomedical devices for children.

Last fall, Godines discovered the fledgling program and set to work on a mission to help Noel bend his arms, something the boy had been unable to do on his own since birth.

Within months, to the delight of Noel's parents and therapists – and Godines himself –, he built a model that worked: twin "exo-arms" made of 3D-printable plastic and elastic bands.

[...]

Now, with his new exo-arms, Noel can write and color. He can pour himself a glass of milk. He can catch himself with his forearms when he falls. But the biggest relief to his mother, Jessica Cuevas, is that he can take off his shoes, get dressed and perform other mundane but essential tasks that will be key to his independence as he grows up.

[...]

Disponível em <www.mercurynews.com/news/ci_29367076/community-college-students-create-device-help-boy-bend>.
Acesso em 23 de abril de 2016.

Habilidades

H5: Associar vocábulos e expressões de um texto em LEM ao seu tema.

H6: Utilizar os conhecimentos da LEM e de seus mecanismos como meio de ampliar as possibilidades de acesso a informações, tecnologias e culturas.

Por meio da criação de um aparelho médico, o estudante Kevin Godines pôde ajudar um menino de 4 anos a dobrar os braços. O que pode ser afirmado sobre o projeto de Godines?

a ☐ Ele faz parte de um programa desenvolvido por uma faculdade para a criação de aparelhos biomédicos para crianças.

b ☐ O aparelho criado pelo estudante foi feito apenas com materiais plásticos descartados por empresas de impressão.

c ☐ O projeto permitiu que o garoto Noel, após a utilização do aparelho, aprendesse a ler, escrever e desenhar.

d ☐ O uso do aparelho desenvolvido por Godines não permite ao usuário se levantar sozinho caso sofra uma queda.

e ☐ Godines se inscreveu para participar do programa porque, quando criança, sonhava em ter poderes de super-heróis.

Before Reading

1 **Discuss the questions below.**

1 What are rainforests?

2 Are they respected and preserved?

RAINFORESTS ARE THE EARTH'S OLDEST LIVING ECOSYSTEMS

A rainforest can be described as a tall, dense jungle that gets a high amount of rainfall per year. Rainforests cover only 6% of the surface of the Earth, yet they contain more than half of the world's plant and animal species. They are all part of a complex system, each species depending on the others to survive. Therefore, the destruction of one can result in the extinction of the others.

Animals of the rainforest occupy specific microenvironments:

EMERGENT LAYER
The tallest trees (45-55 m tall) are the emergents. Sunlight is plentiful up here. Animals found are eagles, monkeys, bats, and butterflies.

CANOPY LAYER
The canopy layer contains the majority of the largest trees (30-45 m tall). Many animals – snakes, toucans, and tree frogs – live in this area since food is abundant.

UNDERSTORY LAYER
Only about 5% of the sunlight reaches this area, so the plants have to grow larger leaves to reach the sunlight. Many animals live here, including birds, snakes, lizards, jaguars, and leopards.

FOREST FLOOR
The forest floor receives only 2% of sunlight. Almost no plants grow in this area; as a result, giant anteaters and tapirs live in this layer.

About 2,000 trees are cut down per minute in the rainforests.

Based on <www.srl.caltech.edu/personnel/krubal/rainforest/Edit560s6/www/whlayers.html>. Accessed on April 15, 2016.

Vocabulary

anteater: tamanduá
bat: morcego
canopy: dossel florestal

eagle: águia
jungle: floresta, selva
layer: camada

lizard: lagarto
rainforest: floresta tropical
snake: cobra

surface: superfície
tapir: anta
tree frog: perereca

After Reading

1 Check the correct alternatives.

Rainforests...

a ☐ cover less than 10% of the surface of the Earth.

b ☐ contain more than 50% of the world's plant and animal species.

c ☐ are dense jungles.

d ☐ are usually located in areas with little sunlight.

e ☐ only have large animals living in it.

f ☐ house specific microenvironments.

2 Check the correct alternative.

1 The tallest trees are located in the...

a ☐ understory layer.   b ☐ emergent layer.

2 The canopy layer...

a ☐ houses bats and monkeys.   b ☐ contains most of the largest trees.

3 Almost no plants grow...

a ☐ on the forest floor.   b ☐ where sunlight is plentiful.

4 Jaguars don't live in the...

a ☐ highest layers.   b ☐ understory layer.

3 Answer the questions.

1 Why do rainforests have this name?

_____

2 Why do many animals live in the canopy layer?

_____

3 Why do very few plants grow on the forest floor?

_____

4 Write the meaning of the words in bold in the sentences below. Use the glossary.

1 Sunlight is **plentiful** up here. _____

2 About 2,000 trees are **cut down** per minute in the rainforests. _____

Before Reading

1 Discuss the questions below.

1 How would you define the idea of online reputation?

2 Are you concerned about your online reputation? Do you think you should be?

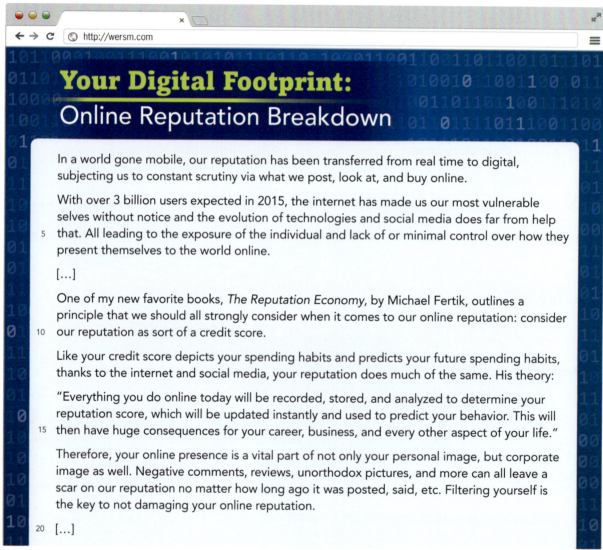

http://wersm.com

Your Digital Footprint:
Online Reputation Breakdown

In a world gone mobile, our reputation has been transferred from real time to digital, subjecting us to constant scrutiny via what we post, look at, and buy online.

With over 3 billion users expected in 2015, the internet has made us our most vulnerable selves without notice and the evolution of technologies and social media does far from help
5 that. All leading to the exposure of the individual and lack of or minimal control over how they present themselves to the world online.

[…]

One of my new favorite books, *The Reputation Economy*, by Michael Fertik, outlines a principle that we should all strongly consider when it comes to our online reputation: consider
10 our reputation as sort of a credit score.

Like your credit score depicts your spending habits and predicts your future spending habits, thanks to the internet and social media, your reputation does much of the same. His theory:

"Everything you do online today will be recorded, stored, and analyzed to determine your reputation score, which will be updated instantly and used to predict your behavior. This will
15 then have huge consequences for your career, business, and every other aspect of your life."

Therefore, your online presence is a vital part of not only your personal image, but corporate image as well. Negative comments, reviews, unorthodox pictures, and more can all leave a scar on our reputation no matter how long ago it was posted, said, etc. Filtering yourself is the key to not damaging your online reputation.

20 […]

Available at <http://wersm.com/your-digital-footprint-online-reputation-breakdown>. Accessed on March 1, 2016.

Vocabulary

breakdown: colapso	**footprint:** pegada	**outline:** descrever	**sort:** tipo
damage: prejudicar	**lack:** falta	**scar:** cicatriz	**store:** guardar, armazenar
depict: retratar, representar	**lead to:** conduzir, levar a	**scrutiny:** exame minucioso	**unorthodox:** ousado(a)

After Reading

1 Based on the text, it is possible to state that…

a ☐ our reputation today is based mainly on our interactions in the real world.

b ☐ we have lost control of our lives because the internet has more than 3 billion users.

c ☐ the only way to control our online reputation is by clearing our internet history.

d ☐ data on what we look at, post, and buy online is constantly collected and analyzed.

2 Decide if the statements are true (T) or false (F).

a ☐ All aspects of a person's life can be influenced by their online reputation.

b ☐ Your past online behavior can be used to predict your future behavior.

c ☐ Internet users should avoid credit scores in order to preserve their online reputation.

d ☐ Negative online reviews are more vital for corporate image than for personal image.

e ☐ The older a negative comment online is, the less harmful it is for the image of a company.

3 Check the correct meaning of the sentences.

1 *"With over 3 billion users expected in 2015, the internet has made us our most vulnerable selves without notice […]"* (lines 3-4).

a ☐ Because of the internet, we have never been as vulnerable as we are today.

b ☐ The internet helps us defend ourselves from privacy violation.

2 *"[…] the evolution of technologies and social media does far from help that"* (lines 4-5).

a ☐ The evolution of technologies and social media makes us even more vulnerable.

b ☐ The evolution of technologies and social media helps make us less vulnerable.

4 Answer the questions.

1 In the context discussed in the text, what kind of information does a credit score comprise? What is this information used for?

_____

_____

2 What kind of information does a reputation score comprise? What is this information used for?

_____

_____

Before Reading

1 Discuss the questions below.

1 Do people usually help others they don't know?

2 Have you ever helped a person you didn't know?

MAKING KINDNESS A DAILY HABIT

An Act of Kindness

She was just 14 and she was very angry with her parents. She had many dreams and wanted to know the world. So she decided to run away from Cleveland, taking a bus to New York.

It was wintertime, so it was very cold in NY. A man noticed that 14-year-old girl wandering in the cold streets and, after hearing her story, took her to the bus station and bought her a ticket back home.

He gave her 20 dollars and wrote his address on a small piece of paper. Then he told her, "Whatever you desire, you can make it happen." The girl went back home.

Time went by; the girl went to high school, to college, then to medical school and became a surgeon. She got married and had two children. She always thought about the man, but she couldn't find the small piece of paper with his address.

One day, when her daughter was 14, they decided to clean the attic. An old box called their attention. Inside it, among old school things, they found the small piece of paper.

The surgeon located her benefactor and sent him a letter with 500 dollars. "Your kindness has no price," she wrote. "I just hope that you come meet my family. Clara."

Ralph Burke accepted the invitation and was welcomed as a long-lost uncle.

Based on <www.lifeway.com/Article/ministry-Making-Kindness-a-Daily-Habit>. Accessed on April 15, 2016.

Vocabulary

attic: sótão	**desire:** desejar	**run away:** fugir	**wander:** perambular
benefactor: benfeitor(a)	**kindness:** bondade	**surgeon:** cirurgião/cirurgiã	**whatever:** o que quer que seja

After Reading

1 **Find in the text words/expressions with these meanings.**

1   o tempo passou _____

2   ela se casou _____

3   um tio perdido há muito tempo _____

2 **What does the text state? Check the correct alternatives.**

a   ☐   The girl lived in New York.

b   ☐   Ralph Burke helped the girl on a cold night.

c   ☐   Her benefactor was a surgeon.

d   ☐   The girl became a surgeon.

e   ☐   The surgeon had a daughter.

3 **What do you think the man meant when he said "*Whatever you desire, you can make it happen*"? Answer in Portuguese.**

_____

_____

4 **Read the information in the box. Then write new words and translate them.**

> **Suffix -*ness***
>
> O sufixo -***ness*** forma substantivos e indica qualidade, estado ou condição.
> kind – kind**ness**   lonely – loneli**ness**

1   sad   _____ sadness _____   _____ tristeza _____

2   bold   _____   _____

3   empty _____   _____

4   lively _____   _____

5 **Complete the sentences using words ending in -*ness*.**

1   _____ is the quality of being polite.

2   _____ is the quality of being good.

3   _____ is the state of being nervous.

4   _____ is the state of being happy.

Before Reading

1 Discuss the questions below.

1 In your opinion, what are the most common feelings among refugees?

2 What do you think their most common wishes are?

REFUGEE CRISES "REFLECT WORLD IN CHAOS"

Political will to stop conflicts missing, with old ones festering and new ones constantly erupting, UN official says.

[…]

On the eve of World Refugee Day, the UN released a new report showing that the number of people forcibly displaced at the end of 2014 had risen to 59.5 million, compared with 51.2 million a year earlier and 37.5 million a decade ago.

[…]

Globally, one out of every 122 people is now either a refugee, internally displaced, or seeking asylum.

Melissa Fleming, UNHCR spokesperson, told Al Jazeera on Saturday that not nearly enough is being done globally to combat the unprecedented crisis.

"Displacement numbers at this scale are a reflection of a world in chaos, where the political leadership to

stop and prevent conflicts is missing in action," she said.

[…]

The large increase in displaced persons has primarily been driven by the war in Syria. Almost four million Syrians are

now refugees, while a further 7.6 million are internally displaced, the UN says.

[…]

Afghanistan (2.59 million) and Somalia (1.1 million) are the next biggest refugee source countries.

[…]

Meanwhile, Pakistan, Iran, and Lebanon are hosting more refugees than other countries.

Internal displacement – people forced to flee to other parts of their country – now amounts to a record 33.3 million people, accounting for the largest increase of any group in the new UN report.

Among all those displaced globally, Fleming told Al Jazeera, more than half are children.

[…]

Available at <www.aljazeera.com/news/2015/06/global-leadership-criticised-refugee-numbers-swell-150620053450428.html>. Accessed on April 12, 2016.

Vocabulary

account for: ser responsável por	**displace:** deslocar, desalojar	**eve:** véspera	**further:** adicional
amount to: equivaler a	**drive:** impulsionar	**fester:** agravar-se	**primarily:** principalmente
asylum: asilo (refúgio)	**erupt:** surgir, vir à tona	**flee:** fugir	**will:** vontade

After Reading

1 **Check the correct option according to the figures presented in the text.**

a ☐ In 2014, an additional 59.5 million people had to leave their places of origin in comparison with 2013.

b ☐ The new report released by the UN interviewed 122 refugees who are seeking asylum in other countries.

c ☐ Afghanistan and Somalia have already given asylum to more than 3 million refugees since 2014.

d ☐ The new UN report showed that more than 7.6 million Syrians can now be considered refugees.

e ☐ According to the UN report, 33.3 million people were forced to move to other parts of their country.

2 **According to a UN spokesperson...**

a ☐ political leaders are trying to solve conflicts in order to prevent displacement.

b ☐ UNHCR is not doing enough to combat the global refugee crisis.

c ☐ the growing number of refugees is the main cause of a world in chaos.

d ☐ political leaders are failing to prevent conflicts, so displacement keeps increasing.

e ☐ Al Jazeera is responsible for this unprecedented crisis that should be fought.

3 **Match the sentence halves based on the text.**

1 The war in Syria...

2 More than 7 million Syrians...

3 Syria, Afghanistan, and Somalia...

4 Pakistan, Iran, and Lebanon...

5 Between 2013 and 2014...

a ☐ are the largest refugee sources in the world.

b ☐ are the countries which receive the largest number of refugees.

c ☐ is the main reason for the increase in displaced people.

d ☐ were forced to flee to other parts of the country.

e ☐ the number of people forcibly displaced increased to 59.5 million.

Before Reading

1 **Discuss the questions below.**

1 What does "social inclusion" mean?

2 Can arts and sports promote social inclusion? How?

**Brazil:
Awakening the Dreams
of Young Slum Dwellers**

By Mario Osava

RECIFE – Left blind in one eye by a bullet wound, 18-year-old Rosinaldo Inaldo admits that he used to be violent, but says he now dreams of becoming a singer of traditional songs from northeastern Brazil like *axé* and *frevo*.

He attributes the change to the Art and Life Association, which, he says, "made me a better person and
5   improved my life."

Thanks to his five years of involvement in the programme, he now enjoys going to school, where he is trying to complete his primary education, while dreaming about making money as a singer, actor or computer operator, "to help my family and to help out other people as well," he tells IPS.

[...]
10   In a three-story building in the city's historic centre, the youngsters take drumming, music, dance, art and literature classes.

[...]

Art as a tool for transformation was the method chosen by the firm, following the example of a number of Brazilian programmes in which art and sports have been successfully used to promote social inclusion
15   and prevent juvenile delinquency among young slum dwellers.

[...]

Danuzia Pereira, 18, was until recently a participant in the programme and now works as an assistant to the teachers who provide tutoring.

The children's academic performance improves after they join Art and Life, because the project
20   "awakens their interest and enthusiasm for learning," says Pereira.

[...]

Available at <www.ipsnews.net/2005/08/brazil-awakening-the-dreams-of-young-slum-dwellers>. Accessed on April 15, 2016.

Vocabulary

awaken: despertar	**dweller:** morador(a)	**tool:** ferramenta
blind: cego(a)	**slum:** favela	**wound:** ferimento

After Reading

1 **Check the correct alternatives about Rosinaldo Inaldo, according to the text.**

a ☐ He was born blind due to a public health issue in northeastern Brazil.

b ☐ He was left blind in one eye after being wounded by a bullet.

c ☐ He is completing his primary education.

d ☐ He is a teacher assistant at the Art and Life Association.

e ☐ He wants to help other people nowadays.

f ☐ He is a violent person because of a bullet wound.

2 **Check the correct alternatives about the Art and Life Association.**

a ☐ It was created by Rosinaldo Inaldo.

b ☐ It is located in the historic center of Recife.

c ☐ It is trying to transform youngsters' lives through art and music.

d ☐ It is trying to buy a three-story building in the historic center of Recife.

e ☐ Its programs have ended up increasing juvenile delinquency.

f ☐ It helps prevent juvenile delinquency among slum dwellers.

3 **Decide if the following statements are true (T) or false (F).**

1 ☐ Rosinaldo Inaldo attributes the change in his life to the Art and Life Association.

2 ☐ Participants in the program can never work as teacher assistants.

3 ☐ The youngsters have drumming, music, dance, art, and literature classes.

4 **Check the correct meaning of the sentences.**

1 *"The children's academic performance improves after they join Art and Life [...]"* (line 19).

    a ☐ The children do better in school after they join the association.

    b ☐ The children join the association because they want to take tests.

2 *"[...] the project 'awakens their interest and enthusiasm for learning' [...]"* (lines 19-20).

    a ☐ People in the association don't focus on students' enthusiasm.

    b ☐ Youngsters are more interested in learning after joining the program.

Before Reading

1 Discuss the questions below.

1 What is more important in a public building: beauty or usability? Why?

2 What do you understand by the expression "form follows function" in the context of architecture?

The Architecture of the Solomon R. Guggenheim Museum

Form Follows Function

"*Form follows function – that has been misunderstood. Form and function should be one, joined in a spiritual union.*"

As a young architect, Frank Lloyd Wright worked for Louis Sullivan (1856-1924) in his Chicago-based architecture firm. Sullivan is known for steel-frame constructions, considered some of the earliest skyscrapers. Sullivan's famous axiom, "form follows function," became the touchstone for many architects. This means that the purpose of a building should be the starting point for its design. Wright extended the teachings of his mentor by changing the phrase to "form and function are one."

This principle is thoroughly visible in the plan for the Guggenheim Museum. According to Wright's design, visitors would enter the building, take an elevator to the top and enjoy a continuous art-viewing experience while descending along the spiral ramp.

Wright's design for the Guggenheim has sometimes been criticized for being inhospitable to the art it displays. However, over the past five decades Wright's design has housed a wide variety of exhibitions, from traditional paintings to motorcycles to site-specific installations by contemporary artists. According to former Guggenheim director Tom Krens, "great architecture has this capacity to adapt to changing functional uses without losing one bit of its dignity or one bit of its original intention. And I think that's the great thing about the building at the end of the day" [...].

Available at <www.guggenheim.org/new-york/education/school-educator-programs/teacher-resources/arts-curriculum-online?view=item&catid=730&id=120>.
Accessed on April 12, 2016.

Vocabulary

axiom: axioma, premissa, máxima	**purpose:** propósito; objetivo	**steel-frame:** que tem estrutura de aço
former: anterior, antigo(a)	**site-specific:** específico(a) para o local	**thoroughly:** completamente
inhospitable: inóspito(a), hostil	**skyscraper:** arranha-céu	**touchstone:** padrão de comparação

After Reading

1 **Decide if the ideas below are from Sullivan (S), Wright (W), or Krens (K), according to the text.**

1 ☐ Form follows function.

2 ☐ Form and function are one.

3 ☐ Architecture should adapt to different uses.

2 **Find in the text the opposite of these words.**

1 praised _____

2 latest _____

3 bottom _____

4 ascending _____

5 ancient _____

6 invisible _____

3 **Check the best option according to the text.**

1 Frank Lloyd Wright believed that...

a ☐ form is more important than function.

b ☐ form and function are equally important.

c ☐ function is more important than form.

2 Some people have criticized the Guggenheim because...

a ☐ it has housed nonartistic exhibitions, such as one about motorcycles.

b ☐ they believe visitors feel tired from having to descend the ramps.

c ☐ they think it is not appropriate for the art exhibitions it hosts.

3 The Guggenheim Museum...

a ☐ has hosted a great variety of exhibitions in more than 50 years.

b ☐ usually hosts several different shows in a single day.

c ☐ loses its originality when it has to adapt to different art exhibitions.

4 **What was Wright's visiting plan for the Guggenheim Museum?**

_____

_____

_____

Before Reading

1 **Discuss the questions below.**

1   Why do people work?

2   Why do some people accumulate more money and goods than they need?

Walden

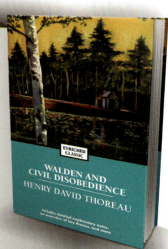

Economy

When I wrote the following pages, or rather the bulk of them, I lived alone, in the woods, a mile from any neighbor, in a house which I had built myself, on the shore of Walden Pond, in Concord, Massachusetts, and earned my living by the labor of my hands only. I lived there two years and two months. At present
5   I am a sojourner in civilized life again.

[...]

I see young men, my townsmen, whose misfortune it is to have inherited farms, houses, barns, cattle, and farming tools; for these are more easily acquired than got rid of. Better if they had been born in the open pasture and suckled by a wolf,
10 that they might have seen with clearer eyes what field they were called to labor in. Who made them serfs of the soil? Why should they eat their sixty acres, when man is condemned to eat only his peck of dirt? Why should they begin digging their graves as soon as they are born? They have got to live a man's life, pushing all these things before them, and get on as well as they can. [...]

15 But men labor under a mistake. [...] By a seeming fate, commonly called necessity, they are employed, as it says in an old book, laying up treasures which moth and rust will corrupt and thieves break through and steal. It is a fool's life, as they will find when they get to the end of it, if not before. [...]

THOREAU, Henry David. *Walden*. Available at <www.gutenberg.org/files/205/205-h/205-h.htm>.
Accessed on April 12, 2016.

Vocabulary

bulk: maior parte
dig: cavar
earn: ganhar, obter

fate: destino
grave: túmulo
moth: traça

peck of dirt: punhado de terra
rust: ferrugem
seeming: aparente

serf: servo(a)
sojourner: morador(a) temporário(a)
suckle: amamentar

After Reading

1 Based on the text, it is possible to affirm that...

a ☐ Thoreau wrote the book after living alone in a house he built near a lake.

b ☐ after his experience of isolation, the writer started working with his hands.

c ☐ Thoreau inherited a farm and some cattle when he was younger.

d ☐ the writer prefers not to accumulate expensive goods or money.

2 Check the best equivalent to the sentences.

1 *"[...] [I] earned my living by the labor of my hands only"* (lines 3-4).

a ☐ Working with my hands I provided for myself.

b ☐ My money was enough to live without working.

2 *"[...] these are more easily acquired than got rid of"* (lines 8-9).

a ☐ It is very difficult to acquire riches in this world.

b ☐ When you have many things, you get attached to them.

3 Which alternative explains the sentence "*But men labor under a mistake*" (line 15)?

a ☐ People say they work for necessity, but they work to accumulate.

b ☐ Thieves will corrupt and steal the treasures only of the fool workers.

c ☐ Men must work because it is their fate to accumulate treasures.

4 What do the words in bold refer to?

1 *"I lived **there** two years and two months"* (line 4).

a ☐ in the woods on the shore of Walden Pond

b ☐ in the woods outside Massachusetts

2 *"[...] for **these** are more easily acquired than got rid of"* (lines 8-9).

a ☐ young men

b ☐ farms, houses, barns, cattle, and farming tools

3 *"Who made **them** serfs of the soil?"* (line 11).

a ☐ young men

b ☐ cattle

Before Reading

1 Discuss the questions below.

1 How would you define a musical instrument?

2 Is it possible to make music without using musical instruments or the voice?

STOMP

Members of Stomp Perform at the Food Bank

By Stephen Hunt, Calgary Herald

Take a mixing bowl. A box of Grape Nuts. A shopping cart. An empty water jug. A biscuit tin, two coffee cups, one bell, one stool, one cake tray, a green plastic garbage bin, a milk crate and a Calgary Food Bank donation bucket, add a few members of the cast of Stomp and what have you got? A lunch-hour concert like no other. Those were the instruments played

Tuesday at the Calgary Inter-Faith Food Bank's 11th Street warehouse, where a few members of the cast of Stomp dropped by to perform an impromptu concert on a bunch of stuff they found lying around in the break room. The result was a brief, brilliant glimpse into the world of Stomp, where everyday objects become musical instruments. [...]

What Is Stomp?

[...]
Stomp is performed in theaters, but it is not a play, musical, or opera. It is not theater in the traditional sense of the word. There is no speech, dialogue, or plot. However, it does have two characteristics of traditional theater: mime and characterization. Each performer has an individual character that is distinct from the others. These characters are brought out through the mime and dance in the show.
[...]

"People drum their fingers on tabletops when they are waiting for something to happen. They tap their feet when they are bored. They walk in rhythm quite naturally when they walk down the street... and jangle keys in their pocket... Yes, everything has a rhythm to it. Everything has music to it!"

Luke Cresswell and Steve McNicholas, creators of Stomp

Available at <www.stomponline.com/news/food-bank-performance.php>; <www.stomponline.com/studyguide/intro.php>; <www.artisttrove.com/artist/241739492548503/Stomp+and+Holler>. Accessed on April 18, 2016.

Vocabulary

bell: sino	**crate:** engradado	**jug:** jarra	**tin:** lata
bowl: tigela	**drum:** batucar	**plot:** trama	**tray:** bandeja
bucket: balde	**jangle:** chacoalhar	**stool:** banquinho	**warehouse:** armazém

After Reading

1 **Check the correct alternative.**

1 The texts are part of...

a ☐ an informative leaflet. b ☐ a newspaper article. c ☐ an advertisement.

2 Stephen Hunt is...

a ☐ a member of the Stomp cast. c ☐ one of the creators of Stomp.

b ☐ the author of the first text.

3 A shopping cart, a biscuit tin, one bell, one stool, a milk crate, and a donation bucket are...

a ☐ considered musical instruments by the members of Stomp.

b ☐ discarded in a warehouse after Stomp performances.

c ☐ everyday objects which can't be used as musical instruments.

2 **Match the words/expressions from the text to their meaning.**

1	tap	a	☐	many things
2	impromptu	b	☐	group of artists
3	cast	c	☐	beat gently
4	a bunch of stuff	d	☐	visit briefly
5	drop by	e	☐	improvised

3 **Find in the text words that match these definitions.**

1 a person portrayed in a play, movie, or novel _____

2 a discourse delivered to an audience _____

3 a quick or partial view _____

4 **Answer the questions.**

1 How are theatrical and Stomp performances different?

_____

2 What do theatrical and Stomp performances have in common?

_____

3 According to the text, when do people make music in their everyday lives?

_____

Before Reading

1 Discuss the questions below.

1 What are the signs of drug addiction?

2 Do you know anyone who is a drug addict?

SIGNS OF DRUG ADDICTION

It is important to stress the fact that drug addicts regularly try to deny their drug-related problems while they hide the symptoms of their addiction.

There are, however, many well-known and predictable "warning" signs of drug addiction that strongly suggest drug dependency. The following list represents some of the most common and recognizable warning signs of drug addiction.

Talking incoherently or making inappropriate remarks.

The inability to limit one's drug use over time or during any given situation.

Inappropriately and frequently wearing long-sleeved shirts and/or sunglasses.

Engaging in secretive or suspicious behaviors, such as making numerous trips to the restroom, basement, garage, or other isolated areas where drug usage can take place.

Withdrawal symptoms that take place when an individual suddenly quits taking drugs. Such symptoms include "the shakes", sweating, headaches, and nausea.

Noticeable degradation regarding one's grooming and physical appearance.

Sudden increase in school absences or work problems, while grades or quality of work diminishes. [...]

Available at <www.drug-addiction-facts.com>. Accessed on April 18, 2016.

Vocabulary

addiction: vício	**grooming:** aparência	**quit:** parar	**the shakes:** tremores
basement: porão	**hide:** esconder	**remark:** comentário	**warning:** alerta
deny: negar	**long-sleeved:** de mangas compridas	**stress:** enfatizar	**withdrawal:** abstinência

After Reading

1 **Complete the sentences with the verbs from the box in the correct tense.**

| limit | deny | stress | hide |

1 The importance of this vaccine needs to be _____ in the media.

2 This is evident, so don't try to _____ it.

3 The boy is _____ the ball from his brother.

4 The school _____ the number of students in each class.

2 **Decide if the statements are true (T) or false (F) according to the text.**

1 ☐ When a person stops taking drugs, withdrawal signs appear.

2 ☐ Restrooms, basements, and garages are the only places where people take drugs.

3 ☐ Drug addiction doesn't impact a person's grades at school.

4 ☐ Talking incoherently might be a sign of drug addiction.

3 **Match the synonyms.**

1 quit   a ☐ visible

2 take place   b ☐ comment

3 noticeable   c ☐ stop

4 remark   d ☐ occur

5 predictable   e ☐ unsurprising

4 **Check the correct alternative.**

1 How do drug addicts behave?

   a ☐ They normally ask their friends and family for help.

   b ☐ They usually deny they have a drug problem.

   c ☐ They rarely try to hide the symptoms of their addiction.

2 Which of the following is <u>not</u> a sign of drug addiction?

   a ☐ Using sunglasses on sunny days.

   b ☐ Not being able to control the use of drugs over time.

   c ☐ Saying inappropriate or confusing things.

Extra Reading 10

Before Reading

1 **Discuss the questions below.**

1 Are there gangs in your school or neighborhood?

2 What makes a teenager join a gang?

http://issues.goodnewseverybody.com/gangs.html

THE BUSINESS OF GANGS, GANG MEMBERS, AND GANG IDENTIFICATION

In our website you will find videos and links that will give you some information on street gangs and prison gangs, gang identification (based on clothing, colors, graffiti, marks, and tattoos), investigations, prosecutions, rivalries, and alliances.

WHERE DO WE FIND GANGS?

Odds are that you have street gangs in your community. Gangs are not confined to the large urban communities anymore. They are now found in many of the smallest towns as well and its members are no longer just low-income, poorly educated dropouts. Gang members are now a mixture of all races, cultures, and ethnicities. They no longer come exclusively from a one-parent family who is never available to show love and guidance to the child. The youngsters of today are sometimes joining gangs even if they live with both parents and are middle- or even upper-class.

Too often the phrase "We don't have gangs in our community" is uttered by the city fathers, the police, the chamber of commerce, or the tourist office. This is often followed by "All we have are a bunch of wannabes". However, nothing could be further from the truth. If a group of young people in your community has banded together and call themselves by a particular name; if they use signs, symbols, and/or colors to identify themselves; and if they are committing crimes, they are a gang, regardless of what members of the community say.

It is easy to understand why any community, large or small, might deny the existence of gangs – no community wants the stigma of having gangs. However, by denying the existence of gang activity, they are doing these gangs a favor – they are allowing them to develop, grow stronger, and create a power base.

Adapted from <http://issues.goodnewseverybody.com/gangs.html>. Accessed on April 18, 2016.

Vocabulary

band together: juntar-se	**income:** renda	**rivalry:** rivalidade
dropout: quem abandona os estudos	**odds are:** é provável	**utter:** dizer
guidance: orientação	**regardless of:** independentemente de	**wannabe:** aspirante

After Reading

1 **Match the words/expressions from the text to the corresponding meaning.**

1	clothing	a	☐	de classe social mais alta
2	prosecution	b	☐	roupas, vestuário
3	no longer	c	☐	não mais
4	available	d	☐	permitir
5	upper-class	e	☐	disponível
6	allow	f	☐	acusação, instauração de processo

2 **Answer the questions according to the text.**

1 What are some elements that identify gangs?

_____

2 Do all gang members have the same race or culture?

_____

3 Do gang members come only from low-income families?

_____

4 Why do communities deny the existence of gangs?

_____

3 **Which of the following topics <u>cannot</u> be found on the website?**

a ☐ Videos about street gangs.

b ☐ Information on gangs' rivals and allies.

c ☐ Discussion about the background of gang members.

d ☐ Videos on how to dress as a gangster.

e ☐ How communities react to gangs.

4 **Decide if the following statements are true (T) or false (F) according to the text.**

1 ☐ Gangs have left large urban centers and moved to smaller towns.

2 ☐ The location of gangs and the profile of their members have changed.

3 ☐ Gang members commonly use some form of identification and commit crimes.

4 ☐ Young people are joining gangs because they don't like living with their parents.

Before Reading

1 Discuss the questions below.

1 What do people usually do when they think they have too much work to do?

2 Have you ever made up an excuse to avoid an obligation?

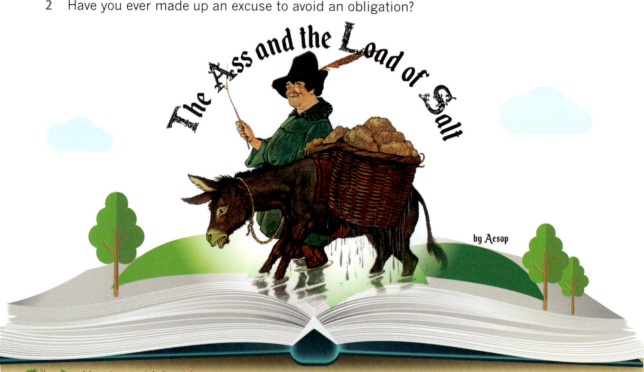

The Ass and the Load of Salt

by Aesop

A Merchant, driving his Ass homeward from the seashore with a heavy load of salt, came to a river crossed by a shallow ford. They had crossed this river many times before without accident, but this time the Ass slipped and fell when halfway over. And when the Merchant at last got him to his feet, much of the salt had melted away. Delighted to find how much lighter his burden had become, the Ass finished the journey very gaily.

Next day the Merchant went for another load of salt. On the way home the Ass, remembering what had happened at the ford, purposely let himself fall into the water, and again got rid of most of his burden.

The angry Merchant immediately turned about and drove the Ass back to the seashore, where he loaded him with two great baskets of sponges. At the ford the Ass again tumbled over; but when he had scrambled to his feet, it was a very disconsolate Ass that dragged himself homeward under a load ten times heavier than before.

Available at <http://americanliterature.com/author/aesop/short-story/the-ass-and-the-load-of-salt>. Accessed on April 13, 2016.

Vocabulary

ass: asno	**ford:** parte rasa de um rio	**melt:** derreter	**seashore:** litoral
at last: finalmente	**gaily:** alegremente	**merchant:** mercador(a)	**shallow:** raso(a)
burden: carga, fardo	**load:** carga; carregar	**scramble:** arrastar-se	**tumble:** cair

After Reading

1 **Check the correct statement about the text.**

a ☐ It is a description of a true event that happened in a distant past.

b ☐ It is a recommendation for how to behave in certain situations.

c ☐ It is an allegory that intends to teach a lesson.

2 **Complete the sentences with the words/expressions from the box. Make any necessary changes.**

slip	drag	purposely	get rid of	delighted	homeward

1 The soap _____ from my hand.

2 She was _____ to hear that we're getting married.

3 They were setting off _____ after a long journey.

4 Why don't you _____ that pile of junk?

5 I was so tired that I had to _____ myself out of bed this morning.

6 She'd never _____ disappoint us.

3 **Check the sentences that are true according to the text.**

a ☐ The merchant and the ass lived on the seashore.

b ☐ The ass was glad to travel carrying less weight after the fall.

c ☐ The ass made a decision after something that happened by accident.

d ☐ After the second loss, the merchant noticed the ass's intentions.

e ☐ The ass fell four times while carrying the salt.

f ☐ In the end, the ass was praised for his attitude.

4 **Which alternative best represents the moral of the fable?**

a ☐ Do not attempt too much at once.

b ☐ It is easy to kick a man that is down.

c ☐ Little friends may prove great friends.

d ☐ The same measures will not apply to all circumstances.

e ☐ Quality is better than quantity.

Before Reading

1 Discuss the questions below.

1 How much does a person's appearance influence his/her success in life?

2 What do poor people worry about in life? How about the rich: are their worries different?

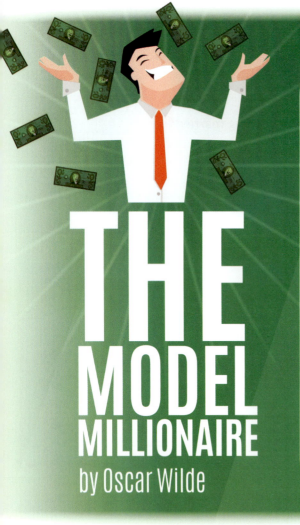

THE MODEL MILLIONAIRE
by Oscar Wilde

Unless one is wealthy there is no use in being a charming fellow. Romance is the privilege of the rich, not the profession of the unemployed. The poor should be practical and prosaic. It is better to have a permanent income than to be fascinating. These are the great truths of modern life which Hughie Erskine never realised. Poor Hughie! Intellectually, we must admit, he was not of much importance. He never said a brilliant or even an ill-natured thing in his life. But then he was wonderfully good-looking, with his crisp brown hair, his clear-cut profile, and his grey eyes. He was as popular with men as he was with women, and he had every accomplishment except that of making money. His father had bequeathed him his cavalry sword, and a *History of the Peninsular War* in fifteen volumes. Hughie hung the first over his looking glass, put the second on a shelf between Ruff's Guide and Bailey's Magazine, and lived on two hundred a year that an old aunt allowed him. [...]

Available at <http://americanliterature.com/author/oscar-wilde/short-story/the-model-millionaire>. Accessed on April 14, 2016.

Vocabulary

allow: dar, reservar	**income:** renda	**realise:** perceber
crisp: crespo(a)	**looking glass:** espelho	**sword:** espada
fellow: rapaz	**prosaic:** prosaico(a), trivial	**wealthy:** rico(a)

After Reading

1 **Write the words/expressions from the box next to their meaning.**

| bequeath | ill-natured | there is no use | accomplishment | clear-cut | unless |

1 a menos que _____

2 não adianta _____

3 deixar como herança _____

4 feito, realização _____

5 desagradável, maldoso(a) _____

6 bem delineado(a) _____

2 **Check the correct statement about Hughie Erskine, according to the text.**

a ☐ He was an important intellectual who attracted both men and women.

b ☐ His priority in life was to work, not to earn a permanent income.

c ☐ His largest accomplishments were making money and buying a sword.

d ☐ He was handsome and popular, but he could not make any money.

e ☐ He lived off his father's allowance because he wasn't intellectually relevant.

3 **Decide if the following statements are true (T) or false (F) according to the text.**

1 ☐ The author thinks it is important to be both wealthy and charming.

2 ☐ It is only useful to be charming if you are wealthy.

3 ☐ The author thinks that the unemployed aren't romantic enough.

4 ☐ Unemployed people should focus more on finding a profession than on finding romance.

5 ☐ Poor people have to worry about earning a living, so they are more practical.

6 ☐ Hughie Erskine discovered fascinating truths about modern life.

4 **Do you agree with the "great truths of modern life" presented in the text? Why?**

_____

_____

_____

Glossary

A

a bit: um pouco

a bunch of: um monte de

a few: alguns/algumas

a little: um pouco

a lot (of): muito(a), muitos(as)

ability: capacidade, habilidade

able: hábil, capaz

about: sobre, a respeito de

above: acima

abroad: no exterior

accompany: acompanhar

accomplish: realizar

accomplishment: feito, realização

account for: corresponder a, responder por; ser responsável por

acknowledge: reconhecer

active: ativo(a)

actually: de fato, realmente, na verdade

ad: anúncio, propaganda

adapt: adaptar

addict: viciado(a)

addiction: vício

additionally: além disso, ademais

address: endereço; abordar

adjust: ajustar

adult: adulto(a)

advertise: anunciar, fazer propaganda

advertising: publicidade

afraid: com medo

again: de novo, novamente

against: contra

age: idade; era, época; envelhecer

ageless: que não envelhece

aging: envelhecimento

ago: atrás (tempo)

agree: concordar

ahead of time: com antecedência

aimed at: voltado(a) para

allow: permitir; dar, reservar

ally: aliado(a)

aloud: em voz alta

already: já

also: também

although: embora

always: sempre

amount: quantia, quantidade

amount to: equivaler a

ancient: antigo(a)

and: e

and so forth: e assim por diante

another: outro(a)

answer: atender (ao telefone, à porta); resposta; responder

anteater: tamanduá

antique: antiguidade

any: algum(a); qualquer; nenhum(a)

apparel: vestimenta

appliance: aparelho, utensílio, eletrodoméstico

appointment: compromisso

approach: aproximar-se; abordar; abordagem

apricot: damasco

archery: tiro com arco

around: em volta de, ao redor

as: enquanto; quando; tão... quanto; uma vez que; como (na função de)

ascend: subir

ass: asno

assistant: assistente

assume: supor, presumir

asylum: asilo (refúgio)

at an early age: cedo na vida

at last: finalmente

at least: pelo menos

athlete: atleta

athletics: atletismo

atmosphere: atmosfera

attach: anexar; atribuir

attack: atacar

attempt: tentativa; tentar

attend: frequentar, comparecer

attentively: atentamente

attic: sótão

audience: público, espectadores

aunt: tia

available: disponível

avoid: evitar

awaken: despertar

awesome: impressionante; muito bom/boa

axiom: axioma, premissa, máxima

B

background: formação; experiência

bad: mau/má; ruim

bakery: panificação

balance: equilíbrio

band together: juntar-se

bank: banco; margem

bare: descoberto(a), desnudo(a); descalço(a)

barrier: barreira

basement: porão

basin: bacia

bat: morcego

be able to: ser capaz de

be caught: ser pego(a)

be down: não funcionar

beat: bater

because: porque

become: tornar-se

bed: cama

beet: beterraba

before: antes

behind: atrás

belief: crença

bell: sino

belong: pertencer; fazer parte de

below: abaixo

benefactor: benfeitor(a)

bequeath: deixar como herança

best: melhor

betrayal: traição

between: entre

beverage: bebida

beyond: além; do outro lado

birthday: aniversário

blank: espaço em branco

bleed: sangrar

bless: abençoar

blind: cego(a)

blood: sangue; sanguíneo

boat: barco

boccia: bocha

bold: negrito

bone: osso

book: livro; agendar

bookstore: livraria

bored: entediado(a)

boring: entediante

boss: chefe

both: ambos(as), os dois/as duas

both… and…: tanto… quanto…

bottom: parte de baixo

bow: curvar-se; fazer reverência

bowel: intestino

bowl: tigela

brain: cérebro

brand: marca

brawl: briga

breakdown: colapso

breath: respiração; sopro

breed: criar (animais)

bucket: balde

bug repellent: repelente de insetos

bulk: maior parte

bully: pessoa que pratica *bullying*

bullying: intimidação, assédio moral

burden: carga, fardo

business: negócio(s)

but: mas; exceto

buttock: nádega

by bus: de ônibus

by car: de carro

by plane: de avião

cabbage: repolho

cake: bolo

campaign: campanha

can: lata

cane: vara

canopy: dossel florestal

care for: cuidar de

career: carreira

careless: descuidado(a), negligente

carrot: cenoura

cartoon: história em quadrinhos

cast: elenco

caste: casta, classe social

cattle: gado

cauliflower: couve-flor

ceiling: teto

century: século

challenged: desafiado(a)

challenging: desafiador(a)

champion: campeão/campeã

championship: campeonato

change: mudar; mudança

character: personagem

charming: charmoso(a)

chat: conversar; conversa

cheap: barato(a)

cheese: queijo

Chemistry: Química

cherry: cereja

chestnut: castanha

chew: mascar

chicken: frango

chief: chefe

child: criança

child labor: trabalho infantil

choir: coral

Christmas: Natal

circle: circular

citizen: cidadão/cidadã

citizenship: cidadania

city: cidade

class: aula; classe

clear-cut: bem delineado(a)

clenched: fechado(a), cerrado(a)

clothes: roupas

clothing: roupas, vestuário

coal: carvão

coffee: café

cofounder: cofundador(a)

cold: frio(a)

college: faculdade

colorful: colorido(a)

column: coluna

come: vir

come across: encontrar por acaso

come down with: adoecer, ficar doente

come out: ser publicado(a); estrear

come up: surgir

come up with: inventar

comeback: retorno

comment: comentário

committee: comitê, comissão

companionship: companheirismo

comprise: englobar, incluir, abranger

comrade: companheiro(a), camarada

concealed: escondido(a), oculto(a)

conceive: imaginar, conceber

concerning: no que diz respeito a, relativo a, referente a

conductor: maestro/maestrina

confectionery: confeitaria

conference: conferência, congresso

confined: confinado(a), preso(a)

conquer: conquistar

consciousness: consciência

consent: consentir

consequently: consequentemente

contemporary: contemporâneo(a)

continue: continuar

continuous: contínuo(a)

convey: comunicar, transmitir

cool: legal

core: núcleo, centro

costume: fantasia

couch: sofá

counterpart: correspondente, semelhante

country: país

couple: casal

cousin: primo(a)

cover letter: carta de apresentação

cover up: cobrir

coverage: cobertura

cramp: cãibra

crate: engradado

crazy: louco(a)

crisp: crespo(a)

criticize: criticar

crop: safra

crossfire: fogo cruzado

crouched: agachado(a), encolhido(a)

crowded: cheio de gente, lotado(a)

cry: chorar

cuisine: culinária típica de determinado local

culprit: culpado(a)

cure: curar

current: atual

currently: atualmente

customer: cliente

cut down: derrubar

CV: *curriculum vitae*

dairy: laticínio

dam: represa, barragem

damage: prejudicar, danificar

dangerous: perigoso(a)

dark: escuro(a)

darling: querido(a)

data: dados, informações

date: data; encontro

daughter: filha

dead: morto(a)

deal with: lidar com

dealer: comerciante

dear: caro(a), prezado(a), querido(a)

decay: deterioração

decision: decisão

decline: cair, decair

deference: deferência, respeito

deforestation: desmatamento

delay: retardar, atrasar

delighted: alegre, contente

demand: demanda, procura

deny: negar; recusar

depict: retratar, representar

deprive: privar, desprover

descend: descer

desire: desejar

despair: desespero

despite: apesar de

destroy: destruir

determined: determinado(a)

developing: em desenvolvimento

development: desenvolvimento

diagnosis: diagnóstico

dialogue: diálogo

dictatorship: ditadura

die: morrer

dig: cavar

diminish: diminuir

dinner: jantar

direct calls: transferir ligações

disability: deficiência

disappointment: decepção

discover: descobrir

discrimination: discriminação

disease: doença

dish: louça; prato

dishwasher: lavador(a) de pratos; máquina de lavar louça

displace: deslocar, desalojar

displacement: deslocamento

display: expor, mostrar

disturb: perturbar

disturbingly: perturbadoramente

divert: mudar o curso ou destino, desviar

divide: dividir

do: fazer

do well: sair-se bem, ir bem

doctor: médico(a)

donate: doar

door: porta

doubt: dúvida

downpour: aguaceiro, chuva forte

draft bill: projeto de lei

drag: arrastar

drawer: gaveta

dress: vestido; vestir(-se)

drive: impulsionar; dirigir

drop: gota

drop by: visitar, dar uma passada

drop out: abandonar

dropout: quem abandona os estudos

drought: seca

drum: batucar

dry: seco(a)

dubious: duvidoso(a), questionável

due to: devido a
dump: despejar
dweller: morador(a)

eagle: águia
earliest: mais antigo(a), primeiro(a)
earn: ganhar, obter
earth: terra; Terra (planeta)
eastward: na direção leste
easy: fácil
easygoing: tranquilo(a)
eat: comer
eating disorder: distúrbio alimentar
economic: econômico(a)
effect: causar, provocar; afetar, impactar; efeito
effort: esforço
either: também (frases negativas)
either… or…: ou… ou…
elderly: idosos(as)
embarrass: envergonhar
emission: emissão
emphasize: enfatizar
employee: empregado(a)
employer: empregador(a)
employment: emprego
empty: vazio(a)
enclosed: anexo(a)
encourage: encorajar, estimular
end: final
engage: envolver-se em
enjoy: gostar
enough: suficiente(mente)
ensure: garantir, assegurar
environment: meio ambiente, ambiente
erupt: surgir, vir à tona
especially: principalmente
evaporation: evaporação

eve: véspera
ever: alguma vez; jamais
every: todo(a), cada
every other day: dia sim, dia não
everything: tudo, todas as coisas
examine: examinar, verificar, analisar
exchange: trocar
excited: empolgado(a)
exciting: empolgante
exercise: exercício
exhibit: exposição; expor
expensive: caro(a)
eye: olho

face: enfrentar; rosto
facility: instalação, aparato
fail: ser reprovado(a)
fairly: razoavelmente
fairy: fada
fairy tale: conto de fada
far from: longe de
farm: fazenda
farmer: fazendeiro(a)
fast: rápido(a)
fat: gordo(a); gordura
fate: destino
father: pai
fathom: compreender
feel down: sentir-se triste
fellow: rapaz
fester: agravar-se
few: poucos(as)
field: campo, área
fig: figo
fight: combater; brigar
finger: dedo
finish: terminar
firefighter: bombeiro(a)

first-aid kit: *kit* de primeiros socorros
fish: peixe; pescar
fisherman: pescador
fist: punho, mão fechada
fit for purpose: adequado(a), pertinente
fit muscle: músculo exercitado
fitness center: academia de ginástica
fix: curar, consertar
flaw: falha, defeito
flee: fugir
flight: voo
flight attendant: comissário(a) de bordo
flooding: enchente
flower: flor
fly: voar
focus: foco, enfoque
follow: seguir
food: comida, alimento
footprint: pegada
for ages: há muito tempo
ford: parte rasa de um rio
forecast: prever
forefront: frente, vanguarda
foreign: estrangeiro(a)
forest: floresta
forge ahead with: seguir adiante, fazer progresso
forget: esquecer
forlorn: abandonado(a), desprezado(a)
former: anterior, antigo(a), ex
fossil fuel: combustível fóssil
frame: moldura
free: libertar; livre
freshwater: água doce
friend: amigo(a)
friendly: amigável
frightened: assustado(a)
from: de (origem)
from now on: daqui em diante

fruit: fruta

fumble: sair de forma desajeitada; tatear

functioning: funcionamento

furniture: móveis, mobília

further: mais longe; adicional

furthermore: ademais, além disso

gaily: alegremente

garbage: lixo

garden: jardim

German: alemão/alemã

Germany: Alemanha

get away with: escapar, ficar impune

get married: casar-se

get out: sair

get ready: arrumar-se

get rid of: livrar-se de

get sick: ficar doente

get to: chegar a

get together: juntar(-se)

give: dar

give in: ceder

give out: distribuir

give rise to: causar, originar, dar origem a

give up: desistir

glass: vidro

glasses: óculos

glimpse: relance, vislumbre

glow: brilho

go about: abordar, lidar com

go after: ir atrás de

go ahead: prosseguir, seguir adiante

go back: voltar

go by: passar por, passar (tempo)

go down: baixar, descer

go fishing: ir pescar

go on: continuar

go out: sair

go over: examinar, verificar, analisar

goal: objetivo, meta

gold: ouro

good: bom/boa

grade: nota (em uma avaliação); série/ano (escolar)

graduate: graduado(a), formado(a); formar-se

grandma: vovó

grandpa: vovô

grape: uva

graph: gráfico

grass: grama

grave: túmulo

grooming: aparência

grow: crescer

grow older: envelhecer

grown-up: adulto(a), crescido(a)

growth: crescimento

grumble: resmungar, lamentar

guava: goiaba

guess: achar, supor; adivinhar

guidance: orientação

guilty: culpado(a)

guitar: violão

gunman: pistoleiro

H

hair: cabelo

half: metade; meio

hand: mão

handle: lidar com

handsome: bonito(a)

hang: enforcar

happen: acontecer, ocorrer

happiness: felicidade

happy: feliz

harass: perturbar; assediar

hard: duro(a); intensamente

harm: prejudicar, causar dano a

hate: ódio; odiar

have: ter

have fun: divertir-se

head: cabeça; chefe, dirigente

headache: dor de cabeça

heal: curar

healthcare: cuidados com a saúde

hear: ouvir; ficar sabendo

heart: coração

heat-trapping: que retém o calor

heat wave: onda de calor

herb: erva

heritage: patrimônio, herança

hidden: escondido(a)

hide: esconder

high: alto(a)

high school: Ensino Médio

hiking: caminhada

hire: contratar

hold: segurar, guardar; realizar, promover

hold up to: sair-se, desempenhar

holiday: feriado

homemade: caseiro(a)

homeward: para casa

homework: lição de casa

homophobic: homofóbico(a)

honeymoon: lua de mel

hook: fisgar

hope: ter esperança/expectativa

hopeful: esperançoso(a)

horse: cavalo

hot: quente

housework: tarefas domésticas

How is it going?: Como está indo?

however: entretanto

huge: enorme

hunter: caçador(a)

hurry: apressar(-se)

husband: marido

hydroelectric: hidrelétrico(a)

I

ice: gelo

if: se

ill-natured: desagradável, maldoso(a)

illiteracy: analfabetismo

impact: impacto

impossible: impossível

impromptu: improvisado(a), de improviso

improve: aumentar, melhorar

improvement: melhoria

in: em, dentro de

in front of: na frente de

in the same way: da mesma forma

inappropriate: inadequado(a)

income: renda

increase: aumentar

indie: independente

inequity: injustiça

inflexion: inflexão, mudança no tom de voz

inhabit: habitar, morar em

inhospitable: inóspito(a), hostil

in-house: interno(a)

injury: lesão, ferimento

injustice: injustiça

innate: inato(a)

inside: dentro

instead of: em vez de

intelligent: inteligente

intend: pretender

interested: interessado(a)

interesting: interessante

interview: entrevista; entrevistar

interviewer: entrevistador(a)

introduce: apresentar

invisible: invisível

issue: questão, assunto; problema

J

jangle: chacoalhar

jewelry: joia

job: trabalho

join: ingressar

judge: julgar; juiz/juíza

jug: jarra

jump: pular

jungle: floresta, selva

just: justo(a); simplesmente; apenas

K

keep: guardar, conservar

key: chave; central, fundamental

kick: chutar

kind: bondoso(a), gentil; tipo

kindness: bondade

kinesthetic: cinestésico(a)

knee: joelho

know: conhecer, saber

knowledge: conhecimento

L

labor: trabalho

lack of: falta de

lake: lago

land: terra, território

landfill: aterro sanitário

landing: aterrissagem

landlord: senhorio, proprietário

large: grande

last: último(a); durar

latest: mais recente

laugh: rir

law: lei

lay: pôr, colocar

layer: camada

lead to: conduzir, levar a

learn: aprender

leave: partir, deixar

lecture: palestra

left: esquerdo(a)

leg: perna

leisure: lazer

length: comprimento, duração

level: nível

library: biblioteca

lie: mentir; deitar-se; jazer; encontrar-se, situar-se

lifeblood: força vital

like: gostar; como se fosse, como, do mesmo modo

limit: limitar

listen: ouvir

livelihood: meio de vida

lizard: lagarto

load: carga; carregar

lock: trancar

lodging: acomodação, hospedagem

logo: logotipo

long-lost: perdido(a) há muito tempo

long-sleeved: de manga longa

look: olhar; parecer

look after: cuidar, tomar conta

look at: olhar para

look for: procurar

look into: investigar

look up: consultar (uma lista, um dicionário)

looking glass: espelho

lose: perder

loss: perda

low: baixo(a)

luck: sorte

luggage: bagagem

lunch: almoço

lyrics: letra de música

M

made-up: inventado(a)

magazine: revista

main: principal

mainstream: predominante

maintain: manter

maintenance: manutenção

major: formar-se (em curso universitário)

make: fazer

make fun of: caçoar de, ridicularizar

make up: constituir

makeover: transformação estética

makeup: maquiagem

mall: *shopping center*

malnutrition: desnutrição

management: administração

mango: manga (fruta)

manufacturing: fabricação

many: muitos(as)

married: casado(a)

match: combinar, ligar, relacionar

maybe: talvez

maze: labirinto

mean: maldoso(a); querer dizer

meaning: significado

measure: medida; medir

meat: carne

medicine: medicina; remédio

meet the needs: atender as necessidades

meeting: reunião

meld: fundir, misturar

melt: derreter

mend: consertar

merchant: mercador(a)

mess: bagunça

milk: leite

misinformation: informação incorreta

Miss: senhorita

miss: sentir falta

mistake: confundir; erro

mistaken: equivocado(a)

misunderstand: entender errado

monkey: macaco

moreover: ademais

mostly: principalmente

moth: traça

mother: mãe

mother tongue: língua materna

movie: filme

movies: cinema

much: muito(a)

multiply: multiplicar

muscle: músculo

mushroom: cogumelo

N

name-calling: xingar

narrow: estreitar, apertar

near: perto de

news show: noticiário

NGO: organização não governamental (ONG)

nightmare: pesadelo

nip and tuck: cirurgia plástica

no longer: não mais

nonsensical: absurdo(a), sem sentido

notice: notar, perceber

noticeable: notável, perceptível

novel: romance

nowadays: atualmente, hoje em dia

nurture: cultivar, promover

nut: noz

O

oatmeal: aveia

occur: ocorrer

ocean: oceano

odds are: é provável

of: de (posse, parte)

official: oficial; funcionário(a) público(a)

often: geralmente

on: sobre, em cima de

on foot: a pé

only: apenas, somente

orange: laranja

ordinary: comum, corriqueiro(a)

outline: descrever

outside: fora, do lado de fora

outstanding: excepcional

over: demais; excessivo(a); por cima

overload: sobrecarregar

own: próprio(a)

ownership: propriedade

P

package: pacote

packaging: embalagem

palm wine: vinho de palma

papaya: mamão

parents: pais

part: peça

partner: parceiro(a)

pass: passar

path: caminho, trilha, via

pay: pagar

peach: pêssego

peck of dirt: punhado de terra

peer: colega

people: pessoas; povo

perform: realizar, executar

perhaps: talvez

permitted: permitido(a)

persecute: perseguir

personnel manager: gerente de recursos humanos

Phew!: Ufa!

pick: escolher
plant: fábrica
plentiful: abundante
plenty of: muitos(as)
plot: trama
plow: arar
plum: ameixa
plump: rechonchudo(a)
poised: preparado(a), pronto(a)
police: polícia
policy: política
ponder: refletir sobre, considerar
pose: representar
possible: possível
potato: batata
pound: libra
pour: derramar, transbordar
PR: relações públicas
precipitate: chover
precipitation: precipitação atmosférica, chuva
predictable: previsível
prejudice: preconceito
prepare: preparar
pretend: fingir
pretty: bonito(a)
prevent: prevenir, evitar
primarily: principalmente
printed: impresso(a)
proceed: proceder, prosseguir
production: produção
prohibited: proibido(a)
proper: adequado(a)
prosaic: prosaico(a), trivial
prosecution: acusação, instauração de processo
proud: orgulhoso(a)
provide: fornecer; propiciar
provided that: desde que
pull: puxar
pumpkin: abóbora
punish: punir
purpose: propósito; objetivo

purposely: propositalmente
push: empurrar; promover
puzzle: charada, quebra-cabeça

quantity: quantidade
quit: abandonar; parar; desistir

rainforest: floresta tropical
raise: criar, despertar
range: alcance
rate: taxa, índice
readership: público leitor
realize: perceber, ter consciência de
realm: reino, mundo
recall: lembrar(-se)
recognize: reconhecer
recycle: reciclar
recycling: reciclagem
reduce: reduzir
refuse: recusar
regard: considerar
regardless of: independentemente de
relative: parente
release: ser lançado(a)
remain: permanecer
remark: comentário
remarkable: notável, extraordinário(a)
remember: lembrar(-se)
repair: conserto
replenish: repor; substituir
request: solicitação
require: requerer, necessitar
research: pesquisa
resource: recurso
respect: respeito

résumé: currículo
retain: reter, manter
reuse: reutilizar
revenue: receita, rendimento
review: resenha, crítica
reward: recompensa; recompensar
rewarding: gratificante
rewrite: reescrever
rice: arroz
riddle: enigma, charada
right: direito(a); certo(a)
rivalry: rivalidade
root: raiz; origem
Rubenesque beauty: beleza curvilínea
rule: regra
run: correr; administrar
run after: correr atrás de
run away: fugir
run out of: ficar sem
running water: água corrente
rust: ferrugem

safety: segurança
sail: navegar, velejar
save: salvar; economizar
savvy: especialista
scar: cicatriz
scary: assustador(a)
scholarship: bolsa de estudos
school: colégio, escola
schoolyard: pátio da escola
scramble: arrastar-se
screen: tela
scrutiny: exame minucioso
seashore: litoral
secure: garantir
seek: procurar, buscar
seem: parecer, aparentar
seeming: aparente

self-esteem: autoestima

self-portrait: autorretrato

self-taught: autodidata

sentence: frase

separate: separar

serf: servo(a)

set up: preparar, configurar

sever: cortar

several: alguns/algumas; vários(as)

shack: cabana

shadow: sombra

shaky: trêmulo(a)

shallow: raso(a)

shantytown: favela

share: dividir, compartilhar

sheltered: protegido(a), escondido(a)

shift: mudar

shine: brilhar

shopping: compras

shortcoming: defeito, deficiência

shove: empurrar

showcase: exibir

side: lado; aspecto

Sign me up!: Contratem-me!

silver: prata

since: desde; visto que, uma vez que

single: solteiro(a)

sink: afundar

site-specific: específico(a) para o local

skin: pele

skinny: muito magro(a)

skyscraper: arranha-céu

slang: gíria

slap: estapear

slim-waisted: que tem a cintura fina

slip: escorregar

slum: favela

smart: esperto(a), inteligente

snake: cobra

soap opera: novela

sojourner: morador(a) temporário(a)

solve: resolver

son: filho

soon: logo, em breve

sort: classificar; separar; tipo

soul: alma

soundtrack: trilha sonora

source: fonte

soy: soja

special: especial

speech: discurso

spinal cord: medula espinhal

spokesperson: porta-voz

sponsorship: patrocínio

spread: espalhar

stabilize: estabilizar

stage: palco; fase

stalk: perseguir

standard: padrão

starch: amido

starvation: inanição

statement: declaração

stay: ficar

steady: contínuo(a), estável

steal: roubar

steel-frame: que tem estrutura de aço

stem cell: célula-tronco

stereotype: estereótipo

still: ainda

stool: banquinho

stop: parar, interromper

store: guardar, armazenar

story: história

strawberry: morango

stream: fluxo, corrente

strength: força; ponto positivo/forte

stress: enfatizar, reforçar

stroke: pancada

stuff: coisas (informal)

subject: assunto; disciplina escolar

such as: tal/tais como

suckle: amamentar

suffering: sofrimento

sunscreen: filtro solar

supplier: fornecedor(a)

supply: fornecer

suppose: supor

surface: superfície

surgeon: cirurgião/cirurgiã

sustainability: sustentabilidade

sustainable: sustentável

sweep the floor: varrer o chão

swim: nadar

sword: espada

T

take care of: tomar conta de

take part: participar

take place: ocorrer, acontecer, ser realizado(a)

tap: bater de leve

tapir: anta

target: ter como alvo/objetivo

tarpaulin: tipo de lona

tea: chá

tear: lágrima

tease: provocar; implicar com, fazer pouco de

the shakes: tremores

then: então

there is no use: não adianta

therefore: portanto

thoroughly: completamente, meticulosamente

thoughtfully: refletidamente

threat: ameaça

threaten: ameaçar

throughout: ao longo de, no decorrer de

thus: assim, dessa forma

time: tempo

tin: lata

tip: dica

tissue: tecido

to: para

to sum up: em suma, resumindo

together: juntos(as)

tomato: tomate

tone: tom

too: também; demais

tool: ferramenta

top: parte de cima

top of the hill: topo da colina

touchstone: padrão de comparação

tourist: turista

town: cidade

trapped: confinado(a), preso(a)

trash: lixo

tray: bandeja

tree frog: perereca

trend: tendência

tributary: afluente

triple-A: de ponta, um(a) dos(as) melhores

truth: verdade

tumble: cair

tuna: atum

turn: girar; virar(-se)

turn against: voltar-se contra

turn around: virar-se

turn away: expulsar, afastar

turn back: voltar

turn down: recusar

turn into: transformar(-se) em

turn off: desligar

turn on: ligar

turn out: resultar; acontecer

twist: girar, rodar

unattended: desacompanhado(a)

unavoidable: inevitável

uncle: tio

under: embaixo de

underage: menor de idade

undergo: submeter-se a, passar por

undermine: minar, solapar

understand: entender

unfortunately: infelizmente

unhappy: infeliz

unless: a menos que

unmistakable: inconfundível, evidente

unorthodox: ousado(a)

unpaid: não remunerado(a)

unreliable: não confiável

unsuitable: inadequado(a)

unsurprising: que não surpreende

untrained: não treinado(a)

unwanted: indesejado(a)

upper-class: de classe social mais alta

utter: dizer

vegetable: verdura, vegetal

venue: local, espaço

vicious: cruel, maldoso(a)

visible: visível

voluptuous: curvilíneo(a)

waif-thin: muito magro(a)

wander: perambular

wannabe: aspirante

warehouse: armazém

warm: esquentar

warn: avisar, alertar

warning: alerta

wash: lavar

waste: lixo; desperdiçar

water: água

watermelon: melancia

weaken: enfraquecer

weakness: ponto negativo/fraco

wealthy: rico(a)

weight: peso

well-exercised: bem exercitado(a)

What about me?: E eu?

What's going on?: O que está acontecendo?

What's up?: E aí?

whatever: o que quer que seja, qualquer coisa que

wheelchair: cadeira de rodas

when: quando

whenever: sempre que

wherever: onde quer que

whether: se

while: enquanto

whoever: quem quer que

wildfire: incêndio florestal

wildlife: vida selvagem/silvestre

will: vontade

withdrawal: retirada; abstinência

witness: testemunhar

wonder: imaginar

word: palavra

work: trabalho; trabalhar; funcionar

wound: ferimento

you guys: turma, pessoal

youngster: jovem

yup: sim (informal)

zoo: zoológico

Irregular Verbs List

Infinitivo	Passado simples	Particípio passado	Tradução
to be	was/were	been	ser; estar
to become	became	become	tornar-se
to begin	began	begun	começar, iniciar
to break	broke	broken	quebrar
to bring	brought	brought	trazer
to build	built	built	construir
to buy	bought	bought	comprar
to catch	caught	caught	pegar
to choose	chose	chosen	escolher
to come	came	come	vir
to cost	cost	cost	custar
to cut	cut	cut	cortar
to do	did	done	fazer
to drink	drank	drunk	beber
to drive	drove	driven	dirigir, guiar
to eat	ate	eaten	comer
to fall	fell	fallen	cair
to feel	felt	felt	sentir
to fight	fought	fought	lutar, brigar
to find	found	found	achar, encontrar
to fly	flew	flown	voar
to forget	forgot	forgotten	esquecer
to forgive	forgave	forgiven	perdoar
to get	got	got/gotten	obter, conseguir
to give	gave	given	dar
to go	went	gone	ir
to grow	grew	grown	crescer
to have	had	had	ter
to hear	heard	heard	ouvir
to hide	hid	hidden	esconder
to hit	hit	hit	bater, chocar-se
to hold	held	held	segurar; realizar
to hurt	hurt	hurt	ferir, machucar
to keep	kept	kept	manter

to know	knew	known	saber
to lead	led	led	conduzir; liderar
to learn	learned/learnt	learned/learnt	aprender
to leave	left	left	partir, deixar
to lend	lent	lent	emprestar
to let	let	let	deixar, permitir
to lose	lost	lost	perder
to make	made	made	fazer
to mean	meant	meant	significar, querer dizer
to meet	met	met	encontrar(-se); conhecer
to pay	paid	paid	pagar
to put	put	put	pôr, colocar
to read	read	read	ler
to run	ran	run	correr
to say	said	said	dizer
to see	saw	seen	ver
to sell	sold	sold	vender
to send	sent	sent	enviar
to show	showed	showed/shown	mostrar, demonstrar
to sing	sang	sung	cantar
to sit	sat	sat	sentar
to sleep	slept	slept	dormir
to smell	smelled/smelt	smelled/smelt	cheirar
to speak	spoke	spoken	falar
to spend	spent	spent	gastar; passar (tempo)
to steal	stole	stolen	roubar
to sweat	sweated/sweat	sweated/sweat	suar
to swim	swam	swum	nadar
to take	took	taken	pegar
to teach	taught	taught	ensinar
to tell	told	told	contar; dizer
to think	thought	thought	pensar
to throw	threw	thrown	jogar, arremessar
to understand	understood	understood	entender, compreender
to wake	waked/woke	waked/woken	acordar
to wear	wore	worn	vestir, usar
to win	won	won	vencer
to write	wrote	written	escrever

Track List

① Apresentação